MUSLIM IDENTITY
IN THE 21st CENTURY:
Challenges of Modernity

International Conference on Muslim Identity in the 21st Century:
Challenges of Modernity School of Oriental and African Studies,
University of London,
October 31-November 1 1998

Institute of Islamic Studies-London

MUSLIM IDENTITY IN THE 21st CENTURY:
Challenges of Modernity

First Published in Great Britain, 2000
© Institute of Islamic Studies
(Affiliated to Islamic Centre of England – London)
All Rights Reserved.

Edited by
M. S. Bahmanpour
H. Bashir

Published by

BookExtra
INTERNATIONAL PUBLISHERS & DISTRIBUTORS

P.O.Box: 12519
London, W9 1ZA, UK
Tel: (44) 020-7604 5523
Tel: (44) 020-7604 5508
Fax: (44) 020-7604 4921

E-mail:
sales@bookextra.com

Home Page:
www.bookextra.com

ISBN: 1 900560 75 5

In the name of Allah,
The Compassionate The Merciful

Institute of Islamic Studies
(Affiliated to Islamic Centre of England – London)

140 Maida Vale, London, W9 1QB, UK

Tel: (44) 020-7604 5544
Fax: (44) 020-7604 5545
E-mail:

iis@islamic-studies.org

Home Page:
http://www.islamic-studies.org

Contents

Introduction 1

Chapter 1: *Muslim Umma* 35

Social Identity According to Islamic Sources 37
    Mohsen Araki

Beyond Westphalia: Nations and Diasporas 47
    S. Sayyid

Muslims of Asia; with special reference to China and Chinese
Central Asia 71
    Michael Dillon

Negotiating British Muslim Identity 89
    K. H. Ansari

Chapter 2: *Muslim Identity in a Rationalized World* 103

Muslim Identity and Civil Society: Whose Islam? Which
Society? 105
    Ali Paya.

Rationalization and Muslim Identity 125
    Muhammad Saeed Bahmanpour

Cultural Globalization and Muslim Identity 151
    S. R. Ameli.

The Future of Young Workers under Islamic Versus Western
Economic Systems 171
    Karen Pfeifer.

Human Rights and Muslim Identity 193
    Azzam Tamimi.

Chapter 3: ***The Impact of Education and Communication***
Technology on Muslim Identity 203

Education, Sacred Authority and the Religious Imagination in
Contemporary Muslim Societies 205
    Dale F. Eickelman.

Cyber Muslim and the Internet: Searching for Spiritual
Harmony in a Digital World 219
    Bahman Bakhtiari.

Covering Islam: Media and its Impact on Muslim Identity 237
    Hamid Mawlana

Mass Media and the Changable Identity of the Youth 267
    Hadi Khaniki.

Index 287

Acknowledgment

The articles in this book are the result of the conference on *Muslim identity in the 21st Century: Challenges of Modernity*, held in SOAS (University of London) on the 31st October - 1st November 1998. The organisers of the conference are deeply indebted to Dr. Ahmed Jalali for his constant endeavour on the minute details in the planning aspects of the conference; deep gratitude to Professor Baktiari for his continuous guidance and support. Also, with utmost sincerity to our dearest colleagues Mr. Ameli, Mr. Bahmanpour, Mr. Safavi, Moafi, Mr. Sotodeh, Dr. Bashir, Dr. Nojumi and Dr. Khush-Khu, whose enthusiasm and tireless efforts made the conference success. Also we acknowledge, with deepest respect, the spiritual guidance and sincere support of Ayatollah Araki, without which the conference would not have achieved its goals.

With highest sincerity, we would like to express our deepest gratitude to those who pioneered the implementation of the conference. Also, our appreciation to the speakers who participated in the conference with their deep intellectual and academic papers in the arena of religious identity in the modern world and the age of globalization. The speakers have manifested the theoretical approach of analysing and understanding Muslim identity at the dawn of the 21st Century.

Institute of Islamic Studies (London)

INTRODUCTION

This book is a collection of articles presented at the International Conference in London on "Muslim Identity in the 21st Century: Challenges of Modernity", organised by the Institute of Islamic Studies, from October 31 to November 1, 1998. The Conference was meant to discuss and put forward solutions for the challenges facing Muslims, as believing people and as people trying to follow a written *shari'a,* on the thresholds of the 21st century and amidst the dramatic social, economic and political changes brought about by modern society.

Islam, according to Gellner, is the only global faith to maintain its potency in the age of secularization[1]. However, although three general traits of Islam, as identified by him, i.e. egalitarianism, literacy and sense of identity, makes it, of the three great monotheistic creeds the one closest to modernity[2], it has proved "to be more resistant to the forces of secularization than the other global religions"[3].

It was only after the Islamic Revolution in Iran and a high pitched pronunciation of religious identification by Muslims throughout the world that attention was paid to this very new and vigourous phenomenon. Manuel Castells calls it a cultural-religious revolution.

> "The 1970s, the birthdate of the information technology revolution in Silicon Valley and the starting point of global capitalist restructuring, had a different meaning for the Muslim world: it marked the beginning of the fourteenth century of the *Hijra,* a period of Islamic revival, purification and strengthening, as at the onset of each new century.

Indeed, in the next two decades an authentic cultural-religious revolution spread throughout Muslim lands."[4]

This is why a definition of the Muslim *Umma* has become very pressing both for Muslims and non Muslims alike. For Muslims, since *umma* does not only mean community but also implies a sense of identity, it has become the most urgent priority for Muslim individuals, especially the younger ones, to know who they are; and for non-Muslims, because misunderstanding is always dangerous, and the degree of misunderstanding between the Islamic and the Western worlds remains dangerously high.[5] However, due to the vast diversity of Muslim communities, in terms of ethnic, political and ideological factors, defining the Muslim *Umma* or Muslim identity is not an easy task to shoulder. Indeed to define such an identity in a globalized world with its own values and ethos, permeating all aspects of social and individual life and crunching all kinds of resistance put forward by any specific culture and identity, is near to impossible.

It is outside the scope of this introduction to give statistical figures about the diversified nature of Muslim communities throughout the world, but with a speedy overview one may attain a concise picture. Muslims, ethnically, cover a wide range from Slavs in the Balkans to Arabs in the Middle East, to white and black Africans, to Persians, Indians, Malays and Chinese, each of which embrace, in their fold, a large spectrum of smaller ethnicities. According to one estimate, Islam includes, under its banner, over 4000 ethnic groups.[6] Needless to say, each of these groups, while adapting Islam to their own culture, give different spirits, meanings and interpretations to it.

Politically speaking, Muslims, except for less than a couple of centuries after the emergence of Islam, have not been a united entity. Some parts of Muslim lands, like Indonesia are so geographically aloof from other parts that it becomes prevented from developing any kind of political identification, and those parts which neighbour each other have been so enmeshed in constant wars and disputes, that any kind of unified political identity would be unimaginable..

Although the situation is better ideologically, it is, still, not free from troubles. There are among Muslims, Sunnis, Shi'ites, Sufis and

Wahhabis, each of which comprises in itself a wide range of theological and jurisprudential differences.

Therefore, while talking about Muslim identity, one should be careful not to ignore such manifold differences and should try to find some kind of definition by which all diversities could be covered.

Identitiy in one definition, is the way people think and behave, and the history of behaviour and thought to which they belong, or taking Manuel Castells definition - which goes one layer below this definition - it is the "peoples' source of meaning and experience."[7] Religion also, in one definition, is a symbolic structure that generates meanings for people, a worldview capable of providing answers to human problems, and an ethos telling people how they should act.[8] Therefore religion in itself could confer identity.

To define Muslim identity, however (and not Muslim identities), we have to ignore all specifics attached to different Muslim ethnicities and find an all-encompassing source to which all Muslims refer for their behaviour. Keeping this in mind, Muslims could generally be defined as the people who believe in the Holy *Qur'an* and the *Sunna* (practice) of Prophet Muhammad (p.b.u.h.) as the source of, and as the frame of reference for their belief and behaviour. Of course, the *Qur'an* and the *Sunna* could accept different interpretations and meanings, but as long as all these interpretations and meanings are returned and referred to those sources, their holders could be identified as Muslims.

The most general ideas and the core of all Islamic doctrines elaborated in the *Qur'an* and the *Sunna* in which all Muslims believe - whereby anybody not believing in any one of them, would not be considered Muslim - are as follows:

1. There is only One God Who is the Creator of the Universe and the creatures *(al- Tawhid)*.
2. All worship should be offered to Him and only to Him *(al- Ikhlas)*.
3. All Prophets of God have preached only one religion, which is Islam (submission to God alone), and Muslims must believe in all of them and "make no difference between the Prophets",[9] the

last of whom is Prophet Muhammad (p.b.u.h.) and no other
prophet has or will ever come after him *(al-Nabuwwa)*.

4. This life is transient, temporal and instrumental, and there comes
    after this a life which is the real life, perpetual and everlasting,
    and is molded and created by what we do in this world *(al-Ma'ad)*.

5. Every Muslim should act according to the injunctions of the
    Prophet Muhammad (p.b.u.h.), the most important of which are
    salat (prayer, five times a day), *zakat* (poor-due), *sawm* (fasting) in
    the blessed month of Ramadhan, and Hajj (pilgrimage) to Mecca
    for those affording it once during their lifetime.

    There is a sixth idea which, though not very central to and not
    very explicit in the Islamic doctrine, has occupied the
    background of every Muslim mind, that is:

6. Acting in accordance with the Islamic laws and precepts would
    guarantee the prosperity and superiority of Muslims in this world
    as well as in the Hereafter.

Although the concept of God and the amount of attention and
worship which is due to Him has been challenged to a great extent
during the past two centuries, I think it is the last three themes that
have caused much problems for Muslim identity in the contemporary
era. The idea of instrumentality and transience of this world has given
its place to fascination with it. It has, at the same time, become the
means and the ends. It is the realization of the deceit of Satan when
he came to Adam and told him: *"O Adam! Shall I guide you to the tree of
immortality and a kingdom which decays not?"*[10] It is really turned to a
kingdom without decay. Obviously, keeping up with the teachings of
the Holy *Qur'an* and, simultaneously, dealing with such a transient
world, are not wholly compatible and would, therefore, cause
problems with respect to Muslims' sense of identity.

The fifth and sixth themes have been even more problematic.
Until recent centuries, Muslims would not have even been questioned
on the validity and credence of such axioms. It was not until the late
18th and early 19th century that Muslims – due to the occupation of
their countries by non-Muslims and the setbacks suffered by them
from scientific, technological and military advances of the West -
started to rethink the superiority and rightfulness of their ideas and

behaviour over others, and to reconstruct the picture they had in mind about themselves for several centuries.

As Ali Paya states in his paper:

> *"It is only since the encounter of the Islamic societies with modern western civilization in the early 19th century that the symptoms of an acute and comprehensive identity crisis in the Islamic belief - ecosystem has become evident."[11]*

The defeat of the Ottoman empire by Russia in 1769, the separation of Crimea from Islamic lands, the conquest of Egypt by Napoleon in 1798, France's attack on Lebanon in 1860, the collapse of the Moghul Empire and the gradual subjugation of the Indian Muslim states by the British in the 19th century, the Russian advance into Central Asia in the 19th century, the occupation of Egypt by the British in 1883, the defeats suffered by the *Qajarid* dynasty of Iran at the hands of Czarist Russia as well as the occupation of Iran's southern islands by the British, and finally, and most crucially, the fall of the central government of Islam, that is the Turkish caliphate in 1924, all caused the Muslims to rethink and try to revitalize their system of beliefs. As Hamid Enayat puts it:

> *"The military defeats by the West shook the conscience of the Ottoman Turks and their leaders who were for several centuries proud of the strength of their territory and the righteousness of their way of life. It drove them to think about the cause of their incapability. Obviously, thinking about how to make up for their military failures, their first exigency was to rebuild and renovate their military apparatus. But it soon became clear that renovation of the army would not be possible without renovation of other aspects of social life, like the system of education, the economic infrastructure and introduction of basic factors for social change. So the wave of reformism gradually permeated into other fields of social life."[12]*

These reforms created so much change in the social structure of Muslim societies that they completely alienated them from their traditional legal, political and social systems - systems which were mainly based on Islamic jurisprudence. However, despite all these changes the belief in Islam persisted, but it was difficult "to be modern and Islamic at the same time,"[13] and therefore a crisis of identity appeared in full force. This unbearable situation pushed faithful thinkers and thoughtful *ulama* to try to devise ways by which conformity could be created between new social structures and institutions on the one hand and Islamic belief and legal systems, on the other.

Since such efforts have been, and still are, a very crucial and vital factor in maintaining Muslim identity in the past few decades and will continue to influence the course of Muslim societies in the 21st century, I shall elaborate on some instances of such an effort by Shi'ite *ulama*. I have chosen the Shi'ites because less is known about such intellectual efforts within the Shi'ite world, although I do not discount the enormous amount of effort and contribution by the Sunni world. Moreover, I have chosen the *ulama* because they are "the formal arbiters of Islamic opinion,"[14] i.e. beliefs and behaviours would not be considered Islamic unless approved by them, and Muslim intellectuals who have discussed these matters have not been very scrupulous about the *shari'a*.

The first such attempt, as far as I know, was the book *'Tanbih al-Umma wa Tanzih al-Milla'* (Awakening the *Umma* and Purifying the Creed) by one of the greatest Shi'ite ulama of the 19th century, Allamah Saiyyid Muhammad Husayn Na'ini, (1856-1936), in which he tried to develop a compatibility between the modern constitutional system of government and the traditional Islamic legal and political system. The amount of resistance and disagreement that was created by this book, amongst other *ulama*, is a good indicator of the difficulty of such efforts.

In his book, Na'ini has tried to answer the argument of those who thought that as long as the laws of the shari'a existed, there would be no need for a legislating body or parliament, for if those legislations were the same as that which is expressed in the Qur'an and Sunna, then there was no need for parliament and moreover, if they were contrary to the *shari'a* law, then they would be seen as dubious innovations and rulings and according to them, unlawful or haram. The most expressive, though not the most prominent, propagater of such ideas was Shaykh Fadhlullah Nuri (1842-1909), a well known alim of Tehran who "found the idea of constitution unacceptable because it provided for a legislative body, which would infringe upon divinely revealed law."[15]

Na'ini answered these arguments with the complex style of jurisprudential writing of his time, which makes reading his book very difficult. He argued that the functions and responsibilities of a government, such as establishing law and order, fending off the enemies, and regulating the affairs of society are included into two catagories. Either they are included in the religious text whereby, as a result, the practical duty of every one is defined and its ruling, in *shari'a*, is expressed, or they are not included and hence could not be defined by a specific rule or special criteria and become subsequently delegated to the opinion and decision of the ruler.[16]

It is evident that, contrary to the first type of rules, that is the "expressed" *(mansoos)* rules that cannot be changed on a spatial-temporal basis and for which no other duty but obedience has been envisaged, the second type (i.e. the "not-expressed" *(ghayr-e mansoos)* rules) are the ones that are affected by time and place and undergo compulsory changes. Even during the time of the Prophet (p.b.u.h.) and the infallible Imams, the judicial issues, that came across in various parts of the Islamic lands and were specific to the said areas and which did not fall into the purview of the "expressed" rules, depended on the discretion and judgement of the one who was appointed in the specific area by the Prophet (p.b.u.h.) or Imam. Such type of rules during the occultation *(ghayba)* of the Imam (p.b.u.h.) undergo change which is consistent with the period and place, and the discretion, of jurisprudents who are deputies of the last Imam (p.b.u.h.) or those who are authorised by them to do so. These individuals can take into consideration any type of time-fitting legal system, which is in accordance with social conditions or is not in contradiction to the "expressed" rules.

Having proved this point that was "crystal clear and obvious" in his view, Allamah Na'ini deduces several subsequent results:

First, the laws and regulations which should be in conformity with religious decrees are restricted to the first type, and to talk about such a conformity with the second type, is out of context.

Secondly, the principle of consultation - as ordained by the Qur'an and Sunna - serves as a basis of the Islamic government[17], and on the basis of which the National Islamic Consultative Assembly has been formed, fits in with the second type of rules while the "expressed" rules are beyond its jurisdiction and no consultation can be forecast for them.

Thirdly, the rules which are determined on behalf of the Imams by those appointed by the Imams or by those who are authorized by them during the occultation, fall into the second category of rules and are compulsory both during the presence and occultation of the Imam. "This exposes the false claims of those who regard implementation of such legal obligations not religiously compulsory. Denying the implementation of such rules has no other reason but lack of knowledge and sufficient awareness on the part of the objectors about the exigencies of religious principles."[18]

Fourthly, most of the social regulations, which have been referred to as *'siasat-e now'ieh'* (policy of expediency) by the late Na'ini, are covered by the second type of rules, that is the "non-expressed" rules, and fall within the jurisdiction of the authority of the Master of the Affairs (*Waliy Amr* - the Infallible Imam) and the power of discretion of his special or ordinary deputy. These regulations are bound by time, place and circumstances, and according to the *shari'a*, the council or *shura* under whose jurisdiction the explanation and elaboration of such rules falls, is based on this principle. Such rules, which are formulated through prudence and wisdom of those elected by the people, would be officially recognized and implemented as obligatory, once ratified by representatives at the National Consultative Assembly *(Majlis)* and duly endorsed by qualified *mujtahids* who are authorized by the authority of the Imam (p.b.u.h.)

Fifthly, since the second type of rules are categorized under *'siasat-e nowieh'*, and do not follow a precise order and would change consistently with different interests and exigencies - and this is why they are not expressed in the holy religion - they depend on views and attitudes of related authorities, and are prone to change and abrogation. Contrary to the first type of regulations, that are the "expressed" rules - which on no account could be altered irrespective of the time and place - such regulations are transient.[19]

Thus, Allamah Na'ini, who was among the greatest jurisprudents of his age - and many contemporary jurists in Iran and Iraq are considered as the students of his special jurisprudential school - succeeded in presenting a dynamic solution for harmony between the social changes and the stable legal system of the *shari'a*.

Allamah Na'ini criticized those who could not see such realities of the legal system and who wrongly persisted on the unchanging character of all aspects of the legal system of the Islamic society.

> "*It is amazing to see how those in non-Muslim societies who are ignorant of accurate Islamic rulings are actually basing their laws on the precepts called for by Islam. But in Islamic societies, it is a matter of astonishment to see the extent of the plagiarists' ignorance of the requisites and exigencies of the principles of Islam and their mistaken doubts whether any change and abrogation would be a kind of deviation from an obligatory duty towards a forbidden act, or vice-versa or from a permitted act to another permitted one.*"

Would it not be a wise idea to take out these misgivings from the sphere of doubts, undue fears and self interests, that distort public opinion, and make them conform with the real objective of safeguarding the system and the political affairs of the *umma* which is obligatory?[20]

The next *alim* after Na'ini who has deliberated over the issue is Allamah Sayyid Muhammad Husayn Tabatabai (d.1982) who had also held the view that communities of human beings cannot be ruled by a single legal system.

> "*In the times when people traveled by-ways and moved from one place to another on foot or by horse, donkey and mule, there was not much need to bother about routes, whereas today many bewildering devices have come up, requiring elaborate and minute regulations concerning urban, land, sea and air*

*transportation. The early Man led a simple life... but today,
due to a complexity of tasks, work has become technical, and
as a result has been divided into various specialized branches.
Jobs or modes of work have been sub-divided and are
characterized by thousands of regulations devised for them.'*[21]

On the other hand, Allamah Tabatabai believes that Islam is a
religion that can address all requirements of Man in all ages.

"*The invitation by Islam has foreseen certain methods and
a number of regulations that guarantee prosperity of the human
community in the best possible manner and ensure the various
needs of modern life.'*[22]

Allamah Tabatabai, by taking the above-mentioned two
principles into consideration, divides the laws governing human
community as follows:

"*The laws, which change in place with time and in tune
with progress of civilizations, and concern special status and
conditions. And laws which are irrevocable and are related to the
unchangeable essence of humanity, which is common between all
human beings in all ages, all conditions and all environments.'*[23]

Likewise, Islamic regulations are either revocable or
irrevocable. In fact Allamah Tabatabai holds the same view that
Allamah Na'ini did.

But the problem with the late Tabatabai and late Na'ini was
that they took all regulations included in the text of *shari'a* as fixed
rules, whereas many such rules are related to special states and
conditions. For example, one should ask whether fixing a camel, a
cow or a sheep as blood-money for man is related to the essence of
humanity or is a rule issued on special occasions and certain
conditions. Are *muzare'ah* (contract for leasing a farm), *musaqat*
(letting a farm or vineyard for part of the produce) or *muzareba*
(limited partnership or selling the goods of others for a portion of
the profit) related to the essence of humanity? Is the Arabic formula
of marriage or other contracts such as security-ship by a mature
individual *(Zaman Aqela)*, related to the principle of humanity? Such a

word looks more like a convincing answer rather than a serious debate.

At any rate, Allamah Tabatabai like the late Na'ini believes that revocable rules and regulations fall within the jurisdiction of a ruler and are interpreted as *Wilayat-e Ammah.*

> *"This very Islamic principle addresses the transient needs of people in any age, time or place, and caters to their changing necessities without tampering with the fixed and primordial laws of Islam."*[24]

But, according to Allamah Tabatabai, the authority of the *Wali* is not more than the authority of the head of a family in his daily decision-makings depending on spatial-temporal conditions and is not related to the drastic structural and legal changes in society.

> *"A person, living in an Islamic community, can make use of anything (of course on the basis of virtue and through observation of law), and can spend of his property as much as he deems proper in order to improve his life standard. Likewise, the Waliy Amr of Muslims, who is duly recognized by Islam, can on the basis of his general authority, determine whatever he deems necessary in the area of his jurisdiction. He can set regulations, for example, concerning roads, passes, houses, residential buildings, bazaar, transportation, labour and relations among various classes of the society, in light of the fixed rules. He can issue orders for defence on army mobilization and necessary preliminary tasks, enforce them on time and conclude pacts in the interests of Muslims."*[25]

As mentioned, what Allamah Tabatabai refers to as revocable regulations, are in fact the measures adopted by the *Wali* in accordance with spatial-temporal conditions, and are not the revocable legal rules, which are necessitated by changing social structures. To sum up, it is apparent that he has not explained the deep link between legal laws and social structure. His ideas are quite similar to those of Rashid Redha who thought that the community has the authority to create positive and man-made laws, as long as these laws, do not contradict, and are subsidiary to the *shari'a*.

Allamah Tabatabai's views were promoted by his student, Martyr Ayatollah Murtedha Mutahhari (d.1979). In his debates on 'Islam and Time Exigencies', Mutahhari upholds the view that:

> "*the problem with the issue of Islam and time exigencies is the problem of co-existence and coordination between two objects that are against each other in their natures. Of the two, one is fixed and irrevocable in nature, while the other is revocable, not fixed and fluid. Since Islamic decrees could not be abrogated, they are unchangeable and permanent, and since time exigencies or any other issue related to time, including human necessities and living conditions, are not fixed, it is but natural for them to undergo changes.*

In such a case how can two things, one of which is fixed and permanent by its nature while the other is everchanging by its nature, co-exist and coordinate with each other?"[26]

Mutahhari, having raised the question, provides the answer by expressing the same view as Allamah Tabatabai but in another form. He says that neither Islam is absolutely fixed in that no change could ever enter its rules and regulations nor do the time exigencies and conditions undergo absolute change. In Islam, there are both fixed and transient factors, as there are fixed and changing elements in time.

However, the big difference between student and teacher is that, as mentioned earlier, the late Tabatabai, like Allamah Na'ini, does not favour changes within the "expressed" laws of Islam, whereas Mutahhari breaks this barrier and this is a turning point in Islamic thought, in this field. From the viewpoint of Mutahhari, Islam has a mechanism inside its legal system, which ignites internal changes of its own without the need of any person to bring about such a change.[27] It is only for the *ulama* to discover those changes.

This mechanism of change, according to the late Mutahhari, consists of the following components:

1. Enactment of laws, in Islam, fall in the category of factual propositions and not actual proposition. This means that rules are of a general nature and do not pertain to specific events.
2. The way rules are set, open the door for contradiction between certain rules, that is, doing something can be obligatory as much as forbidden. For example, a non-*mahram* Man saving a woman who is about to be drowned, is an obligatory task under factual proposition, which says that "saving the life of a human being is obligatory." But the action would be forbidden under a factual proposition which states that "touching the body of a non-*mahram* woman is forbidden."
3. In the case of contradiction between rules, it is advisable to follow the rule which is more important and ignore the one which is less important, as is evident in the light of the following phrase: *"Idha ijtama't hurmatan turehat-al-sughra lil-kubra"* (If two issues overlap, leave the less important one for the sake of that which is more important).[28]

In view of the above-mentioned formula, Mutahhari concludes that people's duties might differ in the course of time. It is possible that an issue which might be forbidden during certain times to turn into a lawful and even obligatory issue at another time, due to the nature of the changed conditions i.e. change in laws and legal regulations under various social conditions. According to Mutahhari:

> *"This is the point, which prompts jurisprudents and mujtahids to be fully aware of time and circumstances, in order to make a distinction between minor and major important things at various times... This is a way of harmonizing Islam with time requirements i.e. an evolution in Islamic law, but in a way that does not mean abrogation, rather it is something allowed by Islam. Islam has set its rules in a way they could be changed in accordance with different periods and places."[29]*

But what is the reason behind such laws and why is there such a mechanical instrument in Islam? Ayatullah Mutahhari believes that Islamic regulations are heavenly as much as they are attributed to the earth. This means that "they are consistent with the interests and exigencies of human beings," and have no secret or hidden aspects. For Islamic regulations, one should not say that "divine injunctions have no connections with such statements. God Almighty has set a law and He Himself is fully aware of the reason behind it."[30] Since rules are made on the basis of real human interests and exigencies and since all rules are not defined by the Holy Qur'an and the Sunna, therefore the system of Islamic legislation has kept its door open for common sense.

> '*Kullo ma hakam behi-al-aql hakam behi al-shar'a'*, that means wherever sense discovers a necessary exigency we get to know that divine law concords with it even if there is basically no word on the issue in the holy Qur'an, *hadith* or the expressions of the *ulama*."[31]

He who is authorized to alter the rules is a qualified *mujtahid* - not with the restriction that the late Tabatabai believed in, but, rather, with more authority. Conformity of Islamic rules with a series of so-called temporal interests (the ones which are related to Man and the ones which can be discerned through Man's sense and knowledge) on the one hand, and on the other hand the legislative system of Islam, which falls in the realm of factual propositions (the rules which are of a general nature and not applicable to specific individuals), present the *mujtahid* a wonderful opportunity to issue, in accordance with Islamic injunctions, different fatwas under various spatial-temporal conditions. It is, in fact, an opportunity to determine the conditions under which something lawful, would become forbidden in a time, or obligatory or recommended in other times.[32]

All these views had been raised before the triumph of the Islamic Revolution in Iran, in 1979. The climax came in the post-revolution era, when Islamic regulations were being practically implemented in Iranian society and when the structures and institutions of modern society refused to accept the laws and regulations which were feared to be Islamic. This climactic point manifested itself in the late Imam Khomeini's (1902-1989) viewpoint on *Wilayat-e Faqih* or "the absolute authority of the supreme jurisprudent."

Absolute authority here does not mean an absolute or despotic form of government, rather it is possessing the authority - which the late Tabatabai and the late Nai'ini believed should be within the jurisdiction of the *mujtahids* - not in a limited mode, but rather in absolutely terms. The late Imam Khomeini, himself, often used to say that the concept of *Wilayat-e Faqih,* has not yet been clearly understood. In one of his speeches in 1979, after entrusting the task of restricting private ownership to the government, he said "this is one of the authorities that emanates from *Wilayat-e Faqih* but unfortunately our intellectuals do not understand what *Wilayat-e Faqih* is?"[33]

In fact, *Wilayat-e Faqih,* in Imam Khomeini's opinion is the solution for making Islamic laws and regulations compatible with structural changes in the society, in an absolute manner and not simply within the framework of "expressed" and indubitable Islamic injunctions. A glance at the statements of Imam Khomeini on this issue would make it fully clear that *Wilayat-e Faqih* actually means absolute authority to devise and make laws and regulations in accordance with social exigencies. His views on these issues are fully explicit, candid and free from any ambiguity. For example, in a message sent to the ulama on February 22, 1988, he said:

*'Time and place are two key factors for **ijtihad**. The issue which had a ruling in the past might urge a new ruling in the political, social and economic context of a new system. This means that with accurate identification of economic, social and political relations the first subject, which has apparently not differed from its former form, might really be a subject, which warrants a new rule.''*

On September 24, 1988 Imam Khomeini wrote in response to an *alim* who had questioned him about his ruling concerning chess:

> *"As per your excellency's inquiry,* **rahan, sabq** *and* **ramayah** *and martial arts which were used during battles in the past are exclusive to bow and arrow and horse riding and so on, as is the case with* **anfal** *(spoils), which has been stipend for Shi'ites. Can Shi'ites today freely ruin forests with such and such a machinery, destroy whatever that protects the environment, and endanger the life of millions of people with no one having the right to prevent them of such a doing? Based on your excellency's estimation of* **hadith** *and the sayings of the Prophet (p.b.u.h.) and his Household, modern civilization and its amenities should be discarded completely, and people should dwell in ruins or live for ever in forests."*[34]

This reveals that Imam Khomeini had been in full agreement with the sociological aspects of law on the issue concerning legal regulations being affected by social structure. The only exception to the rule is that Imam Khomeini lays greater emphasis on the role of government in this regard, i.e. a government, led by a qualified jurisprudent. Wherever there is a word on *Wilayat-e Faqih*, Imam Khomeini defines *wilayat* as a government system, led by a jurisprudent, and not the *wilayat* of a single person. The decisions made at the Islamic Consultative Assembly or the government cabinet or the State Expediency Council or the Guardians Council would be considered legitimate, only, through their reliance on absolute *wilayat*, even if, in certain cases, they appear to be against some indubitable rules.

Thus, it is the government and not the person that determines which of the indubitable rules of Islam should be momentarily overlooked and replaced by a new law.

> *"It is the government which determines practical philosophy of confrontation against blasphemy and idolatry or internal and external problems. The theological debates raised at schools within the framework of theories are not only impractical but could lead us into deadlocks, which would be an apparent violation of the constitution."*[35]

In the face of a government which is a manifestation of absolute *wilayat*, none of the "expressed" and indubitable rules of Islam can offer resistance. Such a view would undoubtedly create many theoretical problems in the minds of most pious people. When Imam Khomeini's views on powers possessed by the government system, based on absolute *wilayat*, were announced to the Council of Guardians, the then Iranian president (present leader), Ayatollah Saiyyid Ali Khamenei told the Friday prayer congregation that what the Imam meant was the authority of government within the framework of the *shari'a* and the indubitable rules. Imam Khomeini immediately wrote a letter, in which he outlined his views as such:

"You are mistaken if you do not believe that the government, which on the principle of absolute **wilayat** *was entrusted by Almighty God to Prophet Muhammad (p.b..u.h.), enjoys precedence as an important divine commandment over all jurisprudential rules. The comments on my remarks do not at all conform with my view that the government has the authority within the framework of divine rules. If the powers of the government are limited to the framework of the jurisprudential rules of Islam, then it should be said that divine government and absolute* **wilayat** *entrusted by God to Prophet Muhammad (p.b.u.h.), would be meaningless and devoid of any content. As a token of my remarks I would like to refer to the consequences of such an issue to which no one can adhere. To cite an example, the case of broadening streets, which requires the taking over of a house or part of it, does not fall within the framework of jurisprudential rules. The military service and dispatch of forces to battlefronts, ban against hoarding - except in two or three cases - customs duties, taxes, coding and control of prices, measures against distribution of narcotic drugs, banning addiction in any form, other than alcoholic drinks (which are divinely prohibited), bearing of arms in any form, and hundreds of such cases, which fall within the realm of government authority, would be beyond state jurisdiction as per*

> *your remarks. What has been or is said results from lack of sufficient knowledge about absolute **wilayat**. What has been said to the effect that with such authority issues such as **muzare'ah** contract for cultivation or leasing of land) or **muzarebah** (limited partnership) would be forsaken, even if they are presumed to be so, I would like to state explicitly that they are among authorities of government.*

There are even more important issues, which I do not like to dwell upon now.[36]

As is evident, Imam Khomeini had, in mind, the necessity of change in social laws and regulations and he sought the solution in absolute divine *wilayat* (authority) in changing or abrogating laws on the basis of special social conditions as was the case when the task was entrusted to the Prophet, and after him fell within the jurisdiction of the ideally just government. Imam Khomeini's reference to issues urged by new social parameters such as military service, taxes, price coding, etc., reveals the dynamic way in which he dealt with these developments. The reason for the late Imam's emphasis on the necessity of supervision of government affairs by a just jurisprudent, was his refusal to ignore the principled values of Islam. He believed that if a government, enjoying such authorities was willing to be labeled Islamic without restricting itself to the jurisprudential framework of rulings, then it should at least be faithful to the principles that from the viewpoint of Islam ensure the spirit of an Islamic society. And this would be impossible, unless the one, who guides such a system, is, himself, aware and committed to such principles.

The point worth noting here is that, for the late Imam, the rules devised by such a government are not secondary rules, i.e. it does not mean ignoring principles due to social exigencies, rather they are the rules which are based on principles. Due to the same reason, Imam Khomeini emphasized that "government rulings are amongst the prime and fundamental rules."[37]

Thirty years ago, N.J. Coulson, saw this kind of approach to Islamic laws as a radical approach, but also viewed that Islamic jurisprudence should have such a solution in dealing with issues caused by new social conditions. It would be worthy to include his conclusion and final judgement on Islamic jurisprudence :

> *"It cannot be denied that certain specific provisions of the Qur'an, such as that which commands the amputation of the hand for theft, pose problems in the context of contemporary life for which the solution is not readily apparent. But, generally speaking, the Qur'anic precepts are in the nature of ethical norms - broad enough to support modern legal structures and capable of varying interpretations to meet the particular needs of time and place. And on this basis it would seem that Islamic jurisprudence could implement, in practical and modernist terms, its fundamental and unique deal of a way of life based on the command of God. Freed from the notion of a religious law expressed in totalitarian and uncompromising terms, jurisprudence would approach the problem of law and society in a different light...*
>
> *Radical though the break with past tradition which such an approach involves might be, it is nevertheless a break with a particular construction of the religious law and not with its essence... Law, to be a living force, must reflect the soul of a society; and the soul of present Muslim society is reflected neither in any form of outright secularism nor in the doctrine of the medieval text books."*[38]

The method which Coulson envisions for jurisprudence is justly speaking, a bold method. It seems that absolute authority of government or absolute guardianship of the just jurisprudent would set such conditions. If laws are superstructures and are dictated by such deep-rooted aspects like economy, culture, the natural and social environment, then one cannot uphold a forceful campaign in such affairs; but an infrastructure can necessitate different superstructures. That which a jurisprudent does in order to make society Islamic is setting up a framework on different superstructures and selects the one which best fit or most suitable.

At any rate, Imam Khomeini presented a bold and unprecedented method in Islamic jurisprudence, that was fully novel when compared with the traditional approach. His views should be considered as more progressive compared to that of Ayatollah Baqir Sadr (martyred 1980), who is regarded as the most enlightened Shi'ite thinker of the contemporary era. Ayatollah Sadr has referred to this issue in his book "Our Economy" where he speaks of the economic laws and regulations of Islam. After categorizing the economic system in a society, as infrastructural, and civil rights and laws as its superstructure,[39] to understand the Islamic system, he starts to study its superstructure, i.e. Islamic civil rights. However, he believes that to study the issue one should not suffice looking at static elements of the legal system, rather he should take up the dynamic elements into consideration as well. The static elements are those rules that are set by the Holy Legislator and are not open to any change. The dynamic elements in turn are the ones, which fall within what he calls "the realm of legal freedom" and which "should be regulated by the guardian, i.e. government, in tune with spatial-temporal needs and exigencies."[40]

"The decisions taken by Prophet Muhammad (p.b.u.h.) in the realm of legal freedom" was not intended to be everlasting because the Prophet (p.b.u.h.), in such cases, had acted not as the propagator of fixed divine rules nor as political leader and head of an Islamic government. Due to the same reason, his decisions in such cases should not be included within the static elements of the Islamic economic system.[41] According to this view, the Prophet's (p.b.u.h.) move in confirming such rules as *muzarebah* (limited partnership), *musaqat* (agreement on fruit trees with common share), and proving claims through *qasama* (oath taking) as were valid during his prophethood, or his move in formally recognizing the then existing rules by adding to them or omiting some of them, should not be taken as something made to make a rule permanent. Rather, one should think that the Prophet (p.b.u.h.) had done such a thing within "the realm of legal freedom", and the ones who assume political leadership or government of the Islamic establishment after him are free to follow or abandon such rules as per spatio-temporal exigencies.

Apparently, all confirmed rules of Islam (i.e. the rules which existed before the Prophet (p.b.u.h.) and were confirmed by him) and some of the ordained rules fall in the same category. Although such a view is bold in its kind within the framework of traditional jurisprudence, it cannot address the legal problems of the society in pace with the view on "absolute guardianship of the jurisprudent", because as Ayatullah Sadr has said the "realm of legal freedom" could only be extended to an area where it would not contradict the fixed and legislated rules. Therefore, absolute wilayat, which Imam Khomeini considered for government due to the structural needs of a society should be restricted in Ayatullah Sadr's view. It seems that Ayatullah Sadr has neglected the invisible changes in subjects, which predicate religious decrees. Imam Khomeini had been fully aware of such an issue.

> "*The same subject that a rule had been issued about it in the past might in a different political, social and economic system, be the issue of a new ruling. This means that a careful look at the economic, social and political relations would reveal that the same subject, that is not apparently different with its former form, might turn into a new issue, which deserves to be subject of a new ruling.*"[2]

There were some solutions provided for the challenging problems of how to be a Muslim in a new environment. All these solutions - after admitting the legal difficulties which has entangled the Muslim society and the need for legal reforms - have one thing in common i.e. any change in or abrogation of jurisprudential laws, must be supervised by a jurisprudent who is authorized for this purpose by the Prophet (p.b.u.h.) or the infallible Imam. This idea is, in fact, rooted in the Shi'ite belief of (the continuation of) Imamate.

The idea of the "absolute authority of the jurisprudent" *(Wilayat-e Faqih)* is not only the most conclusive of all these solutions, but also is the most progressive of them compared to the traditional approaches. It would not recognize any limit for change in the Islamic legal system as long as it is based on broad Islamic principles. To meet this condition, these modifications should be supervised by somebody who has both religious commitment and knowledge, otherwise it would end in secularism.

It is interesting to note that a considerable number of laws enacted or reformed after the victory of the Islamic Revolution in Iran are beyond the realm of traditional jurisprudence. For instance, the laws concerning women are not consistent with the jurisprudential framework of traditional Islamic regulations. For example, the right to choose or be chosen are, of course, offshoots of more general developments in the field of the society's political laws and its economic structure. It should be said that within the framework of Islam, presentation of such rights to women was impossible before the Islamic Revolution.

Even after the triumph of the Islamic Revolution and at the time when the said rights were compiled for women, some wrote a letter to Imam Khomeini, protesting that they were against the transmitted texts of Islam.[43] Other changes were observed in family rights, especially on the subject of the right to divorce. The family support law, which had been devised before the revolution, by non-Islamic jurisprudents, was abrogated immediately after the revolution, but the social conditions and the structure governing the family institution within the entire society, underwent change to such an extent that the former laws concerning divorce stirred social disorder and were found to be not on par with the changes in the rights of women, in other fields. Therefore, the Supreme Judicial Council arranged, in a ratification called on the Public Notary and the Statistics and Registration Department, to place in the marriage register set conditions during a marriage contract.[44]

Excerpts of such conditions are as follows:

1. Transfer of half of the husband's property (the portion earned during matrimonial life) to the wife, in case the request for divorce was initiated by the husband and was not due to the wife's refusal to abide by her duties or maltreating her spouse.
2. Irrevocable attorney-ship granted to the wife by the husband with the legal right to refer to the court, concerning matters related to divorce settlement - under the conditions mentioned in

the marriage contract - including maltreatment by the husband, refusal to give alimony for a period of six months, engagement in a vocation which is against the interests of the family and woman's dignity, addiction and marriage with another woman without obtaining permission of the first wife.

It is true that the conditions are not compulsory and the bridegroom can refuse to sign the contract, but since the conditions mentioned in the register concord with the type of justice accepted by people of his generation, the man cannot oppose them and they are automatically included as conditions of the marriage contract. It is also true that inclusion of any condition which is not against religious laws, is allowed during the final enactment of the contract; but inclusion of such conditions in the marriage contract, as a general rule, is indicative of the changes in the law of marriage and divorce as well as the fundamental alterations in the marriage contract - to the effect that no official marriage would take place without full justification. In other domains, the laws - ranging from the principle of ownership (of property) to the labour law, political rights and public rights, that were formulated after the Islamic Revolution - fall beyond the jurisdiction of traditional jurisprudence.

These adjustments and similar efforts, launched by *ulama* in the Sunni world, are all attempts for finding solutions to be *modern* and *Muslim* simultaneously i.e. to worship God and to take heed of His words, while living in societies with structures and institutions completely different from those of the society at the time of Divine Revelation, over fourteen centuries ago.

However, in recent decades, the process of globalization has added fuel to the flames and has created more problems for Muslim identity; not only because globalization and identity are two conflicting trends[45], and not because of the fact that with the acceleration of the pace, extension and complexity of modern societies, identity becomes more and more unstable and fragile[46], but, rather, because globalization is an institutionalization of materialism which is in conflict with all religions. With globalization, the question is no longer the adjustment of the Islamic legal system with new social structures, rather, it is, in fact, challenging the whole value system of Muslims. This is why religious fundamentalism - though it has existed throughout human history[47] – is, surprisingly, stronger at the end of the 20th century.

This book includes 13 articles which discuss the present situation and the future of Muslims in the face of globalization.

Faced with the ever-increasing onslaught of globalization, Muslims theoretically have three alternatives before them: either to accept the process and allow their identity to undergo a metamorphosis of the most severe kind, or to resist all aspects of the process and hold fast to their identity and launch a *jihad* against all aspects of modernity. These are two extremes of the theory put forward as "Mecca or Mechanization."[48]. The third alternative, for Muslims, is to accommodate the process to their own value system and produce, out of this conflict, a new breed of moral, modern society.

The increasing fervent of Islamization all over the world – which includes Muslim minorities living in the West, the Islamic Revolution in Iran, the situation in Afghanistan, Algeria, Turkey and Palestine - all prove that the first alternative is certainly and most definitely out of the question. The problems and difficulties presently experienced by Muslim societies in economical, political, cultural and social issues establish enough evidence to show the futility of the second alternative. It is only the third way which is open to Muslims and to the West, at the same time, and which could constitute a viable solution to the problem. This is what I have tried to demonstrate in the preceding paragraphs i.e. that Muslims are willing and are able to do so.

In his paper, in this book, Ali Paya also believes that this process is already underway. He writes:

> *"In the past two decades ... many thinkers have striven to develop more refined models of civil society in which the rights and liberties of the individual are reconciled with a partnership between the state and the society. In such models, great emphasis has been placed on the priority of morality as a method for conducting the affairs of the state and the individual."[49]*

This process of mutual understanding and adaptation could be accelerated by co-operation and mutual learning, otherwise it may be impeded by misunderstandings, mistakes and mis-management as well as efforts, by each side, to globalize its own culture. This is, unfortunately, the option which the West has chosen to aim. This is why Hamid Mawlana claims vehemently that numerous studies during the last several decades have demonstrated that the process of modernization is "a one way traffic from the West," and "even the dichotomy of 'Occident versus Orient' was pushed aside, since the worldwide diffusion of modernization, which was now creating the new world of the so called 'globalization' had rendered 'East' and 'West' irrelevant".[50]

According to S. Sayyid, "McWorld, emerges not as a 'rainbow formation' where all human cultures find a home, but rather, as an attempt to make the whole world a home for one way of life, one cultural formation. The difference between McWorld and *jihad* comes down to a matter of scale rather than content, for both projects seem to be about making the world familiar, making the world home." [51]

As long as the West looks upon its culture as the superior culture in all aspects - endeavouring to humiliate other cultures without making efforts to understand them, and tries to globalize one, and only one, culture - the world will not come out of its present difficulties. Muslims have tried their best to adopt new scientific, social and philosophical ideas from other cultures, especially from the West, and adapt it to their own value system. They have not, generally, treated their *shari'a* as "an invariable, rigid command, but [as] a guide to walk towards God, with the adaptations required by each historical and social content."[52] It is now the West which should participate in this mutual effort of understanding and cultural interchange.

ABOUT THE BOOK

As I have mentioned previously, this book consists of thirteen articles which have been arranged in three chapters.

Chapter 1 includes four articles relating to the Muslim *Umma*. In the first article, 'Social Identity According to Islamic Sources', Ayatollah Araki tries to give us a definition of social identity as he finds it in authentic Islamic sources. According to him the first discernable attempt made to define social identity was by Amir al-Mu'mineen, Ali B. Abi Talib (d. 40/663) who gave a nice and neat criterion for it, that is satisfaction, dissatisfaction towards good/bad actions. Based on this, Ayatollah Araki opines that adherence to Islamic ideals and obedience towards a Muttaqi (pious) Leadership are found in the Islamic sources to be the cornerstone of Muslim social identity.

In the second article, entitled *'Beyond Westphalia: Nations and Diasporas'*, S. Sayyid tries to define and locate the Muslim *Umma* in the global age. To define what the term Muslim *Umma* means, the article first determines what the Muslim *Umma* is *not*. It is not a nation, it is not a common market and it is not a civilization. By redefining the notion of diaspora and divesting it of its three co-ordinates i.e. homeland, displacement and settlement, Sayyid has tried to categorize the *Umma* as a diaspora. Diasporas are anti-nations and because of globalization of world societies, which is characterized by five main processes - the emergence of a nascent global civil society, the emergence of supra national formations, the rise of cosmopolitan centers, the generalization of the experience of distant travel and the integration of the worlds political economy - nations are being replaced by diasporas."What is involved in a diaspora is the de-concentration of power and subjectivity."

Of course, the logic of diaspora is not only anti-national, rather, if a particular national or cultural formation like the Mc World takes a global form, diaspora also becomes anti-global. Therefore, the Muslim *Umma* (in its present situation) is anti-national and anti-global, at the same time. In his article, Sayyid successfully comes to an identification of the Muslim *Umma* in spite of those who consider the notion to be little more than an exercise of wish fulfillment.

In the third article of this chapter, Michael Dillon discusses, briefly, the Muslims of Asia in general and goes into detail about the little-known Muslim communities in China. It shows the diverse identities of the small population of Muslims in China - believed to be about 18 million - which are usually classified into ten ethnic groups. Over the centuries, it was thought that these small and far away communities were assimilated into the Chinese culture. However, the identification of these small and remote communities with the Muslim *Umma* ,rather than with the Chinese culture, became clear from the 1980s onwards when after the death Mao Zedong, the control of the central government was relaxed and a rapid programme of building and rebuilding mosques and shrines was initiated.

The final article of the chapter deals with British Muslim identity, in which K. H. Ansari provides an assessment of emerging British Muslim identity in an historical perspective. He attempts to explore themes with regard to the evolving relationships between Muslim communities in British and wider society in a way that questions the existing presuppositions about Muslims. He tries to explain what it means to be a Muslim in Britain in the 1900s.

Drawing on a range of research and analysis about the experience of Muslims in Britain he also examines the various dynamics of change in the attitude and behaviour of diverse groups of Muslims, and touches on the existence of alternative interpretations, which may have had the potential for evolution, and the reasons why they have failed to blossom.

The second chapter covers articles concering Muslim Identity in the new and rationalized world. In the first article titled: *'Muslim Identity and Civil Society: Whose Islam? Which Society?'* Ali Paya talks about a crisis of identity which has been pervasive in Muslim societies since the encounter of the Muslim societies with modern Western civilization. This crisis is the result of threats which Muslim individuals or communities perceive against their ideas and doctrines and which has led to very difficult questions concerning the very fundamentals of the Islamic belief system. After listing some of these questions, he tries to identify the solution to the existing problem i.e. how to be an Islamic model of civil society. He argues that among different interpretations of Islam and its belief system, only the rational approaches will benefit from some *bona fide* model of civil society.

Naturally, both orientalists and Muslim traditionalists have argued against the possibility of such a model. While orientalists have based their argument on what they call the "stationariness of Islamdom," Muslim traditionalists have argued that since Islam does not accept moral pluralism, it could not endorse civil society. Paya argues that civil society is based upon universal ideas such as responsibility, freedom, equity and pluralism, all of which are "indigenous ingredients of Islamic mystical belief system." Therefore, he says, from among many interpretations of Islam, it is only the mystical interpretation which is well equipped to produce viable answers to the challenges facing Muslim communities in a rationalized world.

The second article is my own, entitled *'Muslim Identity in a Rationalized World'*, in which I have tried to clarify the notion of rationality as it is used in authentic Islamic texts. Rationality and rationalization are two concepts which are part of the Islamic belief system and are used abundantly in Islamic literature. This has led many Muslim thinkers to the supposition that Islam had advocated social rationalization. Though I believe that social rationalization is not in contradiction to Islam, nevertheless, the rationality which is talked about in any religion, generally, and in Islam, particularly, is different in nature. To explain this point, I have elaborated on different kinds of rationalities ranging from theoretical to practical, formal, normative, instrumental and communicative. Although all these rationalities could be approved by the Islamic belief system, the rationality advised in Islam, looks at a different angle of human intellect. The religious rationality, as I call it, tries to cultivate and nourish in people *that* aspect of reason which deals with the philosophy of life and its Creator and which is usually the most ignored corner of human reasoning.

In the third article of this chapter, *'Cultural Globalization and Muslim Identity'*, S.R. Ameli first makes a brief reference to the early formation of Islamic Identity and then examines the general differences that exist between religious identities in the traditional, modern and post-modern societies. He then gives a detailed analysis of globalization and the relevant concepts and by using Castells categorization, explores the types of identities which Muslim individuals and communities may behold in such an environment. He tries to show that the effects of globalization trends are not uniform on Muslim identity and not only would it not, necessarily, lead to the assimilation of an Islamic identity into a global culture, rather, in most cases, Islamic Identity has resisted the prevailing universal culture.

The fourth article of this chapter deals with moral aspects of Muslim identity in a rationalized economy. In her study in a small, selective sample of 25 firms in Egypt, Karen Pfeifer found that the eight non-Islamic firms as a group had a significantly higher rate of profit and that the Islamic firms who paid significantly higher wages, had a lower profit/ wage ratio and were more likely to share profits with workers. This means that "Homo Islamicus", contrary to "Homo Economicus" pursues the subject of profits within moral and religious constraints. She concludes that the Islamic business sector can make a contribution to economic growth by improving its innovative-ness and productivity performance, thereby raising profitability to fund greater investment in the future. At the same time, it should not sacrifice its superior equity performance in a false "trade-off equity for efficiency", but use the profit-sharing system to include the workers in investment for growth and new employment opportunities.

Finally we have the article of Azzam Timimi concerning human rights and Muslim identity in which he relates Muslim identity to the issue of human rights via three ways. The first is the emphasis that Islam has put on the issue of human rights from the outset, by asserting the supremacy of the value of justice and of the principle of human dignity. The second is the violations of basic human rights of Muslims whether in Islamic countries or where Muslims live as minorities, which have led to adverse effects on Muslim identity; and the third, in which he goes into some detail, is the secularist discourse on human rights which in some parts clash with some of the characteristic features of Muslim identity and, in the name of universalism, undermines the rights of Muslims to any cultural specificity. This is why some Muslims regard the human rights movement as a post-colonial tool of cultural imperialism.

The third chapter explores the impact that education and communication technology have had in Muslim societies and communities. It also comprises four articles, the first of which is a very good contribution by Dale Eickelman. His article explores the relationship between the massive expansion in higher education, in the Muslim world, since the 1950s and its implication for ideas of religious knowledge and authority. He suggests that mass communication and higher education have virtually given rise to conceptual innovations, open-ended debates and new senses of religious and political authority in the Muslim world which is ignored by many observers. Like Abdul Karim Soroush, he opines that this happens not in established intellectual circles but within background understandings, against which the beliefs and practices, in any given society, are formulated. In fact, a large number of believers are engaged in the reconstruction of religious thought, and this is because of the unprecedented access that believers have to sources of information and knowledge about religion and other aspects of life.

Eickelman's article produces statistics about the great boom in higher education, in some Muslim countries, and mentions books and writers giving new opinions about religious doctrines which stand outside the traditional interpretations produced by clerics, the result of which is collapse in the earlier, hierarchial notions of religious authority. As the formal institutions of religious thought are being overpowered by new contributions to religious and political debate, a religious public sphere is showing up which contributes to the creation of civil society.

The second article, *'Cyber Muslim and the Internet'* , by Bahman Bakhtiari, examines the Internet's impact on Muslim identity, in the 21st century. Besides the interesting information and statistics provided in the article about "The Network Society" in general and the "Muslim Network Society" in particular, Bakhtiari discusses three consequences of the Muslim sites on Muslim identity. The first consequence is the evaporation of geographical borders making possible the creation of virtual communities of Muslims who live as far apart as Indonesia and Iceland. This has changed the informational environment of Muslim individuals and, hence, has affected the processes of their identity formation. The second consequence is the establishment of alternative sources of learning and education; and the third effect is pluralism and enhancement of local democracies by creating a kind of electronic participation? The number of Islamic parties which have set up websites, like the *Ikhwan al-Muslimeen* (Muslim Brotherhood) in Egypt, the *Jama'at-e Islami* in Pakistan, the Islamic Movement in Palestine, *Hamas*, and the Hizbollah in Lebonan illustrate how Muslims are using technology for creating a virtual pluralistic community.

In the third article of this chapter, titled *'Covering Islam: Media and its Impact on Muslim Identity'*, Hamid Mawlana informs us about a crisis in Muslim identity created by the modern nation-state system which is inconsistent with Islamic values. This crisis is further enhanced and promoted by distorted images portrayed of and for Muslims through western-controlled media. He argues that print and electronic media in the Islamic world has helped the centralization of the modern state apparatus in the hands of westernized and secular rulers; however, in parallel to this, the *ulama* and religious groups - while using the traditional oral modes of communication to decentralize and diffuse the power of the state - have also made use of modern communication technologies. As an example of this, Mawlana suggests the impact of news media, especially television, on Muslim identity in Iran. He suggests that the important feature of television in Iran is its integration into the vast and complex system of traditional and oral channels of communication. Although his illustrations about the role and the contents of television broadcast in Iran are interesting, they should be viewed with some caution. Also, it is true that, as Piscatori puts it, "the contept of modern international relations, particularly the concept of the nation-state, have no equivalents in traditional Islamic political theory"[53], but there is no evidence that such new notions are not able to be harmonized with Islamic tenets, like many other notions which were not in existence during the time of Prophet Muhammad (p.b.u.h.). In any case, the practice of Mawlana's exemplar Islamic state, i.e. the Islamic Republic of Iran, is a good example of the adaptation of this notion into Islamic ideology.

In the last article of this chapter and of the book, entitled *'Mass Media and the Changable Identity of the Youth'*, Hadi   Khaniki postulates that the problem of identity is peculiar to societies and peoples in the process of transition. In traditional societies, where social status is stable, the problem of identity does not exist; and since most Islamic societies are societies in transition, suffering from the identity problem, Khaniki examines the role in which the media could play in this identity information, especially with regards to the youth, of these societies. Taking Iran as a case study, Khaniki argues that in the sensitive process of identity formation, within these societies in transition, the mass media could have constructive or destructive roles. Of course, before being influenced by the mass media, the concept of identity is influenced by those social variables that the media, in one form or another, reflect. The article then goes into detail, explaining these variables in post-revolutionary Iran.

Endnotes:

1 Triston James Mubry - *Modernization, Nationalism and Islam: An examining of Ernest Gellner's writings on Muslim society with reference to Indonesia and Malaysia* in "Ethnic and Racial Studies", No. p.119

2 Ibid

3 Ibid, p.113

4 Manuel Castells - *The Power of Identity*, Blackwell, 1997, pp13-14

5 H.R.H. The Prince of Wales - *Islam and the West*, Oxford Centre for Islamic Studies, 1993, p.9

6 Bahman Bakhtiari - *Cyber Muslim and the Internet: Searching for Spiritual Harmony in the Digital World*, in this book, p.

7 Castells - Opt. cit., p. 6

8 Clifford Geertz - *Religion as a Cultural System: The Interpretations of Cultures*, New York, 1973, p. 90

9 Holy Qur'an, Surah al-Baqarah, Ayah 285

10 Holy Qur'an, 20/120, Cf. The story in the Bible. It is interesting to note that in the Qur'anic version of the story, Eve plays no role between Adam and satan, and it is the temptation for immortality and "a kingdom which decays not" that brings the calamity to Adam and his wife.

11 Ali Paya - *Muslim Identity and Civil Society: Whose Islam? Which Society*, in this book, p.

12 Hamid Enayat - *Seyri Dar Andisheh Siyasi Arab* (A Review of Arab Political Thought), Tehran, 1358 SH, p.20.

13 James P. Piscatori - *Islam in a World of Nation States*, Cambridge University Press, 1986, p.77.

14 Ibid. P.98.

15 Dale F.Eickelman and James Piscatori - *Muslim Politics*, Princeton, 1996, P.27.

16 Sayyid Muhammad Husayn Na'ini - *Tanbih al-Umma wa Tanzih al-Milla*, with a preface by Ayatullah Sayyid Mahmoud Taleqani, p. 98

17 Ibid, p.99

18 Ibid, p.101

19 Ibid, p.102

20 Ibid, p.104

21 Saiyyid Muhammad Husayn Tabatabaie - *Majmua-e Maqalat wa Pursish-ha wa Pasukh-ha*, published by Sayyid Hadi Khosrow Shahi, Dafter-e Nashr-e Farhang-e Islami, Tehran, 1371 SH, p.75

22 Ibid, p.62

23 Ibid, p.70

24 Ibid, p.80

25 Ibid, pp. 80-81

26 Murtedha Mutahhari - *Islam va Moqtaziyat-e Zaman* (Islam and the Needs of the Time), Intesharat-e Sadra, Tehran, 1370 SH, p.11

27 Ibid. p.14

28 Ibid. p.22, on the authority of a *hadith* from the Prophet.

29 Ibid. p.26

[30] Ibid. p.27
[31] Ibid. p.30
[32] Ibid. p.31
[33] *Sahifeye Nur*, vol. 10, p.139
[34] Ibid. vol. 21, p.34
[35] Ibid. vol. 21, p.98
[36] Ibid. vol. 20, pp. 170-171
[37] Ibid. vol. 20, p.174
[38] N.J. Coulson - *A History of Islamic Law*, Edinburgh University Press, pp.224-225
[39] Saiyyid Muhammad Baqer Sadr - *Iqtesaduna* (Persian translation - Abdul Ali Ispehbodi, Intesharat-e Islami, Tehran 1357 SH, vol. 2, p.22
[40] Ibid. p.34
[41] Ibid. p.35
[42] Sahifeye Nour, vol. 21, p.98
[43] Abbas Abdi & Samira Kalhor - *Mabahithi Dar Jame' Shinasi Huquqi Iran*, Intesharat-e Amuzesh-e Inqelab-e Islami, Tehran, 1371 SH, p.74
[44] Ibid. p.75
[45] Castells - opt.ct. p.1.
[46] D. Killner, quoted from S.R. Ameli, *Cultural Globalization and Muslim Identity*, in this book, p.
[47] Castells, opt. ct. p.12.
[48] Daniel Lerner - *The Passing of Traditional Society: Modernizing the Middle East;* New York, Free Press, 1964, p.405.
[49] Ali Paya - *Muslim Identity and Civil Society: Whose Islam? Which Society?*, in this book, p.
[50] H. Mawlana - *Covering Islam: Media and its Impact on Muslim Identity*, in this book, p.
[51] S.Sayyid - *Beyond Westphalia: Nations and Diasporas*, in this book, p.
[52] R. Garaudy, quoted from Castells, opt.cit. p.14.
[53] Piscatori, opt. cit. p.42.

Chapter 1

Muslim Umma

Social Identity According to Islamic Sources

*Mohsen Araki**

Identity occupies a central place in our social system. It helps trace not only Man's anthropological roots but also determines his/her present and future behavioural patterns. Scholars and Men of Literature have attempted to formulate different definitions for *identity*. That denotation which seems most accurate - context-wise - beholds *identity* as an explicitly precise value-system, within which goodness and badness, musts and must not, each are allocated a specific position. It acts as a discriminator between our do's and don'ts - dealing even-handily with both. It is a sort of kaleidoscope, which exhibits human reactions towards blessings and calamities. It is this very *identity*, which shapes our feelings towards other individuals and societies.

Identity inculcates in us the awareness of being individual. It prevents an individual from being an ordinary figure 'drowned' in a crowd of blind followers. It sharpens our judgement and enables us to assess the course of ongoing events from a truly genuine perspective. It helps us clearly distinguish between the 'tyranny of majorities' and the 'righteousness of minorities'.

I believe that the first discernible attempt made to define social *identity*, was by *Amir-al Mu'mineen* 'Ali (peace be upon him), who said:

* Islamic Centre England - London

"يا أيها الناس انما يجمع الناس الرضا والسخط، وانما عقر ناقة ثمود
رجل واحد، فعمهم الله بالعذاب، لما عموه بالرضا، فقال سبحانه:
فعقروها فاصبحوا نادمين" **(خطبة: ٢٠، نهج البلاغة)**

> *O people, certainly, what unites people together (in*
> *categories) is, (their) agreement (to good and bad) and (their)*
> *disagreement. For only one individual killed the camel of Thamud*
> *but Allah held them all in punishment, because all of them joined*
> *him through acquiescence; thus Allah the Glorified, said, 'then*
> *they hamstrung her, and turned themselves regretful.¹*

That which constitutes a society's *identity* (social *identity*) are
criteria which prevail/dominate a society with respect to its
acceptance/agreement or rejection/disagreement, satisfaction or
dissatisfaction - towards good/bad actions - hence formulating its
value-system. This system is not alluding to an existing system of
values, usuallytaken for granted by a people, but it is, rather, referring
to that system which directs the actions of a people (in society),
leading them, *en masse*, towards taking a fortified position - with
respect to that action. This has been further elaborated by *Amir-al
Mu'mineen* 'Ali (peace be upon him),who stated:

"الراضي بفعل قوم كالداخل معهم فيه وعلى كل داخل في باطل إثمان: اثم
العمل به، واثم الرضا به" **(نهج البلاغة، تحقيق صبحي الصالح، ص: ٢١٩)**

> *He, who agrees to the actions of a group of people, is just*
> *like a blind camp-follower; for he commits two sins: one, he does a*
> *wrong thing; and two, he is in agreement with it'².*

One observes from the aforementioned statements - as well as
other Islamic sources which demonstrate the same concept – that
(one's) satisfaction towards a social behaviour is on par with (one)
being in unison with that society i.e. the *identity* and disposition of any
society is shaped by the criteria of (the people's) satisfaction,

dissatisfaction, acceptance, rejection and general stances, taken, with respect to deeds; being acquiescent in matters of social *identity* is tantamount to extending an indirect consent (or tacit acceptance) towards *that* activity which is carried out by the public at large. Even though one may be spatial-temporally distanced from that society, he/she is united with it with regards to social *identity*.

EFFECIENCY OF SOCIAL IDENTITY AND ITS LIMITS

This may be examined from two dimensions:
(i) *vis-à-vis* individual **identity** (in this case, that identity which is in opposition to, or inimical towards, social *identity*) and
(ii) in relation to other social **identities**.

Both these aspects have been the subjects of cardinal analysis within Islamic texts.

EFFICIENCY OF SOCIAL IDENTITY WHEN IN OPPOSITION AGAINST INDIVIDUAL IDENTITY

As for the relationship between social **identity** and individual **identity**, it has been emphasised that the latter can, only, resist the former - by preventing and disabling it from destroying their stronghold - under two circumstances:

(a) by employing means which fortify their position when confronting social *identity*, namely *i'tiradh* (objection) - which has been diversely expressed, as *jihad, amr b'il ma'ruf* (commanding towards goodness)and *nahy ani'l munkar* (forbidding badness), throughout the Holy Qur'an. The primary stage of *i'tiradh* is that of unspoken/unexpressed disapproval whilst its most elevated degree involves institutionalised demonstrations/protestations together with organised propagation and political centralization.

(b) By distancing oneself away from society and deciding to situate oneself within a different social environment - such a concept is denominated as "*Hijrah*" (migration) by the Qur'an.

"فضل الله المجاهدين بأموالهم وانفسهم على القاعدين درجة...
ان الذين توفيهم الملائكة ظالمي أنفسهم، قالوا فيما كنتم؟ قالوا كنا
مستضعفين في الأرض، قالوا: ألم تكن ارض الله واسعة فتهاجروا فيها، فأولئك
مأواهم جهنم وساءت مصيرا، الا المستضعفين من الرجال والنساء والولدان لا
يستطيعون حيلة ولا يهتدون سبيلاً" (القرآن الكريم، سوره النساء: ٩٥ ـ ٩٨)

Allah has made the strivers with their property and their persons to excel the holders back a (high) degree. Surely as for those whom the angels cause to die while they are unjust to their souls, they shall say; in what state were you? They shall say; we were weak in the earth. They shall say: Was not Allah's earth spacious, so that you would have migrated therein? So these it is whose abode is hell, and it is an evil resort;

Except the weak from among the men and the children who have not in their power the means nor can they find a way to escape.[3]

These verses illustrate that when a society's social identity is condemned to corruption and (moral) deterioration, choosing to live within such an environment is tantamount to accepting the prevailing social identity; moreover, one must select one of two ways in order to evade the dissolution of such a social identity i.e. those of objection (*i'tiradh*) and migration (*hijrah*).

I'tiradh makes one resistant and steadfast when in confrontation with the social pressures emanating from a society's corrupt *identity*; and like an impenetrable shield, it secures the individual - as well as individual identity – from the social evil of that identity. In the event of all possible channels/mechanisms, of *i'tiradh*, becoming obviated, *hijrah* becomes the only solution in dealing with the undesired environment.

EFFICIENCY OF A SOCIAL IDENTITY WHEN IN OPPOSITION AGAINST OTHER SOCIAL IDENTITIES

Where two social *identities* are in rivalry - each intending to negate the other and to, subsequently, achieve absolute domination over the other's social foundations – the victorious identity will be that which possesses a more superior, stronger and durable resistance. Clear and profound references on the elements/causes of resistance with respect to the social character of muslims are seen in the Holy Qur'an, Prophetic *ahadith* (narrations) and *Nahj-ul Balagha*; according to the Qur'an and *ahadeeth*, the two essential solid pillars of muslims' social *identity*, or even the identity of all followers of divine civilisations, are portrayed as ideals/aims and they comprise :

1) *Imaan* (faith) and *taqwa* (piety), and
2) Obedience to (divine) leadership.

Amir-al-Mu'mineen *stated:*

"لا يهلك على التقوى سنخ اصل و لا يظمأ عليها زرع قوم"
(نهج البلاغة: خطبة: ١٦)

He who is strong rooted in piety does not suffer destruction, and the plantation of a people based upon piety never remains without water.[4]

The Qur'an reads:

"ولو ان أهل القرى آمنوا واتقوا لفتحنا عليهم بركات من السماء والأرض ولكن كذبوا فأخذناهم بما كانوا يكسبون" (القرآن الكريم: ٧: ٩٦)

*And if the people of the towns had believed and guarded
against evil, We would certainly have opened up for them blessings
from the heaven and the earth, but they rejected, so we overtook
them for what they had earned.⁵*

"الم تر كيف ضرب الله مثلا، كلمة طيبة كشجرة طيبة اصلها ثابت وفرعها في
السماء، توتي اكلها كل حين بأذن ربها ويضرب الله الأمثال للناس لعلهم
يتذكرون. ومثل كلمة خبيثة كشجرة خبيثة اجتثت من فوق الأرض ما لها من
قرار، يثبت الله الذين آمنوا بالقول الثابت في الحياة الدنيا وفي الآخرة، ويضل
الله الظالمين، ويفعل الله ما يشاء" (القرآن الكريم، ١٤: ٢٤ - ٢٧)

*Have you not considered how Allah sets forth a parable
on a good word being like a good tree, whose root is firm and
whose branches are in heaven. Yielding its fruit in every season by
the permission of its Lord? And Allah sets forth parables for men
that they may be mindful. And the parable of an evil word is as
an evil tree pulled up from the earth's surface; it has no stability.
Allah confirms those who believe with the sure word in this
world's life and in the hereafter, and Allah causes the unjust to go
astray, and Allah does what he pleases.⁶*

Directing the believers, the Holy Qur'an recommends:

"ولا تهنوا ولا تحزنوا وانتم الاعلون ان كنتم مومنين"
(القرآن الكريم، ٣: ١٣٩)

*And be not infirm, and be not grieving,
and you shall have the upper hand if you are believers.⁷*

Several verses and narrations have stressed upon this truth that
the purpose behind faith and taqwa is in attaining a practical

stronghold towards the divine ideals and in obeying divine leadership; this truth is illustrated in 2:285:

"آمن الرسول بما انزل إليه من ربه والمومنون كل آمن بالله وملائكته وكتبه ورسله لا نفرق بين أحد من رسله وقالوا سمعنا واطعنا غفرانك ربنا واليك المصير" (القرآن الكريم، ٢: ٢٨٥)

> *The apostle believes in what has been revealed to him from his Lord, and so do the believers; they all believe in Allah and His angels and His books and His apostles; We make no difference between any of His apostles; and they say: We hear and obey our Lord! Thy forgiveness do we crave, and to Thee is the eventual course.*[8]

One can find numerous such examples within the Islamic texts, all of which point to the fact that, that society whose *identity* constitutes faith to ALLAH and obedience towards the commands of divine leaders (and leadership) is, indeed, resistant, fortified and victorious; it shall remain strong even if slightly dispossessed - materially - and victorious, by destiny, throughout life's battle; and, it will eventually grasp the reins of leadership - world-wide – and become the Leader of Mankind.

LEADERSHIP–CRYSTALLISATION OF SOCIAL IDENTITY

According to Islam, leadership is the crystallisation of social *identity*, in any society. Hence, this is the reason why social *identity* is inseparable from the concept of leadership; moreover, this is why - according to Islamic sources – knowledge of one's leader is regarded as a criterion of one's muslim-hood i.e. if one were to die and not know the *Imam* of his/her Era, that person would become void of any Islamic *identity* and would, rather, behold an *identity* of ignorance (*jahili*), or as Islamic terminology terms it, 'an alien *identity*'

The Almighty Allah says in the Qur'an:

"يوم ندعو كل أناس بإمامهم" (القرآن الكريم، ١٧: ٧١)

'Remember the day when We will call every nation through (the identity of) their Imam.[10]

A widely quoted *hadeeth* reads:

"من مات لا يعرف امامه مات ميتة جاهلية"
(اصول الكافي، ج: ١، ص: ٢٧٧) و (صحيح مسلم، ج: ٣، ص: ٢٧، كتاب الامارة) و (مسند احمد بن حنبل، ج: ٤، ص: ٩٦)

The one, who died without having embraced awareness about his Imam, died as ignorant.[9]

Commenting on *Fir'aun*, in the Qur'an , **Allah** notes:

"يقدم قومه يوم القيامة فاوردهم النار" (القرآن الكريم، سوره هود، آية: ٩٨)

"He, on the day of resurrection, will lead his nation-guiding them to the Fire".[11]

There are several other verses and quoted (Islamic) traditions on this subject, highlighting the significance of leadership in Islam .

ISLAMIC SOCIAL IDENTITY

From what has been written, we may conclude the following:

(a) the *identity* of an Islamic society depends on two principles:

(1) Adherence/compliance to Islamic ideals (as laid down in the Holy Qur'an and the *Sunna*), and

2) Obedience towards leadership

(b) Leadership, in Islam, is the crown (and true manifestation) of Islamic *identity* and, hence, the crystallisation of any society's *identity* lies in its leadership.

(c) The *identity* of an Islamic society is inseparable from the Islamic political system; that which is granted to a society with an Islamic identity, is a political system.

(d) Muslim societies become possessors of an Islamic *identity* once they are ruled by a political system and whose government is governed by Islamic aims and ideals - dependent on the concept of *Imamate* - which back up society and the Islamic political system.

Endnotes:

[1] *Nahj-ul Balagha;* Sermon No.201.

[2] *Ibid;* Sermon No. 154.

[3] *Qur'an; Surat al-Nisa,* Verse No. 95—98.

[4] *Nehjul Balagha;* Sermon No.16.

[5] *Qur'an; Surat al-A'raaf,* Verse No. 96.

[6] *Ibid; Surat al-Ibra'heem,* Verse No. 24—27.

[7] *Ibid; Surat A'lay Imra'n,* Verse No. 139.

[8] *Ibid; Surat al-Baqa'ra,* Verse No. 285.

[10] *Qur'an; Surat al-Isra'* , Verse No. 71.

[9] *Hadeeth quoted by Imam Ja'far al Sadiq (a.s.);* For this see, *Usool-e-Ka'fi:* Vol.1, p.371. See also, *Sa'hee Muslim,* Vol.3, p.27. See also, *Mus'neday Ahmad bin Humbul,* Vol.4, p96.

[11] *Ibid; Surat al-Huud,* Verse No. 98.

Beyond Westphalia: Nations and Diasporas

The Case of the Muslim Umma

S. Sayyid*

INTRODUCTION

Even though the nation was invented perhaps only two hundred years ago, as an invention it has proved to be fairly durable and highly mobile. Its durability is manifested by the way in which it has continued to undermine empires and other forms of political community. Its mobility is shown by the way in which it has spread to cover all parts of the planet. Despite its apparent success, however, there are reasons for thinking that the days of the "nation-thing" are numbered. Samuel Huntington's much hyped *Clash of Civilisations* sums up the anxieties about the nation, by arguing that nations are being replaced by quasi-primordial constructs such as civilizations. Despite the problematic nature of defining a civilization, what is clear is that these entities are the manifestations of an "a-national logic". Despite the many difficulties with Huntington's thesis, what is interesting is that there is an implicit recognition of the relationship between the nation and the form that the political has taken. This means that the question of the nation also involves the question of the political itself.

* Department of Sociology, University of East London

The "nation-thing" was conceptualized as a homogenous indivisible body. Recent critiques of the logic of the national have highlighted its empirical deficiencies (multiplicity of identities), its ethical difficulties (the possibility of genocide and totalitarianism) and its theoretical limits (the impossibility of eradicating differences). These studies have been very important in undermining the logic of the national and suggesting a multicultural alternative i.e. a normative stance arising from the recognition and celebration of the variety of cultural forms and practices that exist within the body of the nation. Critics of normative multiculturalism point to the way in which such valorisation may lead to the Balkanisation of the nation.

According to Carl Schmitt, the political is founded upon the distinction between friend and enemy. Schmitt's agnostic notion of the political does not necessarily involve the nation. He, himself, points to the example of how conflict between Muslims and Christians was a political conflict that did not take the form of national conflict. It is fair, however, to note that since the invention of the nation, most political conflicts have taken the national form. Either the conflict has been visualised as a conflict between nations or it has assumed the form of the nation. The reason for this, as Schmitt makes clear, is that for the friend-enemy distinction to operate there must be a capacity for combat (Schmitt, 32). This capacity means that within the political there is the possibility of war as a means of negating the enemy. War is a group activity and since the invention of the nation, it is an activity restricted to the national. The friend-enemy distinction not only constructs the political but also helps to necessitate that the political takes the form of the national. Thus, any attempt to contest the logic of the nation implies a transformation of the political. In other words, the relationship between the Westphalian model of political order and contemporary identity formation requires an examination of the nation and its future. In the rest of the paper, I want to examine this implication by focusing on contemporary Muslim subjectivity.

OVER-STATING THE NATION

The assertion of Muslim subjectivity presents a serious challenge to the idea of the nation. As Manuel Castells writes, '(F)or a Muslim, the fundamental attachment is not to the *watan* (homeland), but to the *Umma*, or community of believers, all made equal in their submission to Allah'.[1] I want to explore the implications of this watan/*Umma* distinction in the next section. Firstly, Castells' reading of Muslim subjectivity reproduces Orientalist and neo-Orientalist accounts of Islam.[2] As a consequence, he positions Islam as an anachronistic presence in today's world, almost a monolith in a world of flows. It is also interesting that he perceives that Muslim identity is articulated in terms of a diffuse Islam rather than a spatially bounded unit.[3] The effect of this is to include Islam as a reaction to the world of flows where 'the search for identity becomes the fundamental source of social meaning'. For Castells, an uncertain world produces crises that require the solitude of "primary identities", be they religious, ethnic, territorial or national. This is interesting because the way in which we have talked about collective identities has relied on the use of stable bounded spaces. Castells' general argument is that, for a variety of reasons, we are now living in a world of flows. He argues that these flows are unsettling because they disrupt the continuities that allowed collective identities to be formed, maintained and projected.

Globalization is one way of summing up the transition to this world of flows. It is a process that is intrinsically linked to the formation of dislocated communities: populations that no longer fit within the Westphalian "container". The container is unable to contain not only because of increased mobility but also because its own walls are becoming blurred. It is possible to identify five main processes which seem to be characteristic of globalization.

- There is the emergence of a nascent global civil society. Not only do we have a proliferation of NGOs which operate across national state boundaries, we are also seeing the beginnings of an attempt to construct a "consensus" on issues such as human rights, economic management, gender issues and so forth... The institutional framework for this consensus is provided by elements that are not restricted to a particular national space; these elements often take on roles such as "intellectual and moral leadership" - often being highly critical of Westphalian notions of state sovereignty.

- The emergence of supranational state-like formations such as the European Union also points to a way in which the Westphalian container is being superseded. One can note similar tendencies in the formation of NAFTA and ASEAN. These "superstate" structures serve to undermine the relationship between national forms and sovereignty. In the European Union, we see the attempt to articulate a pan-European identity which subsumes (to some extent) the national identities of member states.

- The rise of cosmopolitan centres such as London, New York, Paris, Los Angeles, etc. provides the terrain where many of the trends associated with globalization can be manifested. Not only are these world cities nodal points in the international economy, but they are also the spaces from which attempts to articulate a global culture are sited. These global cities are, to a large extent, cut off (or at least have an exceptional relationship with) from the nation-states in which they are situated. In many ways, however, they have a distinct identity.

- The generalisation of the experience of distant travel (whether it takes the form of labour migration, the compulsory movements of refugees or tourism) has created a situation in which very large numbers of people are on the move or have moved. Within this movement, one can trace the implosion of the Western colonial empires as well as the imperatives of the world economy.[4]

- The development and increasing integration of the world political, economy acts to suture disparate economies and societies and, at the same, limit the ability of nation-states (with few powerful exceptions) to regulate their economies.

It is in the context of these processes of globalization, that the need to find a vocabulary to describe political/cultural communities that transcend the limits of the Westphalian model becomes necessary. One such community is that of the Muslims.

THE MUSLIM UMMA

There are three factors that point towards the formation of a Muslim *Umma*. First, there is the phenomenon of the assertion of an explicit Muslim subjectivity. This process has reached all Muslim communities. There are no significant Muslim communities in which visible indicators of the assertion of Muslim subjectivity are absent. Second, Muslims are heavily represented in various immigrant communities throughout the developed world. This has occurred partly because of migration that has been attended upon decolonisation, but it is also the case that since 1979 a large percentage of refugees have been Muslims. Thirdly, like most recent migrants, Muslims have tended to concentrate in urban areas. These areas are in the nodes of the new developing planetary networks (Castells, 1997). The net effect of these developments has been to produce situations in which Muslims from different traditions converge around commonalties. This juxtaposition of various Muslim populations has the effect of producing the conditions for the articulation of a Muslim *Umma*. Islam interrupts the logic of the nation by highlighting the problem of integration – i.e. how to include various populations within the boundaries of a nation, and at the same time it focuses on the problem of their loyalties to an edifice larger than the nation. In other words, Islamism undermines the logic of the nation and at the same time it seeks to transcend the logic of the nation. How can we conceptualize this collective? What kind of a structure is the Muslim *Umma*, which is a community of believing women and men unified by faith and transcending national state boundaries?

The Muslim *Umma*, however, is not the nation writ large. One of the main qualities that distinguishes the nation from other forms of collectives is its limited and restricted nature. The nation is, at best, an enterprise based on an exclusionary universalism. It is a bounded entity - not open to everyone. Thus, the problem of integration has poignancy for the nation in a way that it does not for other groupings. Unlike other formations, the nation does not imagine itself to be a composite or melange. The only universalism that the logic of nation can articulate is one that is based on exclusion rather than inclusion. The universal nation can be an exceptional grouping, an incarnation of all that is considered to be great and good; it can be infinite in a temporal sense but, spatially, it has to be bounded, it cannot expand forever.[5] The idea of the *Umma* rejects all such limits; its universalism and implicit expansionism is constantly reiterated. Clearly, the *Umma* is not a nation.

Nor is the Muslim *Umma* a common market. It has been pointed out many times, despite pious statements that occasionally emerge from organizations such as the ICO, Muslims do not trade with each other, nor do they co-operate with each other about other economic matters. We cannot conceptualize the *Umma* as a structure emanating from economic integration. The unity of the *Umma* is not built upon trading contacts and global networks of labour and capital flows. This is not to deny that such flows exist, as clearly the relationship between the Gulf States and Muslim labour exporting states (such as Egypt, Bangladesh, Pakistan and Yemen) is clearly based on such flows. These flows are not, however, strong enough or extensive enough to suture the *Umma*.

Nor is the Muslim *Umma* a common way of life or a linguistic community. There is no doubt that once upon a time an argument could have been made for the *Umma* to be seen as a collective based around a fairly homogenous, elite culture. Books of *fiqh* collected in Delhi would be commented upon in Madrass in Maghreb. Arabic functioned as the *lingua franca* of the elite. There are still some practices which are uniform among Muslims (e.g. all Muslim pray towards the direction of Mecca), however, it is difficult to conclude from these examples that that which constitutes the unity of the Muslim *Umma* is its uniform way of life. (Of course, it is precisely this idea of a Muslim/Islamic civilization that animates people such as Huntington; nevertheless, like all attempts which conceptualize civilization as an unity, these flounder since they rest upon an eclectic collection of observable and generalised features).[6]

If the Muslim *Umma* is not a nation, a common market or a civilization - is it anything at all? Does not the difficulty of identifying the *Umma* suggest that the idea of a Muslim identity is nothing more than a chimera? Analysts have tended to treat "Muslims" as a phenomenon of other more sturdy bases of identity formations (such as class, kinship, caste and ethnicity). This analytical tendency is not only the product of Orientalism, but also of the way in which nationalist discourses within Muslim communities have served to undermine the idea of a distinct Muslim identity. If Muslim identity is so fragmentary, how can we conceptualize it? One way might be to think in terms of a Muslim diaspora.

REDEMPTION SONGS

Diaspora may be used in a descriptive manner to refer to an empirical situation in which settler communities are relocated from their ordinary homes. Extrapolations from the experience of the Jewish and African diasporas have become templates for the understanding of what constitutes a diaspora. Both involve the forced mass removal of people(s) from a homeland to a place of "exile" and the construction of cultural formations premised on territorial dispersal and political fragmentation. As one study of the impact of diaspora on international relations considers - '(M)odern diaspora are ethnic minority groups of migrant origins residing and acting in host countries but maintaining strong sentimental and material links with their countries of origin - their homeland'.[7] The notion of diaspora rests on three co-ordinates: homeland, displacement and settlement. In other words, a diaspora is constituted when communities of settlers articulate themselves in terms of displacement from a homeland. The homeland acts as a horizon around which the community enframes its collective subjectivities. A diaspora is formed when a people are displaced but continue to narrate their identity in terms of that displacement. For example, the Jewish diaspora is possible because unlike other groups that were deported by various ancient conquerors (Assyrians, Neo-Babylonians...), the Jews managed to maintain their collective identity even when they were territorially displaced and politically subordinated. The pre-condition for diaspora is the articulation of a demotic ethnos (or if you prefer nationalism) that is a mechanism to bind a community in terms of its vertical linkages. This is the reason why diaspora refers to Jewish experiences i.e. because it is one first instance when a demotic notion of *ethnos* was circulating (Smith, Armstrong, 1983). The Jews were not the only people deported *en masse* by the Assyrians and the Neo-Babylonians; that which distinguishes their experience, however, is that they continue to hold on to their Jewishness. The Jewish diaspora is made possible by the development of a proto-nationalism, which prevents its assimilation into other cultural formations.

The idea that nationalism of sorts is a pre-condition for the construction of diaspora is given added credence by the way in which diasporas tend to take the form of the nation (for example, Palestinians, Armenians, Assyrians). In other words, diaspora refers to a nation in exile. The boundaries that the discourse of nationalism draws around a community is that which prevents the dissolution of that community once it is displaced from its locality. Nationalism constitutes both nations and diasporas - that is a peoplehood which is territorially concentrated (nation) and territorially displaced (diaspora).

Such a view of diaspora, however, would only be partially adequate to account for the African diaspora. Of course, there are many examples of nationalist or proto-nationalist discourses among the African diaspora, which correspond very closely to the "classic" definition of diaspora (narratives that are organized around the co-ordinates of a homeland (Africa, Ethiopia), a displacement and a horizon of return either as a redemptive gesture or an empirical possibility). There remains, however, the suspicion that in the case of the African diaspora, we are dealing with a process that is not, simply, a nation in exile. Paul Gilroy's notion of a Black Atlantic suggests a more complicated cultural formation than cannot be adequately described in such terms.

Attempts to broaden the notion of diaspora usually take the form of trying to include another population group alongside the classical exemplars of diaspora. So, for example, there is an attempt to speak of an Irish diaspora or a Greek diaspora and so on. While these accounts seek an empirical enlargement of diaspora, they do little to extend it theoretically. The theoretical weakness of the category of diaspora has been the subject of a recent article by Floya Anthias (1998).[8] I want to draw out some of Anthias' concerns as a prologue to suggesting why it may be helpful to think of the Muslim *Umma* as a diaspora.[9]

Anthias argues that diaspora is another way of bringing essentialised notions of ethnicity in the guise of hybridized and syncretic formations. It is possible to identify three main criticisms that she levies against the current conceptualization of diasporas. Firstly, she feels that diasporas, by focusing on soldarities based on transnational commonalties, inhibit the possibility of intra-national trans-ethnic alliances.[10] Secondly, she believes that diasporas, rather than transcending ethnicity are actually continuations and extensions of ethnic identification.[11] Thirdly, she believes that the focus on diaspora forms part of a post-modern neglect of issues such as gender, class and the internal divisions that the notion of homogenous diasporas covers up.[12] In other words, Anthias contends that the way in which diaspora is commonly used, takes no (or little) account of issues of gender or class and continues to be locked within an ethnicity framework. It is useful to divide these specific criticisms into two main arguments. Firstly, there is a theoretical argument about the nature of identities and their relationship to diasporas and, at the same time, there is a political argument about the way in which valorisations of diasporas undermine the possibility of intra-national co-operation among various ethnicised communities.

I have a number of difficulties with Anthias' discussion primarily because of its contradictory and inadequate theorisation of collective identities. At one point Anthias criticises the way in which writers on diaspora seem to focus on the homogenous nature of ethnic ties, ignoring the way in which these ethnicities are riven by divisions and differences; however, at the same time she argues that class and gender are important dimensions that diasporas do not take into account. Although no one could really disagree with such a position, the problem is that "class" or "gender" are no more cohesive or homogenous than "ethnicities". Ethnic unities maybe class-divided and gendered, but genders maybe ethnicised and class-divided, and classes are gendered and ethnicised... Gender, ethnicity or class, however, are not some kind of "holy" trinity of secularised social science: the spirit of which can be seen behind every other form of social identity (e.g identities based on the profession of faith); they do not exhaust all ways of categorising social identities. It is not helpful to think that these are permanent concepts - the building blocks of collective identities; such a limited deployment of anti-essentialism has the effect of turning all social identities into facades, behind which one can find lurking the "real" identities of class or gender or ethnicity... It is more useful to think that identities are constructed through and through: it's "turtles all the way down".

Any attempt to think about social identities is based on an erasure of internal differences and divisions. In this, ethnicity is not exceptional; all attempts to articulate collective subjectivities (including class or gender) will try and erase its constituent elements in an attempt to produce an organic unity. Anthias seems to be aware of this, but appears to consider it only to be a problem when identity takes the form of ethnicity, rather than being a general phenomenon of identity itself. In other words, the formation of all identities is relational and exclusionary. Identities based on faith, gender, class, culture (or whatever) all have this exclusionary and relational logic. Anthias seems to give the impression that ethnic identities are based on "division and difference" and in that they are somehow different from other forms of identification.

It is the case that the most common notions of diaspora are continuations of the ethnic framework, but it does not follow that other identity frameworks are somehow more real and more permanent than ethnicity. How populations are classified and formed into particular clusters is, ultimately, a political process. All social identities are heterogeneous since they do not have an essence that can guarantee their homogeneity. Thus, it would be impossible to empirically ground the homogeneity of social identities (hence, the various ethnographic studies within the field of ethnic relations will always be able to point to divisions and diversities). Homogeneity is an effect of articulatory practices, an articulation that rests upon exclusion and *not* the uncovering of some deep underlying essence. Having said that, one should not confuse the existence of social identities as being necessitated by some essence. The recognition of the 'in-essential' character of social identities demand that we reject the possibility of all social identities. (Or more problematically, that we maintain that the social identities that we do not agree with are merely fictitious, or that we argue that only those social identities that take particular forms (i.e. are ethnically based) are, in fact, essentialist.[13]

I agree with Anthias when she argues that just because a group of people hail from a particular place does not necessarily mean that they then constitute a "valid sociological category". The validity of sociological categories, however, cannot be the product of a practice external to the process by which identities are articulated. Diasporic identities have significance to the extent to which they appear in difference discursive practices. One has to recognise that diasporic imaginings can have an empowering effect, e.g. Marcus Garvey, Malcolm X ... saw in the possibility of diaspora as a way of "out-flanking" some of the constraints on African-American communities. Similarly, the idea of Muslim subjectivity within North Atlantic plutocracies, owes to the possibility of making links between and beyond the sites in which Muslim settler communities have been ghettoised.

Further, I would agree with Anthias when she makes a distinction between diasporas which are simply extensions of ethnic frameworks, and diasporas as conditions (this is a distinction that I also find useful). While I agree with much of her criticisms relating to the difficulty of conceptualizing diasporas as a condition, I do not think that the attempt is so flawed that it needs to be abandoned in favour of a "valid sociology". What is required is to attempt to articulate diasporas as political formations in the context of the erosion of the Westphalian order. In the case of the Muslim experience (which like all collectives' experiences is riddled with division and diversity - but which still forms a unity) the category of diaspora as extended ethnicity is inadequate. While it is the case that there are many Muslims living as minorities throughout the world,

the idea of a diaspora demands both a displaced population and a
homeland - the point from which the displacement originates.[14] Such
a homeland is clearly lacking in the Muslim case. We Muslims do not
have a Zion - a place of redemptive return.   Moreover, the
Universalist urge within many Muslim discourses makes it difficult to
locate a unitary point of origin, and so there *is* no homeland,
imagined or otherwise.   In addition, there is no founding act of
displacement. The Muslim *Umma* is not only reducible to displaced
population groups but also includes the Muslim population in
Muslim countries. It is for this reason, therefore, that the notion of
diaspora seems an unlikely metaphor for describing the Muslim
Umma. Thus to read the Muslim experience as diasporic requires the
reconceptualizion of the notion of diaspora from demographic to
political. Given these limitations, I would like to suggest another way
of understanding diaspora.   It is possible to expand the idea of
diaspora beyond its descriptive core and there are a number of
notions implicit in the descriptions of diaspora that would allow us to
re-consider the idea of diaspora as a political formation.

DIASPORA AS AN ANTI-NATION

Earlier I made the point that diasporas were dependent upon
the discourse of nationalism. It would be difficult to construct a
diaspora without a form of nationalism. The idea that a diaspora is a
nationalist phenomenon is, however, not the only way in which this
phenomenon has been described.   Diasporas have also been
considered as *anti*-national phenomena. Unlike the nation with its
homogeneity and boundedness, diaspora suggests heterogeneity and
porousness. Nations define "home", whereas diaspora is a condition
of homelessness; within the nation, the territory and people are
fused, whereas in a diaspora the two are dis-articulated. The diaspora
is not the other of the nation simply because it is constructed from
the anti-thetical elements of a nation, it is, rather, an anti-nation since
it interrupts the closure of a nation.   The existence of a diaspora
prevents the closure of a nation since a diaspora is, by definition,
located within another nation.

The Jewish experience of diaspora acts as an illustration of the anti-national character of diaspora. Hannah Arendt shows how the *parvenu/pariah* distinction underwrote Jewish integration into European society during the period up to the Second World War and its aftermath. Arendt argues that Jews had two main subject positions open to them. One was based on assimilation. That is, the Jew became part of the "host" society as an exceptional Jew. Somehow, one was a Jew in an exotic sense but, at the same time, was not a Jew. The other option available was that of total alienation. A Jew who was totally distinct from the "host" did not belong to that society. The figures of *parvenu* or *pariah*, both, have problematic relationships with the idea of the nation, as both suggest that the nation is not home. The nation is not the place in which one's identity finds affirmation through the daily mundane rituals of life. The *parvenu* as a figure of obscure origins and recent recognition is a figure who is not settled. She arrives from an unknown place, she gains prominence without trace and she is clearly an exception to the rest of her "race". The *pariah*, as a figure, is clearly and unambiguously someone who is not at home i.e. an outcast. Arendt's reflections on the relationship between identity and belonging, after Nazism, point to the importance of the notion of home as a way in which the nation sutures the subject. It is the nation, as home, that acts as an arena for our everyday practices - practices that provide focus and meaning. If identity is "a way of life" then the nation, by providing a home, is the stage upon which a particular way of life is enacted.

Those without homes face the prospect of trying to enact their "way of life" off-stage. This is a task that they can only accomplish by using either a strategy of alienation and thus becoming a pariah, or by using a strategy of assimilation and thus being considered parvenu. In this sense, those members of a diaspora have a paradoxical relationship to the nation. On the one hand, they demonstrate the possibility of the strength of a nation in their attempt to maintain the sense of nationhood in the context of territorial dispersal; on the other hand, they point to the inability of a nation to be complete by making it difficult to erase differences. It is in this sense that the notion of diaspora is deployed as the anti-thesis of the nation.

Members of a diaspora have an undecidable relationship with the idea of nations and homes. For example, Arendt's opposition to Israeli statehood, stemmed from the privileging of "Jewish homelessness" which allowed Jews to escape the blinkers of belonging to a single nation. In other words, the condition of homelessness is seen as a way of escaping the limits of ethnocentrism. Similarly, Gilroy evokes the Black Atlantic as countering both what he perceives to be the cultural absolutism of black nationalism and closure of the Western project. The Black Atlantic emerges as the name of a space that inhabits the West and that also transcends it. This use of diaspora as anti-nation, as a presence which subverts, hyphenates and hybridises national identity, points to the impossibility of constituting a nation.

It is this undecidability that Arendt privileges in her account of the Jewish experience. Similarly, Gilroy in his description of the Black Atlantic makes an appeal to the experience of the African diaspora as constituting a marginal (undecidable) position within Western modernity - being in the West but not of the West. Both Arendt and Gilroy see in the possibility of "not-quite being a nation", a position that subverts absolutism. In these nations of homelessness there is a certain pathos. Homelessness suggests the possibility of being hyphenated and hybridised. If we understand a diasporic formation as being an anti-nation, then it becomes clear that what is involved in a diaspora is the de-concentration of power and subjectivity. In other words, the concept of diaspora dis-articulates the relationship between the political and the national. The nation focuses power and subjectivity; it makes the national subject the locus of power. Diaspora problematises the possibility of establishing a relationship of coherence between power and subjectivity. What is of critical importance in the formation of a diaspora is the extent to which power and subjectivity are dispersed. This suggests that in many ways, diaspora do not require the trinity of displacement, settlement and homeland. From this perspective, it would be possible to conclude that we are living in an age in which nations are being replaced by diaspora - that is the dream of homogenous, hermetically-contained spaces is being replaced by the idea of hybridised, porous collectives that flow and overflow through any attempt to contain them. However, I would suggest that such an understanding fails to acknowledge the nature of diasporic logic and fails to acknowledge the unevenness by which nations are transformed into diasporas.

The logic of diaspora is paradoxical. On the one hand it emphasises the possibility of a nation, even, in the most difficult circumstances where the Westphalian order does not apply. On the other hand, it suggests the impossibility of a nation - by preventing the nation from being fully formed and by deferring the moment of closure and absolutism.

If diasporas are nations without homes, then the process of homelessness is not generalised; some nations are less likely to be homeless than others. If homelessness is a consequence of the way in which relations of power and collective subjectivities are dis-articulated, then this process is intrinsically political. It is a reflection of broader global struggles. A flavour of these struggles can be gleaned from recent publications such as *Jihad Vs McWorld.*

MCDONALDS AT MECCA: BEING AT HOME IN THE WORLD

In this book, Benjamin Barber makes a distinction between the forces of global disintegration captured in the banalized idea of *Jihad* and the idea of global integration represented by the metaphor of an American fast-food chain. This dichotomy tends to suggest two different conceptions of the articulation of power and collective subjectivity. One, the road of *Jihad* suggests the prospects of "retribalization" and Balkanisation: a global Hobbesian war against all, in which narrow particularities rage against modernity, against technology, against pop culture and against integrated markets - against the future itself. The road of *Jihad* seems to point to an attempt to assert nationhood (i.e. ideas of collectivities bound by cultures of authenticity and the exclusion of the possibility of heterogeneity).

In opposition to the idea of *Jihad*, we have McWorld a place of 'shimmering pastels, a busy portrait of onrushing economic, technological and ecological forces that demand integration and uniformity and that mesmerise peoples everywhere with fast music, fast computers, and fast food - MTV, and McDonald's - pressing nations into one homogenous global theme park, one McWorld tied together by communications, information, entertainment, and commerce' (Barber, 1995).

Although this global theme seems to promise heterogeneity, the form that this globality takes excludes that very possibility. In other words, the homogeneity associated with McWorld is culturally marked and, as such, it is more like the homogeneity associated with "narrow particularism" writ large rather than an escape from particularisms. In this sense, McWorld is the latest trope in the history of exclusionary universalism that has characterised the Western enterprise. As Geyer and Bright (1995) point out, it is this strange mixture of universalism and exclusion that has underwritten the West's relationship to the Rest and it continues to do so. McWorld is based on the domestication of difference and its reduction to superficialities. Underlying the diversity of surface effects, is the idea of homogeneity founded upon the recognition that underneath our cultural skins we are all the same. The form this sameness reflects is our common unity based our being humans. This makes possible our concerns for the "starving" in the Third World, it makes possible our demand and extension of human rights across the planet. It is only by focusing on our common humanity can we avoid the tribalism promised by the advocates of *Jihad.* The snag with this comforting vision is that the notion of what the common human is - together with what constitutes those values and beliefs that arise from our common humanity and those that are incidental to essential humanness - tend to correspond, also, with the boundaries of the Enlightenment project. In other words, features that arise from common humanity, too, often become conflated with features associated with a particular cultural formation. Thus, the West becomes the only place where a human can be truly human, freed from the veneers of superstition and retrograde cultural practices: humans can express their humanness. This conflation between what is essentially Western with what is essentially human, is what excavates the heterogeneity from the globalization of McWorld. McWorld emerges, not as "rainbow" formation where all human cultures find a home, but, rather, as an attempt to make the whole world a home for one way of life, one cultural formation. The difference between McWorld and *Jihad* comes down to matter of scale rather than content, for both projects seem to be about making the world familiar i.e. making the world a home.

If, as a Believer (female or male), you go on *haj*, you may travel to the Red Sea port of Jeddah, from there you will take the road that has taken many believers, before, to the Holy City. The road leads up to the *Haram*, opposite the *Haram* there is an air-conditioned shopping mall - inside the shopping mall, the weary pilgrim who comes from far away will find a McDonalds fast-food restaurant. Like any other shopping mall in any other city - you are never far from a McDonalds. If the city that will not admit any others than believing women and believing men, will admit a McDonalds - is not the world already lost to the Believers?

Of course, it is possible to argue that the establishment of fast-food chains does not really tell us very much about the ways in which global, cultural identities are being transformed. If chicken tikka masala can emerge as one of Britain's most popular dishes, then the appearance of a McDonalds chain in Mecca is equally insignificant. Why consider McDonalds to be more of a sign of cultural imperialism than General Motors or Sony? Is it really possible to make such sharp distinctions between those goods that are considered to be the carriers of cultural values and aspirations and those that are mute on this point? Surely, we have seen that even the Taliban came to recognise that it was not 'television' that was demonic or Western, since once they captured Kabul and they began to broadcast their own programmes, their attitude to television had changed.

The most common way in which a particular form or cultural object is given a specific identity is by privileging its moment of origin. Thus, invention is often the moment at which an identity is attached. The problem with such an approach is that it tends to confuse historiography with history. For example, most accounts of democracy see the process beginning in Ancient Greece (Athens being the model), developing in Europe and finally reaching its fullest form in the North Atlantic plutocracies. Such a sequence ignores the arbitrariness of constructing an origin from many beginnings and it ignores the possibility of other kinds of narratives that could reconstruct democracy as originating from other sites (for example, Sumerian city-states). As the furore over *Black Athena* suggests, the idea of specific historical trajectories is important in establishing the identities of forms and objects. I want to suggest that one sign of being at home is that the narratives that tell tales of origins are also narratives that project one's identity backwards. In other words, being at home means the world is familiar to us, because it institutions, rules and its complex web of relations are the same discursive productions that articulate our identities in terms of being 'at home'. There is then a sense of belonging that is produced through various hegemonic discursive practices. Being at home becomes a condition of the way in which these hegemonic narratives seem to be products of the articulation of our identity. In other words, it is not that hegemonic practices are considered to produce our identity, but that it is when our identity is manifested in those hegemonic practices that we can be considered to be at home. That is, when the world seems to be our mirror.

What I am suggesting is that being at home is no longer simply an empirical experience of the kind that is argued becomes rarer as international movement becomes further restricted due to tighter immigration controls. Just because the movement of people is becoming rarer, does not mean that more people are settled. The process of globalization is an attempt to make a home for some. This settlement implies that others have to be unsettled. In other words, does the re-deployment of the Westphalian order and notions of diaspora on a planetary scale, transform the rules by which we could conceive of diaspora as merely "ethnic minorities" harking back to the lands of their origins? Diaspora is a condition of being homeless - that is of being displaced and territorially diffused. But if this process is global then the only way one can maintain the idea of a diaspora is to make effects of global displacement specific rather than general. Global displacement is not a culturally neutral activity: the process of globalization imposes displacement upon some cultural formations by settling other cultural formations. This means that the logic of diaspora has a cultural specificity (arising out of current historical circumstances). The logic of diaspora includes those who are articulated as homeless in this world. That is, for whom the global hegemonic order is not an echo of their subjectivity. The logic of diaspora is then not simply an interpretation of the logic of the nation, it is also an interpretation of the global hegemonic order: the logic of diaspora is culturally marked. It is cultural marking which prevents the logic of diaspora becoming simply a synonym for an anti-nation. The logic of diaspora is not only anti-national, but in present circumstances, when a particular national formation takes a global form, it also becomes anti-global.

In other words, the logic of diaspora cannot escape the most fundamental distinction i.e. the distinction between the West and the Rest. It is this distinction that underpins the post-Colombian world. Attempts to overcome the West/Rest distinction by pointing to empirical multiculturalism (that is the existence of many cultures and the impossibility of thinking of one culture) and valorising hybridity (the normative celebration of multiculturalism) fail because they ignore the way in which the West/Rest distinction is played out as the distinction between the hegemonic and subaltern and between the culturally unmarked and culturally marked. In the rest of this paper I want to see to what extent this diasporic logic can help us to locate the Muslim *Umma*.

THE UMMA AND DIASPORIC LOGICS

Earlier, I argued that the Muslim *Umma* could not be seen as a nation or common market or a civilization. It can be argued that since the abolition of the Caliphate in 1924, the Muslim *Umma* has been increasingly parcelled out into "nations"- which while consisting of Muslims are not a reflection of a Muslim subjectivity (Sayyid, 1997: 52-83). The nationalisation of the Muslim *Umma* took place in two distinct domains. First, there is development of nationalism within the Ottoman Empire that helped to undermine the Ottoman State. This nationalism had two distinct phases. One was the phase when non-Muslim minorities within the Ottoman Empire began to demand rights of national determination. The second phase was the development of nationalism among the Muslim communities of the Empire. These communities began to identify themselves as Turks and Arabs rather than Muslims and, as a result, the "a-national" logic of Islam had replaced the national logic. In this set of circumstances, nationalism emerged in clear opposition to Islam. The second arena for the development of nationalism was among the Muslim subjects of the European Empire. Decolonisation often took the form of struggles of national liberation in which nationalism was articulated in opposition to European imperialism and thus its relationship to Islam was more ambivalent. Both these forms of nationalisation raise doubts about what exactly the Muslim *Umma* is. It is not clear what kind of relationship is constitutive of the Muslim *Umma*, in other words, what kind of networks or interactions would have to exist for us to accept that there was a Muslim *Umma* and that it had an existence that was not merely rhetorical. There are three main reasons why many consider the idea of Muslim *Umma* to be little more than an exercise in wish fulfilment.

Firstly, it is pointed out that political projects based on the discourses of Muslim subjectivity have failed to make any headway in the Muslim *Umma*. The nationalist regimes of *Dar-ul-Islam* continue and the Islamists have been unable to dis-lodge them even in Algeria or Egypt. The hegemony of the "moderates" in post-Khomeini Iran, is further evidence that even the regime most clearly identified with the articulation of a transnational Muslim subjectivity has retreated from its support of the idea of unified Muslim *Umma*.[15]

Secondly, arguments regarding the integration of Muslim communities into the global economy are seen as signs of the waning significance of Muslim identity. For example, it is argued that the Islamist rejection of modernity flies in the face of the desire of Muslims to have television, Coca-Cola, 501 Levi's, McDonalds, etc.[16] Thirdly, it is argued that any idea of the Muslim *Umma* is undermined by internal conflicts between Muslims. For example, the war between Iraq and Iran, Iraq's invasion of Kuwait, sectarian conflict in Pakistan and even among Muslim communities living in the North Atlantic plutocracies.

These ideas of what should constitute a Muslim *Umma* tend to under-theorise what exactly is involved in the construction of a collective identity. For example, the idea that unless there is total agreement among Muslims, it is impossible to think of a unified Muslim presence would seem to suggest that a unified collective is only possible in conditions of unanimity; that is, a set of conditions in which there should be no possibility of a friend-enemy distinction and the impossibility of the political. Not only is such a set of affairs unlikely to be found among Muslims, it is debatable if they can be found in other cultures or societies. The lack of unanimity does not prevent us for deploying the category of Europe, even though in the last 100 years, intra-European conflicts have been responsible for over 50 million deaths. Muslim unity is, thus, possible in the absence of unanimity.

The notion of diaspora that I am advocating for the Muslim is not based on ethnicity (in the form of a common descent from an originary homeland), nor it merely "metaphoric" in the sense of trying to come to terms with the mis-match between peoples and places. I do not make the claim that Muslim identity is organic, but I do argue that for various reasons it is the subject position, that currently has greater prominence than other forms of identification for those who describe themselves or are described by others as Muslims.[17] I am also aware that there are many among those who would be constituted as Muslims, who would reject the political significance of that appellation and who would refuse to accept the idea that there is Muslim *Umma*. The idea of the Muslim *Umma* is an attempt to come to terms with the limits and the crisis of the nation-state. As forces and developments associated with globalization have weakened the institutional rigidity of the Westphalian State, cracks and gaps began to appear in the international state system that provided terrain for politics. Given the mobile and constructed nature of social identities, these fissures within dominant institutional forms of the nation-state- have allowed different kinds of collectives to be articulated, taking advantages of these gaps.[18] These formations seep through the Westphalian edifice, creating political formations that are neither in nor out of the nation-state but that have an undecidable relationship to it. In this sense, diaspora is the name of this undecidable political formation.

This logic of diaspora suggests an attempt to create a full subjectivity in the form of the nation in the context of when the nation cannot be completed. The Muslim *Umma* also points to a political project which, if it had been successful, would produce a cultural formation which would be as remarkable or unremarkable as Chinese or European but which would remain open - unable to construct itself around an ontological premise. The nationalisation of the *Umma* was an attempt to destroy the possibility of the Muslim *Umma* as a universal cultural formation. Processes associated with globalization have lead to the de-nationalisation of peripheral nation-state forms at the same time as the expansion of central nations. The Muslim *Umma* occupies an undecidable position. As it is clearly located within the periphery, it is subject to a process of de-nationalisation - but this de-nationalisation opens up the possibility of the re-configuration of a cultural formation that is less and less particular and more and more universal. The inability of the Muslim *Umma* to fully articulate itself as universal means that it is caught in the logic of diaspora. The *Umma* interrupts and prevents the nation of finding closure and at the same time it points to another nation that will come into being at some point in the future. In this, the *Umma* is becoming - it is a horizon as well as an actuality. The current world is characterised by two types of de-centring. There is the de-centring of the West that marks the end of the Age of Europe and there is the de-centring of the peripheral nation-state that is associated with globalization. It is in this nexus between these two forms of de-centring that we can locate the Muslim *Umma*, and it is this location which gives its diasporic form.

        I would like to thank Hatoon Al-Fassi, Nasreen Ali, Barnor Hesse, Panedeli Glavanis and Laura Turney for their help with this paper. I am also grateful to the University of Manchester's Faculty Research Fund for supporting the project on "Globalisation and the State: The Challenge of Political Islam."

Endnotes:

[1] Castells, 1997: 15.

[2] Castells places Islamist movements within the genre of religious fundamentalism and suggests that religious fundamentalism has been present "throughout human history". While, we should not take this hyperbole too literally, it is clear that Castells' definition of fundamentalism has been taken without reservation from the flawed "Fundamentalism Observed" Project, which sees fundamentalism as a species of dogmatism that has been a constant in human history. Following this observation, Castells argues that "Islamic identity is constructed on the basis of a "double deconstruction" (ibid.15) in which subjects must deconstruct themselves as national citizens or ethnic groups and "(W)omen must submit to their guardian men". Castells refers to (surah IV, v.34) as a way of justifying this claim. Of course, it is equally possible to pluck other verses from the Qur'an to demonstrate that the Qur'an is one of the few sacred texts that makes continual and frequent references to "believing men and women", "believing woman and man", and so on.

[3] Castells also seems to conflate Ali and Hussein, by giving the date of Ali's assassination as the date of Hussain's martyrdom.

[4] The collapse of the Soviet Union and the attendant population movements being the latest episode of Western decolonisation.

[5] Even the United States, which many would consider to be the most universal of nations, endeavoured to fulfil its manifest destiny - a destiny that was still bounded by the oceans.

[6] See Hodgon's discussion of the difficulties of identifying civilizations.

[7] Sheffer, 1986: 3.

[8] Given our very different epistemological starting points, rather than engage in point-by-point analysis of Anthias's argument, it seems that what I should do is tell a more general story that will by-pass the points that Anthias makes and, at same time, make clear why I think that the notion of diaspora is useful for understanding the current status of the Muslim *Umma*.

[9] Of course, one of the difficulties of someone like me engaging with someone like Anthias is that we belong to different epistemological tribes, we anti-foundationalists do not share the confidence in the neat separations that fundamentalist foundationalists have in positivist sociological categories, nor do we think that we can legislate the use of "sociological categories".

[10] Anthias, 1998, 577.

[11] ibid: 558, 563, 568, and 576.

[12] ibid: 558, 560, 564.

[13] This one-sided anti-essentialism is fairly common, for a critique of this tendency see Sayyid, 1998.

[14] As Anthias, correctly points out. See Anthias, 1998: 561.

[15] See for example, Roy, 1994.

[16] See Sayyid, 1997.

[17] Mandaville, 1998: 19. Mandaville's paper is an insightful overview of some the consequences of the erosion of the Westphalian order within the International Relations community.

Muslims of Asia:
With special reference to China and Chinese Central Asia

*Michael Dillon**

INTRODUCTION: The historical spread of Islam through Asia

Islam spread through Asia, initially, in the wake of the conquering Arab armies, as they marched into Persia, Afghanistan, Central Asia and the Indian sub-continent and later, by the overland and ocean trading routes often known as the Silk and Spice routes that took merchants and their faith to the easternmost points of mainland and island Asia. Arab armies marching eastwards overland had conquered Transoxania (the region of Bukhara and Samarkand) by the 8th century and were only prevented from pushing further eastwards into China by the massive physical barrier of the Tianshan and Pamir mountain ranges which today mark the border between China and the Central Asian republics of the former Soviet Union.[1] In the steppes of Central Asia and the plains of northern China, Islam encountered peoples and cultures of great diversity, from the Turkic nomads to the peasant farmers and confucian scholars of China; and Muslim identities in the region, today, reflect the diversity of the cultures with which Islam came into contact.

---

* University of Durham

In the West, and particularly in the United Kingdom with its colonial ties to South Asia and immigration from the region, the best known contemporary Muslim communities of Asia are probably those of Pakistan, India and Bangladesh. They are so well known that they will be considered only briefly here in spite of their unquestionable importance in the world of Islam as there are many Muslim communities from other parts of Asia who have been neglected in the west, often because their fate has remained little known because of geographical or political isolation. It is a strange fact that the term Asian in the United Kingdom is used almost exclusively to refer to citizens who have family ties with South Asia. Why this does not irritate members of the Chinese, Vietnamese, Filipino and other communities, more than it does, is something of a mystery.

SOUTH ASIA

There is certainly diversity in that part of Islam that lies within the Indian Sub-continent - whether it is the paths of Islam that are followed or the languages and cultures of Muslims but coexistence has been more difficult. The greatest divide is perhaps that between the eastern and western parts of Pakistan, formed as a united Muslim nation in the bitter partition of 1947, but divided after the war between India and Pakistan in 1971 and, in 1974, Pakistan and Bangladesh finally recognised each other as independent states. This division between two Muslim states has a certain logic if one takes into account, as well as the geographical separation, the historical, cultural and linguistic differences between the two – Urdu in the West with its great overlap with the Hindi language but preference in writing for the Persi-Arabic script that is closest to the script used for the Qur'an; and Bengali or Bangla in the East using a script derived from the Devanagari script of Hindi and Sanskrit.

INDONESIA

There is also growing awareness in the West of the role of Islam in Indonesian society (and to a lesser extent in Malaysia although this will not be discussed here). Indonesia now has a population approaching 200 million and is, consequently, one of the most significant Muslim societies in the world. Before the advent of Islam, in the late thirteen century, the territory had derived much of its culture from India. In particular, Hindu and Buddhist religious influences were very important and these are still noticeable throughout the Indonesian archipelago but especially in the island of Bali which never fully accepted Islam. Islam travelled to Indonesia along the sea trading routes of the Indian Ocean, taking root at first in northern Sumatra where there was a thriving trade with India. Although there is some controversy about the precise region of India which influenced Indonesia Islam, there is a strong case for supposing that it might have been the maritime region of Gujerat whose Muslim merchants had established a trading post in Perlac on the northern coast of Sumatra in the thirteenth century.[2]

The islands of Indonesia gradually came under Dutch influence after the Dutch East India Company opened them to trade in the seventeenth century. Indonesia, known then as the Dutch East Indies, was firmly established as a Dutch colony during the nineteenth century and remained so until the Second World War when it was conquered, like so much of Asia, by the Japanese. After the war, independence from the Dutch was achieved but the impetus for this was secular nationalism influenced by Marxism rather than Islam. Indonesia was ruled by nationalists under its founding father President Sucarno until an attempted coup d'etat in 1965 led to the intervention of the army and the Sucarno was replaced by Suharto who remained in power, supported by the military, until his downfall in 1998.[3] Under Suharto's authoritarian rule, Indonesia's Islamic identity has been reinforced, and, with the growth of Islamic village schools and associations there is talk of a new Islamic Century in the archipelago.[4]

CHINA AND CENTRAL ASIA

Much less is known in the West, or indeed in the rest of the Islamic world about the Muslims of Chinese Central Asia and China and it is these communities which will therefore be the main focus of the remainder of this paper.

Central Asian culture, whether in the former Soviet Union or in Xinjiang, remains relatively unknown outside a small circle of specialists as it was subsumed for over a century into a generalised imperial Russian, and later Soviet, culture. Russian became both the official and the everyday working language of the empire and, subsequently, the whole Soviet Union, for all practical purposes, and displaced but did not eliminate - many of the minority languages. There was no encouragement to the Central Asian Muslims to retain their traditional languages and cultures as these were closely connected with Islam and Islam was seen as a major threat, both by the imperial Russian state which was based on the Orthodox Church and its successor, the Soviet Union, which promoted atheism. Central Asian cultures were severely damaged by the process of Russification carried out under the Tsars and under the Communist Party.

After the October Revolution of 1917 and the Bolshevik victory in the civil war which followed, the Union of Soviet Socialist Republics (USSR) was established in 1923, and it lasted until the coup against Michail Gorbachev in 1991. During this period, known as the Soviet era, the Moscow-based government of the Communist Party consistently disregarded and underplayed all the ethnic and religious differences of the USSR in the hope of creating a uniform Soviet culture, which was effectively an authoritarian form of Russian culture imposed on the non-Russian population of the Soviet Union. After the collapse of Soviet power in 1991, the persistence of Muslim traditions in the Turkic and Tajik speaking republics of Central Asia came as a great surprise to many outsiders. It rapidly became clear that Islam had survived in spite of the pressures from the atheist state and the role of Islam has become a key issue in the emergence of the new states and societies of Central Asia.[5]

In China, Muslim communities may have been established as early as the eighth century, but the majority trace their ancestry to the

Mongol conquests of Central Asia in the thirteenth century. One group of Muslims, mostly living in the north western region of China known to the Chinese as Xinjiang but to many of the inhabitants as Eastern Turkistan, have a cultural identity similar to their neighbours in the former Soviet Union, but there is a large group known as the Hui or Huihui who are Chinese speaking Muslims of mixed Central Asian and Chinese descent. There is a heavy concentration of Hui people in north western China, but there are also Hui people with their mosques and community organizations spread throughout the country. Because of frequent religious and political conflicts with the Chinese authorities over the centuries they have coexisted with their Chinese neighbours and have often given the appearance of having been assimilated completely into Chinese culture and society; however, the persistence of a distinctive Muslim Chinese identity became clear in the 1980s onwards when the control of central government was relaxed after the death of Mao Zedong and a rapid program of building and rebuilding mosques and shrines was initiated.

North western China has had a complex history as the ancient remains - that are still visible today throughout the whole territory – testify; and it is a perfect example of a region where diverse Muslim communities have lived alongside each other and with their non-Muslim neighbours. The degree of coexistence has varied: times of peace have alternated with periods of terrible carnage. Over the centuries, the north west has been home to speakers of the Tibetan, Turkic, Mongolian and Chinese language families. Evidence of Manichaean, Nestorian Christian and Buddhist beliefs that preceded Islam survives in works of art such as the Buddhist cave shrines of Maijishan in the south of Gansu province and the cave paintings of Bezeklik, just off the road from Urumqi to Turpan in Xinjiang, just as it does in Afghanistan and other parts of Central Asia. The haunting ruins of the ancient cities of Gaochang and Jiaohe, in the Turpan basin, are a permanent reminder of the ancient pre-Islamic civilizations that flourished in this region. It was in this intricate cultural, religious and ethnic matrix that many of the important developments in Islam, in China, had taken place. This is the part of China that is nearest to the lands of Central Asia and Middle East

where Chinese Islam had its origins and in many ways the existence
of these communities can be regarded as an extension of mainstream
Central Asian culture (as in the present-day states of Uzbekistan,
Turkmenstan, Tajikstan, Kyrgystan and Kazakstan) into China.

Xinjaing, (or Eastern Turkestan as it is known to many of its
indigenous people), which is the largest administrative unit of north-
western China, has been under the control of the Chinese state since
the Manchu Qing dynasty extended its reach westward in the
eighteenth century under the rule of the powerful emperor Qianlong.
It is clearly Central Asian rather than Chinese in language, religion
and culture and the neighbouring Chinese regions of Gansu, Qinghai,
Nixgxia and Shaanxi have also been profoundly affected by Central
Asian civilization.

ETHNIC DIVERSITY AND COEXISTENCE IN CHINA AND CHINESE CENTRAL ASIA

Some explanation of the use of the term Muslim as used in
this paper, and by the Chinese authorities, is necessary. Since the
People's Republic of China was established in October 1949, there
has been no systematic attempt by the state to calculate the number
of followers of Islam, or, indeed, any other religion. For much of the
period since 1949, it was state and party policy to promote atheism
and suppress or ignore religions, which were regarded as feudal and
medieval superstitions. This uncompromising approach was modified
in more liberal times, notably since 1979, to allow the limited
expression of religious beliefs provided that these did not conflict
with the interests of the state. This was primarily a concession to the
rights of ethnic minorities and their beliefs rather than a positive
attitude towards religious freedom. Although religious leaders in
China have their own estimates of the number of their followers,
they do not have the resources that the state has at its disposal to
compile statistics. State organizations have kept records of the
population of different ethnic minority groups in line with the
nationalities policy that the Chinese Communist Party inherited from
the Soviet Union under Stalin. Ten nationalities (*minzu* in Chinese)

have been identified as Muslim, either because of their tradition and culture or their current religious adherence, and Chinese accounts of Muslims use the term in that context. In a sense, the Muslim identity can be considered to have been a hidden identity, masked by ethnic divisions.

The degree to which China's Muslims would be considered pious believers by the rest of the Islamic world varies greatly. There are Imams and their loyal followers in the mosques whose practices are the same as orthodox Muslims anywhere in the Islamic world and there are also devoted members of secretive Sufi brotherhoods who remember Allah through chanting and dancing. There are also Communist Party cadres from the ethnic groups designated as Muslim who were at least officially atheist and there are many people who fall somewhere between the two categories.

There are various criteria for assigning individuals and communities to the officially recognised ethnic groups in China, but one important one is the language that they speak. Six of the ten Muslim ethnic groups whose members live mainly in the Xinjiang Autonomous region (known also as Eastern Turkestan to many non-Chinese) are the Uyghurs, Kazakhs, Kyrgyz, Uzbek and Tatars, all of whom speak a language from the Turkic family, and the Tajiks whose tongue is related closely to Persian. In the region that borders Gansu and Qinghai provinces, there are three smaller Muslim groups: the Salars, the Bao'an and the Dongxiang. The Salars speak a Turkic language which some consider to be merely a dialect of Uyghur and the Bao'an and Dongxiang languages are archaic forms of Mongolian, all heavily influenced by Chinese through centuries of contact. Of all the Muslim ethnic groups, perhaps the most intriguing are the Hui, who are predominantly Chinese speakers. Such is the diversity of Muslim communities that coexist in north western China and although they are very anxious to be identified as Muslims, they also strongly identify themselves as members of their ethnic groups.

Hui: The term Hui, or sometimes Huihui, has been used in different periods as both the name of an ethnic group and as a description of religious adherence, simply meaning Muslim, and it is not always clear from the sources which is meant. In contemporary China, it is a category which includes all Muslims not otherwise identified as Uyghur, Kazakh etc. Unlike other Muslim groups, they have settled all over China in large numbers and can be found in every province and almost every town and city. However, there are significant concentrations of Hui people in two regions of north western China: in Gansu province where an area to the west of the capital, Lanzhou, is designated the Linxia Hui Autonomous Prefecture; and in Ningxia, once part of Gansu, but designated a Hui Autonomous Region, a level of administration equivalent to that of a province, in 1958. According to the 1990 census, the total Hui population of China was 8,602,978.

Hui Muslims are distinguished from other Muslim communities in China by their language. Uyghurs, Kazakhs and other communities which have an Islamic background have their own Turkic (or in the case of the Tajiks, Iranian) language, whereas the Hui use the regional form of Chinese that prevail where they live or where their community originated, but they continue to use a larger number of Arabic and Persian words and preserve an attachment to the Arabic script for decorative and symbolic, as well as religious, purposes. Literature written by Hui people, including poetry, is usually in Chinese.

It is difficult to make accurate generalizations about Hui as there are such great regional variations in their history and culture. In particular, there are great differences between, the Hui communities in Gansu and Ningxia in the Northwest, where Islam is closely woven into the fabrics of everyday life, and the Hui inhabitants of the cities of Quanzhou and Changzhou in Fujian province on the south-eastern coast which, paradoxically, have maintained less of an Islamic identity and have assimilated more closely with the local Han population, in spite of the fact that their Muslim identity goes back much further than that of the Northwest.[6]

Uyghur: The Uyghurs consider themselves to be indigenous people of Xinjaing, where the majority of them live, although there are Uyghurs in Kazakhstan and other parts of the former Soviet Union and small emigré communities in Turkey and Germany. They probably arrived in Xinjaing as part of the great westward migration of Turkic peoples from what is now Mongolia in the eighth and ninth centuries. The total Uyghur population of Xinjaing today is approximately seven million and their language is a member of the Turkic family, close to Uzbek but distant enough from Turkish to make the two mutually incomprehensible. It is now once again written in the Persi-Arabic script after a brief period during which the Chinese tried to enforce a Latin-based script. Uyghurs have a cultural tradition of their own including a literary canon written in Arabic script, a musical tradition of which the famous twelve *muqam* cycles of music and song. In addition to their identity as Muslims and Uyghurs, most tend to identify themselves by the oasis from which they originate such as Kashghar, Yarkand, Karghalik or Turpan. Their dress, and in particular the different designs of the distinctive embroidered caps or *doppa* which they wear, often show which town they come from.

Kazakh: The Kazakhs of Xinjaing are essentially the same people as the inhabitants of the neighbouring state of Kazakhstan, formerly a Soviet Republic. Many families have relatives on both sides of the border, partly as a result of the great migration of 1962 when Kazakhs fled Xinjaing to avoid the programme of collectivisation that was being implemented as part of China's Great Leap Forward. Chinese and Soviet Kazakhs continued to be separated after this by the Sino-Soviet dispute, which began in 1960 but became public knowledge three years later. The dispute effectively closed the borders between China and its Central Asian neighbours, but after the collapse of Soviet power in 1991, old relationships were re-established and many families which had been divided for over thirty years were reunited.

Traditionally, Kazakhs were herdsmen and stockbreeders rather than agriculturalists like the Uyghurs and their lifestyle, culture and physical appearance are close to those of the Mongols; Kazakh mythology claims that they are descendants of Chinggis Khan. There is also a Kazakh minority community in the west of Mongolia. The total Kazakh population of China, almost all of whom live in Xinjaing, was recorded as 1,111,718 in the 1990 census.

Kazakh, like Uyghur, is a Turkic language and was also traditionally written in the Arabic script as modified for Persian. This

script was replaced by Cyrillic, in the Soviet Union, and by Latin
script, in China, in the 1960s; however, Kazakh-language publications
in China gradually reverted to the Arabic script during the 1980s. In
Kazakhstan - where few urban Kazakhs speak it with any degree of
fluency - it has been largely displaced by Russian, and many Kazakhs
in search of a post-Soviet identity look to the Kazakh community in
Xinjaing, with which they are once again in contact, to revitalise their
culture.[7]

Kyrgyz: The semi-nomadic Kyrgyz of Xinjaing are spread
throughout western and southern Xinjaing, but there is a significant
concentration in the Kizilsu Kyrgyz Autonomous Prefecture in the
foothills of the Tianshan mountain range which separates them from
the Kin in the former Soviet Republic of Kyrgyzstan. Most Kyrgyz
are herdsmen with flocks of sheep and camels and, like the close
relatives, the Kazakhs, they move their animals across the mountains
according to the season until the Sino-Soviet dispute closed the
border. The language and customs are closely related to those of their
Kazakh neighbours.

Uzbek: Uzbeks are close relatives of the native population of
Uzbekistan and Uzbeks of Afghanistan live throughout southern and
western Xinjaing. They originate in the great Central Asian oasis of
Samarkand, Bukhara and Tashkent and probably moved into present
day Xinjaing in the eighteenth century. Like the Uyghurs, they are
predominantly farmers and there are also concentrations of urban
Uzbeks in the cities of Ili, Kashghar, Shache, Yecheng and the
regional capital Urumqi; Xinjaing Uzbeks have lived alongside
Uyghurs for so long that there is little difference in lifestyle, food,
clothing and religious practice between the two groups. The Uzbek
language is used with their community, but most are fully conversant
with Uyghur, which is very similar, anyway, in its vocabulary and
structure to Uzbek; they use this language outside their own
communities.

Tatar: The group classified as Tatars, with only 4,872 members
registered in the 1990 census, is one of the smallest ethnic minority

groups in China. Most live in northern Xinjaing near the border with
Kazakhstan and are pastoralists.

Salar: The Salars are an ethnic group speaking a Turkic language,
who trace their ancestry back to migrants from Samarkand region
during the Ming dynasty. Over the centuries, the Salars have acquired
a reputation for fierceness which persists to the present day and
many have followed military careers. Others trade by raft down the
dangerous rivers or by caravan across the high plains and deserts.

Bao'an: The Bao'an, Bonan in their own language, are a small
Muslim ethnic group, only accepted as a separate nationality in March
1952 before which they had been treated as members of the Hui
nationality. They trace their origins to groups of Mongol and Central
Asian troops - sent out during the Yuan dynasty to garrison and
cultivate the border town of Tongren in present day Qinghai
province - who intermarried with local Tibetans, Han Chinese and
other minority groups living in the hills. The Bao'an language is
related to archaic forms of Mongolian but has many borrowings
from Chinese.

Dongxiang: There has been little detailed investigation of the
Dongxiang people and their history, and there is uncertainty about
their origin. Some scholars point to Mongol troops bringing them to
garrison the city of Linxia as the Mongols consolidated their
conquest of China in the thirteenth century (and who converted to
Islam in the sixteenth century), while others argue that they are the
descendants of Muslim Sardars or Sarts brought into China by the
armies of Chinggis Khan as they returned from the great expedition
into Central Asia at the beginning of the Mongol empire. The
Dongxiang language belongs to the Mongolian family with archaic
features similar to those of Bao'an and many loan words are
borrowed from Chinese, Arabic, Persian and Turkic languages.

Tajiks: There is a Tajik population in the Tashkorgan region of
south-west Xinjaing and according to the 1990 census this amounted
to 333,538. Tajiks speak a language related to Persian as do their

kindred in Tajikistan and northern Afganistan. Some Tajik communities live in seclusion high in the Pamirs and have retained their Ismaili Shi'a faith which probably exists nowhere else in Chinese Islam (See below).

As with ethnic groups everywhere, these designated nationalities are far from settled and their use in China has been criticised as crude and mechanical. There is much disagreement over the accuracy of the classification and there are many examples of individuals and communities with ethnically mixed backgrounds; nevertheless, Muslims in China commonly identify themselves and each other by these names.

RELIGIOUS AND SOCIAL DIVERSITY IN MUSLIM CHINA

Almost all Muslims in China regard themselves as orthodox Sunni Muslims who follow the Hanafi school of thought, and regard themselves as being in the mainstream tradition of Islam. In China, this mainstream Islam is usually referred to as *Gedimu*, which is simply the Chinese transliteration of the Arabic *al qadim*, "the ancient", as it is the longest established tradition within Chinese Islam.

There has been a great deal of controversy and confusion about other sects in Chinese Islam. During the late nineteenth and early twentieth century, the most influential western students of Islam in China were missionaries who took a particular interest in the Muslim population. They were aware of different groups within Muslim community which were known in Chinese by names such as the Old Teachings (*laojiao*), the New Teachings (*xinjiao*) and even the New New Teaching (*xinxinjiao*). These terms were not always properly understood or applied consistently by non-Muslim Chinese and some missionaries suggested that the New Teachings were Shi'a groups.

It is now generally accepted that the New Teachings and even the New Teachings were not Shi'a sects but Sufi and Ikhwani organizations. There are, in fact, very few Shi'a Muslims within the

borders of China, although there are two small groups, Tajiks in the
Kashghar region who follow the Ismaili tradition of Shi'ism of which
the Agha Khan is the spiritual leader, and a small community of
Uyghurs in (Yarkand) Shache county to the Southeast of Kashghar
who are Twelver Shi'ites.[8]

Some of the leading Chinese scholars of Islam, including Feng
Jinyuan and Ma Tong, have argued convincingly that although there
is little genuine Shi'a Islam in China, the influence of Shi'a culture on
Sunni Islam in China has been quite profound because of the
influence of Persian Islam. This is especially the case with the Sufi
orders. Ali and his wife Fatima are revered among many groups of
otherwise Sunni Muslims and many Chinese Muslims are given the
names of leading Shi'a figures rather than those associated
conventionally with mainstream Sunni personalities.[9]

The Sufi orders have been more influential in Chinese Islam
than Shi'ism, particularly in the deeply Muslim Northwest of the
country. Sufism probably first arrived in China during the later years
of the Ming dynasty (1368-1644), although it is difficult to find
reliable evidence of this. By its very nature, the mystical and often
secretive heart of Islam does not leave clear traces of its movements
and there have been many attempts to demonstrate that apparently
orthodox *Gedimu* writings have been influenced deeply by Sufi
thought. The inspiration of Islamic movements and individuals who
travelled to China from Persian-speaking Central Asia makes this
seem plausible. Shi'a Islam, therefore, has had a subtle and indirect
influence on Chinese Islam.

Sufi orders or brotherhoods in China, and particularly in
Gansu, Ningxia and Qinghai where they are strongest, are usually
known as *menhuan*, a term of which the origins are still imperfectly
understood, but which is always assumed to correspond to the
Arabic *silsila* or chain of hereditary shaykhs, who trace their authority
back to the Prophet Muhammad or his descendants. In Xinjiang, the
equivalent orders are colloquially referred to as *yichan*, from the
Persian *ishan* (they) and their leaders are known as khojas, rather than
shaykhs. In terms of doctrine and ritual, they are essentially the same
as the *menhuan*, but the two do not mix. *Menhuan* are for Chinese
speaking Hui: *Ishan* are for Turkic speakers, primarily the Uyghurs.

There have been four main groups of Sufi orders in China: the Khufiyya *Hufuye*, the Jahriyya *Zheherenye*, the Qadariyya *Gadelinye* and the Kubrawiyya *kuburenye*. [10] The former two have their origin in the Yemen and the latter two can be traced to Central Asia. The sufi brotherhoods in Xinjaing mainly belong to the Naqshbandiyya, which also has influential branches in Gansu, mainly Jahriyya and Khufiyya.

Members of the Sufi orders, regard themselves as orthodox Sunni Muslims, as do the *Gedimu* and the main brotherhoods trace their origins back to the great Caliphs of early Islam, the Khufiyya to Abu Bakr, the Kubrawiyya to Omar, the Jahriyya to Osman and the Qadariyya to Ali. Chinese Sufis inherited the same tradition but with some variations. Some Chinese Kubrawiyya members, influenced by Persian Shi'ism, trace their line of authority back to Fatima, the daughter of the Prophet Muhammad.

The spread of Sufism across Central Asia played an important part in the strengthening and revival of Islam in China, in the seventeenth and eighteenth centuries, and, as in the Soviet Union, may have been the crucial factor that prevented the absorption and assimilation of Hui Muslims into the Han majority and their mixture of Confucianism, Buddhism, Daoism and folk religions.

The *Gedimu*, as the most orthodox of Muslims in China, came into conflict with the Sufi movements that burgeoned in eighteenth century China. The main doctrinal differences could be expressed in the different emphasis placed on the *Shari'a*, the Holy Law of Islam, which was of greatest importance to the *Gedimu* and the *Tariqa* - mystical pathway - which was the centre of the Sufi belief system. The *Gedimu* held the view that this world and the afterlife were inseparable and that Muslims had to obtain merit in this life if they were to attain happiness in the next world. This made the *Gedimu* very much a this-worldly sect, not averse to compromise with non-Muslim authorities.

There was serious conflict between *Gedimu* leaders and the shaykhs of Sufi orders over the tombs *gongbei* which were venerated by their followers. For orthodox Muslims, this violated the proscription on idol worship but *Gedimu* authorities generally compromised by agreeing that the tombs of saints, many of whom

were of foreign origin, should be respected and that followers could
visit them but opposed the raising of funds to build or repair them.

The *Xidaotang*, or Hall of the Western Pathway is perhaps the
most distinctively Chinese of all Islamic sects in China. Its theology
was based on a number of texts written in chinese and known
collectively as the Han *ketabu*, the Han *kitab*, an interesting Sino-
Arabic juxtaposition as *han* is Chinese for Chinese and *kitab*
(transliterated as *ketabu* in Chinese) is Arabic for book. Because its
followers relied primarily on religious texts translated into or written
in Chinese rather than the Arabic originals, they were sometimes
known as the Sinological Sect, the *Hanxuepai*.[11]

MUSLIM IDENTITY AND THE MODERNITY UNDER THE CHINESE STATE

The diversity of Muslim identities is clear, not only in Asia as a
whole but even in what appears to be a relatively small and self-
contained region of China. While all groups may well identify
themselves primarily as Muslim, the identities of groups and
individuals is complex and multi-layered and, therefore, deeply
interesting in human terms. Part of the identity comes from the
precise form of Islam which the Muslims follow, whether it is the
orthodox mainstream mosque tradition, a Sufi order or the *Xidaotang*
- which is found only in China. Part of their identification is by the
languages that they speak and write, whether it is Chinese or one of
the Turkic languages such as Uyghur or Uzbek. Culture plays a
significant part as do dress, the style of headgear for women or
beards for men (both of which have religious as well as ethnic
significance) and music and literature.

In everyday life, these diverse identities co-exist, as do the
different communities. In the city on China's border with
Kazakhstan which is known as Yinging to the Chinese, Ghulja to the
Uyghurs and Kazakhs and Ili to the Russians, there are two main
mosques. Uyghurs and Kazakhs worship at the Uyghur mosque while
the predominantly Chinese-speaking Hui Muslims attend the Shaanxi
mosque, named after the Chinese province from which the Han

Chinese originated. In the bazaar, Muslims of all sects and ethnic groups rub shoulders with Han Chinese and residents of the old Russian community, who are mainly practising Orthodox Christians.[12] In peaceful times this coexistence works well. In times of social tension, as in societies the world over, the religious and ethnic distinctions can easily become exaggerated and coexistence can rapidly turn into conflict.

The image of modernity that confronts Muslims in China is not the same as that which confronts the rest of Islam. Whereas is Western, - i.e. European and American - values that are presented as modern to most of the Muslim world, Islam in China has been isolated from developments in the West for decades and it is the values of the Chinese Communities Party that are presented as modern and progressive. Young people in the Muslim communities of China are presented with a difficult choice. If they are educated primarily in Chinese, they have access to higher education, employment and official positions but they risk becoming alienated from their families, their religion and their culture. If they are educated mainly in their own language, they risk becoming marginalized. Some manage to be bilingual and bicultural but those who are excluded from mainstream Chinese society are the most likely recruits for the separatist organizations that the Chinese authorities fear.

Endnotes:

1 Joseph Schacht and C. E. Bosworth (ed), The Legacy of Islam, Oxford 1974, p. 116-130.

2 D. G. E. Hall, *A History of South-East Asia*, London (1961), p. 57; Schacht and Bosworth (1974), p. 144-155.

3 Hall (1961) p. 718-724; Fred R. Von der Mehlen, *South East Asia*, 1930-1970, London 1974 p. 57-8; Peter Polomka, *Indonesia since Sukarno*, London (1971).

4 For the first hand, if somewhat idiosyncratic, accounts of Islam in indonesia, see two books by V. S. Naipaul, *Among the Believers: and Islamic Journey*, published in 1981 and *Beyond Belief: Islamic Excursions among the Converted Peoples*, published seventeen years later and revealing the great increase in the influence of Islam.

5 For Islam in Russia and Soviet Central Asia, see Helene Carrere d'Encausse, *Islam and the Russian Empire*, London 1988; laexandre Bennigsen and S. Enders Wimbush *Muslims of the Soviet Empire and Mystics and Commissars*, London 1986, 1985; Ludmilla Polonskaya and Alexia Malashenko *Islam in central Asia* Reading, 1994.

6 On the Hui, see Dru C. Gladney *Muslim Chinese*, Harvard, 1991; Jonathan Lipman *Familiar Strangers*, Washington 1997 and Michael Dillon *China's Muslim Hui Community: Migration, Settlement and Sects*, London 1999 (forthcoming).

7 For recent scholarship on the Kazakhs, see Linda Benson and Ingvar Svanberg *the Kazaks of China: Essays on the minority*, Stockholm 1988.

8 The visit of the Agha Khan to the Pamir Tajiks on the other side of the Chinese border, who are related to the Xinjaing Pamiris and the foundation established to help them survive in inhospitable conditions were recorded in BBC On-Line News May 17 and September 26 1998.

9 Feng Junyuan Zhongguo de Yisilanjiao (China's Islam) Yinchuan 1991; Ma Tong Zhongguo Xibei Yisilanjiao de jiben tezheng (Basic Characteristics of Islam in North-western China) Lanzhou 1991; Ma Tong Zhongguo Yisilan jiaopai menhuan suyuan (Tracing Sects and Sufi Pathways in China's Islam to their Source) Yinchuan 1986; Ma Tong Xhongguo Yisilan jiaopai yu menhuan zhidu shilue (Brief History of Sects and the Sufi Pathway System in China's Islam) Yinchuan 1983.

10 Transcriptions of the Arabic names of these orders into Chinese have not been consistent and there is therefore some variation in the spellings of the romanised Chinese.

11 See feng Jinyuan and Ma Tong (op.cit).

12 Personal observation September 1998.

Negotiating British Muslim Identity

*Dr K. H. Ansari**

This paper provides an assessment of emerging British Muslim identity in an historical perspective; it attempts to explore themes with regards to the evolving relationships between Muslim communities, in Britain, and the wider society, in a way that questions existing presuppositions about Muslims and, hence, help to inform the debate on what it means to be Muslim, in Britain, in the 1990s.

Drawing on a range of research and analysis data, about the experience of Muslims in Britain, it also examines the various dynamics of change in the attitudes and behaviour of diverse groups of Muslims, as well as touching upon the existence of alternative interpretations - which may have had the potential for evolution - and the reasons why they have failed to blossom.

THE CONTEXT

According to current estimates, there are over a million Muslims living in Britain.[1] They are more, in number, than the Jews and only second to members of the Church of England, in terms of active religious observance. While British Muslims have acquired a relatively high profile in the media only recently, they have been part

---
* Royal Holloway, University of London

of the British social and cultural landscape for almost a century and a half. During this time, migrants, of Muslim background, have not just been arriving from South Asia but also – in significant numbers - from South East Asia, West and East Africa, the Middle East and even Cyprus. For decades, there has been a small number of white converts as well. Clearly, then, Muslims in Britain have originated in very diverse historical settings with distinct cultures and languages - even politically antagonistic with Britain at times. The important point to note, however, is that Muslims in Britain are neither ethnically nor ideologically homogeneous. Generalisations about Muslim communities have tended to rely heavily on the South Asian population, predominantly Pakistan and Bangladesh i.e. with their particular socio-economic characteristics, rural origins and religious beliefs and practices which are heavily infused with mystical and 'magical' features. Their socially conservative ways differ greatly, even, from the puritanical and legalistic strands followed by the geographically and educationally different Indian Muslims. Thus, presumptions of Muslim homogeneity and coherence, which claim to override differences between those of rural and urban origins, the rich and poor, educated and illiterate etc. do not correspond to social reality: a Bangladeshi Muslim, apart from some tenets of faith, is likely to have little in common with a Mirpuri from Pakistan, let alone a Somali or a Bosnian Muslim. Their values, symbols and aspirations, their approach to issues of identity, their strength of adherence to ritual ceremony and loyalty to kin networks and the form and nature of their institutions are likely to be extremely diverse. British Muslims are, therefore, connected and separated by a multitude of intersecting and overlapping identifications, namely ethnicity, kinship, national loyalties, geographic location and doctrinal interpretations and denominational traditions and practices.

However, there has been sufficient common experience and context, according to some Muslims, enabling them to view themselves in terms of the 'Muslim Community' in Britain. In terms of the character of Muslim communities and the infrastructure it possesses within public life, there appears to be an adequate degree of underlying unity which lends itself to analysis. On the other hand, there remains a widespread feeling that the 'Muslim Community' is still, very much, in the process of becoming and being established and that its identity remains, somewhat, ambiguous. Indeed, for many economic Muslim migrants, 'the myth of return' has sustained a degree of uncertainty about where they belong: for refugees and political exiles from Africa and the Middle East, the emotional attachment to their homelands has been even stronger.[2] Halliday goes so far as to see little that differentiates it from Christian communities in non-Muslim environments. For him "All Muslims do share certain tenets in common and in this minimal sense there can be said to be a 'Muslim community' in Britain. But, as with Christians, the unity ends there."[3] Nevertheless, the sense of an 'Umma', a community of believers overarching above internal distinctions, remains extremely powerful. Muslims may not be constructed homogeneously or monolithically, as is frequently suggested in the Western- dominated discourses. However, in light of the continuing efforts, globally, to identify areas of common interest and to share experiences and aspirations, the unifying strength of the idea of the 'Umma' cannot be hastily dismissed.

Nevertheless, for as long as there has been a Muslim presence in these islands, Muslims have been grappling with dilemmas concerning aspects of personal morality, codes of behaviour, types of education and forms of religious practices and cultural identity. There has been a continuous engagement - a dynamic interface - with the British social, economic, cultural and political environment. The key questions have been about: the challenge of secularity and modernity; the response to the narrower issue of racism and what impact this has on the politicisation of Muslims; and who should set the so-called Muslim agenda.

THE ISSUE

One of the key issues with which British Muslims have had to engage is the construction of identity. The current thinking on identity seems to suggest that, for a wide variety of people, it is increasingly becoming a less stable notion than in the past. Identity - individual and social - has acquired a degree of malleability and is

susceptible to be shaped by context and change. It is argued that
identity - ethnicity, religion, class, gender- is susceptible to historical
processes and is being constantly re-imagined under the impact of
internal and external forces. The broadly 'secular' and increasingly
plural character of British society has generated an array of
fluctuating and competing identities. Muslims, in Britain, no less than
other groups, have had to reconcile their ethnic and religious heritage
with claims of class, gender and British national identity. They have
been buffeted, at least to some degree, by rapid social and cultural
change, which has forced them to adapt to conscious, as well as
unconscious, ways. Nevertheless, the process of identity construction
has continued and has come to be reflected in the expression, among
them, of a greater solidarity across linguistic and regional differences.
As the influence on attitudes and behaviour of the social and cultural
environment, from which they originated, has faded with the
emergence of larger numbers of British-born and educated Muslims[4],
more commonalities have become identified. These groups of
Muslims are much more 'exercised' than their predecessors with
respect to how they experience British society and how they can
respond to and engage with the issues which are of greatest concern
to them. What seems to govern the behaviour of many of these
Muslims in Britain is their perception that they are part of a worldwide community which does not recognise national or racial
differences - what Muslims call the *umma*. Closely linked to this idea,
is the Muslim belief in the supremacy of the God-given code
enshrined in the Qur'an and the Sunna - despite there being,
arguably, no substantial precedent in Muslim history, when all life has
been subject to divine law. Islamic law, contrary to ideological and
political pretensions has been open to disputation, historically, and its
mutability in changing circumstances has generally been accepted.[5]
Both these apparently unchanging ideals of the Islamist strand
challenge western secular concepts of national sovereignty and law,
and bring them into potential conflict with notions of popular will
and democracy.

Such a fundamental conflict might be expected to pose
problems for many Muslims who find themselves living as minorities
in non-Muslim societies under secular or quasi-secular systems of

law. For many Islamist Muslims, there exists a sense of being a beleaguered minority. They find that they have no clear guidelines on how to arrange their lives in a non-Muslim environment, though some historical precedents have been invoked.[6] One way out of this dilemma, created by apparently irreconcilable contradictions, has been for some Muslims to argue that their minority status cannot be conceived as anything other than a 'transitory phase' *en route* to them becoming the majority, in order for them to be able to lead their lives according to Islamic prescriptions. For Khurram Murad, once leader of a strand of British Islamism, there is nothing to be gained by establishing Islam in Britain with the status of a minority sub-culture, 'grudgingly accepted' by the wider society. He suggests the creation of 'a potent counter-culture'. For him, mere survival is not a realistic option for "intrusion and encroachment of the hegemonic culture is inevitable".[7]

Kalim Siddiqui, the late leader of The Muslim Parliament, also exhorted the creation of a model Muslim community that would act as a beacon to the rest of British society. Its example, he had hoped, would persuade the majority of the British population to convert to Islam presaging the establishment of an Islamic state out of '*darul kufr*' (house of unbelief), thus bringing Muslims - eventually - to power. In this design, 'plugging into the global Islamic grid'[8] and, at the same time, asserting one's Muslim-ness in opposition to the national British identity, clearly signals loyalty to a supra-national entity, and undermines their British credentials in the eyes of Britain's majority community. Nevertheless, as Muslims seem to have gained in confidence, they have come to challenge more and more the attitudes, policies and concerns of the majority social order as part of their re-evaluation of their treatment by the wider society.

Da'wah [invitation to convert], however, is not in reality such a newly discovered impulse among Muslims in Britain. Converts to Islam, in the nineteenth century, were driven by similar aspirations, though their goals were modest and purely religious, in nature, as opposed to the highly political motivation of present-day Islamic groups. Even so, most Muslim communities during the last hundred years or so have been primarily concerned to survive, and, beyond that, to preserve the essential elements of their faith by transmitting these to future generations. For much of this period, they have sought to adjust and to accommodate to existing institutions and practices so long as these have not been viewed as undermining deeply-held core values. They have responded in a variety of ways to achieve the best possible conditions for the continuation of their beliefs and traditions.

Under these circumstances, it might be argued that over-concentration upon the Islamist perspective, widely accepted as hegemonic, downplays the diversity which exists among British Muslims - offering only a partial understanding of the range of beliefs, practices, issues, developments and movements to be found among Muslims who have migrated, settled and emerged in Britain over the last 150 years.

Understandings of Islam which portray it as irreducible, impermeable and undifferentiated, and immune to processes of economic, social, ideological and political change, have for long obscured the complexities of the historical experience of Muslims in different societies. They have also prevented significant meaningful exploration, on the one hand, of the existence of alternative interpretations which may have had the potential for evolution, and, on the other hand, of the reasons why they have not prospered. Western 'Orientalists' and Islamists alike have tended to emphasize what distinguishes Islam from the West and have thus presented it as 'the Other'. On the Islamist side, visible boundaries have been consciously erected to create a sense of religious exclusivity. A past is invented; new sensibilities discovered; particularist institutions established.

The West, meanwhile, has constructed and stigmatised an Islam which resembles little that is of value in ordinary Muslim lives. Islam is conjured up as a danger to be kept at a distance and a powerful force, something which is irrational, fanatical and violent, and which must be tightly controlled. Most recently, the imagery of the Iranian revolution and Ayatollah Khomeini, the public burning of Salman Rushdie's Satanic Verses and the hysteria orchestrated before and in the aftermath of Saddam Hussein's invasion of Kuwait and the Gulf War have combined to confirm an antipathy towards Islam in the Western popular mind. Muslim identity in Britain is thus being constructed very much against the backdrop of negative perceptions i.e. about *who* and *what* they are. It is evolving as an identity of 'unbelonging' in a 'culture of resistance' and in contest with the hegemonic British identity. Alienated from their society and excluded from opportunity, many young Muslims have found a valuable resource in religion to forge an alternative identification in the British context to give purpose and meaning to their lives.

As noted earlier, Muslims in Britain represent a diverse population in their ethnic, linguistic and social constitution. Such immense variation creates problems about how to define these Muslims. For statistical purposes, family background has been thought to be relevant. In addition, the term 'Muslim' has been applied to those for whom Islam is considered to have some significance in the ordering of their daily lives. But as Nielsen tells us, "it is necessary to be aware of the differing factors (social, economic, cultural and generational) which may contribute to vary the application of ideas of Islam to the ordering of that daily life, at both the individual and the collective level".[9] For many of Modood's respondents, for instance, Islam was "a core identity, meaning not that it is always the most prominent aspect in all contexts, but, rather all other significant identities and identity-shaping practices must not be incompatible with it ... [although] what Islam means will be subject to debate and creative interpretation".[10]

These descriptions, however, do not provide a sufficient definition of Muslims and Muslim identity in Britain, for there are also Muslims who, while identifying with a Muslim tradition, do not necessarily possess 'cultural' competence in things Islamic or conscious attitudes towards Islam, as a political or religious system; nor do they necessarily view Islam as a religious system or adhere to a specific form of religious practice. Others have been socialised into and have, to a certain degree, internalised a Muslim cultural tradition. For them, Islam serves as a frame of reference - a pattern of thought and communication - and gives their condition and behaviour meaning. These Muslims may also have very diverse attitudes towards Islam and its practice. But what they *do* have in common is a knowledge of Islam on which they draw, while engaging in discourse, so that they can communicate meaningfully and relevantly. Still, others profess specific beliefs, participate in religious rituals and other practices and adhere to Islamic principles of piety as understood by them. For these Muslims, Islam remains an essentially 'private' and individual matter. A fourth significant group of British Muslims hold specific ideas about the place, role and function of religion in society. They claim that Islam is a political and social phenomenon. The establishment of the sovereignty of God through the implementation of Shari'a is an article of faith for them. They see Islam as a complete way of life which can be fully achieved only in a state run under Islamic law. So, while there are these different varieties of Muslims in Britain, all have had to engage with the realities of living as Muslims under non-Muslim rule. In order to do this, they have had to construct different strategies for two things: firstly to transmit this identity to their children, and, secondly, to create the best possible conditions in which they are able to survive with their identity in tact. This has involved processes of negotiation between themselves and wider society.

The way these strategies have been deployed, of course, has depended on the character of the Muslims and the context in which they have found themselves. Indeed, there is contrast between converts on the one hand and migrant Muslims on the other. The 'problem' is that the vast majority of Muslims, being from outside Britain, have not been seen, primarily, as members of a religious minority but, mainly, in terms of their culture and ethnic background. They have been regarded essentially as 'outsiders' rather than as authentically British, and, as they were predominantly ex-colonial subjects, they and their religion have frequently been perceived as 'inferior'.

As a result, Muslims in Britain have been faced with the challenge of establishing their credentials and proving that they do, indeed, belong to British society. This has not been easy for there lingers a suspicion in the mind of the majority (population) that they do not and perhaps, cannot, fully understand this society and its institutions. This has produced conflict between migrant Muslims and the norms and values of British society. Since the power to decide policy, to distribute resources and to arrange the various affairs of society rest in the hands of the majority community, this means that the Muslims have suffered rejection, disadvantage and exclusion, and, consequently, their identity has developed in response or in reaction to the negative interactions with this society.

MUSLIM IDENTITY AND 'NATIVE' BRITISH CONVERTS TO ISLAM

Such experiences, nevertheless, cannot be said to be shared by white British converts, who, while not many in number, *do* have a tradition which goes back to the late nineteenth century. For large periods of their existence, they have been part of Britain as members of the majority community but have chosen, at some point in their adult life, to take on a Muslim religious identity.[11]

It is interesting, therefore - in the context of current debates about negotiating a British Muslim identity - to see how these converts, who are more firmly rooted in British society, have tried to effect a working balance between the British and the Muslim aspects of their identities.

When we look at these efforts, what we see is that for these converts it has not been a question of simply indigenising Islam but, more urgently, how they can develop innovative ways to reconfigure Islamic ideas so that meaningful connections can be made between Islam and British religious norms. This approach was demonstrated as long as one hundred years ago in the approach of groups of British Muslim converts, for instance, in the practices of the Liverpool congregation led by W. H. Quillium.[12] While this group of Muslims certainly regarded itself as part of an international fellowship of Muslims which demanded expression of support for Muslims from other parts of the world, it also attempted to develop affinities between Islam as a system of beliefs and being British. It endeavoured to spread the message of Islam in the English language. It claimed that true Christianity in essence was no different from Islam, and that, since Jesus like Muhammad was an 'Asiatic', Islam was no more foreign than Christianity to the British Isles. In terms of worship, these Muslims conducted a Sunday service with chairs provided for the congregation, as well as regular Friday prayers; and in this service, popular hymns, suitably modified, were sung to musical accompaniment.[13]

Here it is important to note that, during the Edwardian and inter-war periods, Muslims - whether converts or from outside Britain - continued to try to draw similarities between Islam and Christianity, and to disturb, as little as possible, cultural practices by building bridges. Jesus was accepted as a prophet of God and no distinction was made between any of the prophets - Abraham, Moses, Jesus and Muhammad, as deliverers of the Divine Message. The Woking Mission, established at the Woking Mosque (built in 1889), was referred to as a 'Muslim Church' and those running the Mission often presented Islam as wholly compatible with being 'British' and 'Western'. Islamic celebrations, such as that of Muhammad's birthday, embraced many of the English cultural features. The converts saw themselves as 'better Christians'. The British Muslim Society, led by Lord Headley - an early convert who died in 1933 - and Khwaja Kamaluddin (died in 1932) - the Imam of the Woking Mosque - annually celebrated Muhammad's birthday at plush hotels, to which Muslims and non-Muslims were invited (gatherings were mixed); and after the formal part of the proceedings - with speeches in English - entertainment took a British form. On one such occasion Maulvi Inayat Khan, an Indian sufi, played the sitar and he was followed by English ladies who played the piano and violin.[14]

Converts to Islam, since the Second World War, have formed a significant part of the British Muslim community. They have adopted diverse strategies to sustain their new identities depending on their view of British society and the religious processes by means of which they have converted. By converting to Islam, they have not, simultaneously, radically broken links with their past; research tells us that many ordinary converts have retained their British names, celebrate Christmas with their parents, exchanging presents on the occasion, and are not positively 'puritan' in their outlook. They do not necessarily feel comfortable with the outer trappings of Muslim lifestyle, for example clothing. Recent evidence suggests that while the overwhelming majority of women converts wore clothes which covered their bodies, about a third of the women did not wear a scarf.[15]   A significant minority of them are more at ease with the 'don'ts' rather than the 'dos' of Islamic religious prescriptions. They adhere to prohibitions on alcoholic drink and eschew pork but can find it difficult to pray and fast regularly.[16]

These particular groups of British Muslims seem to be working through ways of retaining their British-ness and combining it with aspects of their new religious identity. The 'convert' way of being Muslim in Britain, therefore, has tended to be different from the way that Muslims of migrant origins have sought to reconcile their religion with being British.

However, it could be argued that what we are seeing nowadays is a convergence between the 'convert' approach and the approaches being made by some of the younger Muslims of migrant origins who have come to share many of the experiences of the British social and cultural life with their white counterparts and to absorb many of the values of the majority community. In this process they have come to recognise the cultural specificity of the religious norms of their parents' generation, and so have began to question the need to retain emotional links with this non-British past. The latter, for instance, have begun to criticise the reluctance of Muslims to use any other language except Arabic for religious worship. The problem for them is that any attempts to move away from what Shabbir Akhtar calls Islam's traditional 'Arab linguistic imperialism' or Arabolatry, has been met with immense resistance.[17]   Any attempt to rupture this linkage runs the danger of being denounced as heresy.   This present day challenge to established convention meshes precisely with what British Muslims converts have unsuccessfully attempted in the past - that is, to cut the umbilical cord that has kept Islam tied closely to its Arab origins - or in other words, to free Islam from its dominant cultural moorings and, in the process, assert its universality while making it connect more organically with particular cultural traditions.

For numerical reasons, apart from anything else, the main groups of Muslims in Britain in search of a British identity which works for them, are Muslims who hold migrant backgrounds. The historical process involved in the construction of the migrant Muslim identity, therefore, has been quite different to that of their convert counterparts. In the making of this identity, the experience of migration has had a significant impact. Vulnerable and uncertain of their bearings in the beginning, these kind of Muslims need to sustain their sense of self in a new and largely unfamiliar environment. As a result, they have imported and transplanted traditions which were established in their countries of origin. As foreigners, they have made little effort to engage with the new realities. They felt no need to make positive connections. Hence, their identity was not 'British Muslim' but 'Muslim from somewhere else'. There was nothing distinctly or consciously 'British' about their Muslim identity.

What seems to have happened since those uncertain beginnings is that the second and subsequent generations, having experienced British society through its education system, in particular, and have increasingly engaged with a different set of values. They have, perhaps, developed more sceptical and enquiring minds tuned into British wavelengths. Thus, a more questioning attitude towards traditional Islam has emerged among sections of these Muslims which has enabled them to be critical of the practices and beliefs of their elders. There has developed among them more of a capacity and a confidence with which to engage with issues that they consider are relevant to their lives. They are, therefore, negotiating new ways of being Muslim in Britain i.e. new forms of British Muslim identity in which the British element is not just tacked on for geographical or legalistic reasons but which is an important part of the equation. They are becoming Muslims who have been shaped by the interaction between Islam and the British environment and who have incorporated 'the British' into their consciousness.

Endnotes:

[1] C. Peach, 'Current Estimates of the Muslim population of Great Britain' [paper presented at the Conference on Statistics and the UK Religious Communities, University of Derby, May 1994]. M. Anwar, on the other hand, using a number of other factors put the figure at 1.5 million in his paper, 'Census Data and Muslims in Britain', given at the same conference.

[2] See M. Anwar, The Myth of Return: Pakistanis in Britain, London, 1979; M. Al-Rasheed, "Political Migration and Downward Socioeconomic Mobility: The Iraqi Community in London", New Community, Vol. 18, No. 4, pp.537-550; D. Griffiths, "Somali refugees in Tower Hamlets: clanship and new identities", New Community, Vol. 23, No. 1, January 1997, pp.5-24; C. F. El-Solh, "Somalis in London□s East End: a community striving for recognition", New Community, Vol. 17, No. 4, July 1991, pp. 539-552; F. Ulug, "A study of Conflicting Cultural Pressures with Particular Attention to the Turkish Cypriot Community and a Small Group of Secondary School Turkish Girls Now Living in North London", unpublished B. Ed. Dissertation, Middlesex Polytechnic, May 1981, pp. 8, 26, 30-31; F. Halliday, Arabs in Exile: Yemeni Migrants in Urban Britain, London, 1992, especially, chapter 6, 'The invisble Arab', pp.131-145.

[3] F. Halliday, Arabs in Exile, Yemeni Migrants in Urban Britain, London, 1992, p.137.

[4] The Runnymede Trust, Islamophobia: A Challenge for Us All, London, p.18.

[5] See F. Rahman, Islam, Chicago, 1979; A. al-Azmeh, Islams and Modernities, 1993.

[6] M.A. Kettnai, Muslim minorities in the world today, London, 1986; M.K. Masud, "Being Muslim in a non-Muslim Polity: Three Alternative Models", Journal of Muslim Minority Affairs, Vol. 10, No.1, 1989, pp.118-129.

[7] K. Murad, Muslim Youth in the West, Towards a New Education Strategy, Leicester, 1986, p.6.

[8] Kalim Siddiqui, "Genertaing Power Without Politics", Speech at Conference on the Future of Muslims in Britain, London, 14 July, 1990, p.8, See also j. Nielsen, "A Muslim Agenda for Britain: Some Reflections", New Community, Vol. 17, No. 3, April 1991, pp.467-475.

[9] J. Nielsen, "Muslims in Britain: Searching for an Identity?" New Community, Vol.13, No. 3, Spring 1987, p.386.

[10] J. Rex and T. Modood, "Muslim Identity: Real or Imagined?: A Discussion", CSIC Papers, No. 12, November 1994, Birmingham, p.11.

[11] See N. Matar, Islam in Britain, 1558-1685, Cambridge, 1998, for evidence of even earlier Muslim presence in Britain. A. Kose, Conversion to Islam, London, 1996, documents some of the prominent conversions in the nineteenth and early twentieth centuries.

[12] Kose, ibid.

[13] See The Islamic World, July 1896, pp.98-99.

[14] S.M. Siddiq, "Islam in England", The Islamic Review, No. 1-2, 1934, pp.14-25.

[15] Kose, <u>Conversion</u>, p.131.
[16] Ibid. p.130.
[17] S. Akhtar, "Ex-defender of the faith", <u>The Times Higher Education Supplement</u>, August 22, 1997, p.15.

Chapter 2

Muslim Identity in a Rationalized World

Muslim Identity and Civil Society: Whose Islam? Which Society?

105

Muslim Identity and Civil Society: Whose Islam? Which Society?

*Ali Paya**

Soul-searching questions concerning identity, either of an individual or a community, usually arise within the context of a crisis. In this paper, the nature of the crisis that is arguably threatening Muslim identity will be briefly discussed, and the possible role in which some model of "civil society" might play in resolving this crisis, will be explored. The paper argues that from among the many existing interpretations of Islam - currently fashionable in different Muslim societies - only a few are potentially well-equipped to produce viable responses to the challenges facing Muslim communities in the next millennium. These privileged interpretations would have no difficulty incorporating a *bona fide* model of civil society.

From a cultural point of view, human beings are, in the final analysis, what they believe and think. As such, it will not be too wide off the mark, for the sake of the arguments of the present paper, to identify "identity", either of individuals or communities, with belief systems. Belief systems are not fixed and rigid entities. On the contrary, like living organisms, they are constantly changing and

---

* Department of Philosophy, University of Tehran

evolving in response to the changing situations within the intellectual and physical environments surrounding them. To stretch the analogy a bit further, we can think of belief systems as residing within belief-ecosystems. Belief-ecosystems, on either part, like natural-ecosystems are shaped by the interaction between the organism and their environment.

Islamic civilization, can be regarded as a geographically vast and historically old belief-ecosystem. Within the context of this belief-ecosystem, one can discern many varied and diverse belief-systems. Each of these systems has taken shape in response to factors (internal and external) that have influenced the Islamic belief-ecosystem since its inception one and a half millenia ago. The emergence of Shi'ism and Sunnism as well as other less comprehensive sects, the rise of various schools of thought and intellectual disciplines, e.g., mysticism (*Irfan*), philosophy, theology (*kalaam*), jurisprudence (*fiqh*) and the appearance of myriad forms of folk-cultures throughout the Islamic lands, can all be attributed to this process of identity-formation.

The responses of Muslims to the changes in their belief-ecosystem can be classified into three general categories, namely, revolutionary transformations and conversions of a gastalt-shift type, evolutionary adaptations and adjustments, and attempts to preserve the *status quo*. These categories, either separately or simultaneously, can be traced in various historical periods in different parts of the Islamic world. The following are a few examples of each of these categories.

Abu-Raihan Biruni, the great Muslim polymath (973-1048) reports that he saw the heliocentric astrolabe made by Abu Sa'id Sijzi, which was as good as the customary geocentric astrolabes, if not better. However, he decided not to use it.[1] Some Muslim scholars have argued that this was a token of a deliberate and conscious decision on the part of our learned forefathers to preserve the fabric of the traditional world-view and to avoid the leap from their closed world to the infinite universe;[2] a leap which took place almost 300 years later in the West with the advent of the Copernican system. The Iranian constitutional revolution (1906), used all this knowledge and socio-political influence to avert the waves of modernism.[3]

In the earlier decades of this century, Seyyed Muhammad Tabatabai and Murtaza Mutahhari, two Iranian philosophers from Qom seminaries, tried to devitalise Marxist doctrines in Iran.[4] During the 1960s and 1970s, Dr. Ali Shari'ati, a Sorbonne educated Iranian sociologist of religion, drawing on the theoretical resources of Existentialism, Marxism and Islam attempted to produce a novel interpretation of Shi'ism which would appeal to younger generations of Muslim activists and would equip them with a modern doctrinal tool to ward off the onslaught of the alien ideologies.[5]

Mustafa Kamal Pasha, Ataturk, in his drive to overcome Turkey's apparent backwardness banished Islamic ideals and ideas from the social scene to the closed circle of private sphere.[6] Seyyed Baab and Ahmad Kasravi in Iran and Gholam-Ahmad Qadiani in Pakistan underwent complete conversion and came out as prophets of new religions.[7]

Belief-ecosystems, as remarked above, are constantly transforming under pressures from internal and external factors, including social, economic, political, environmental, scientific, technological and cultural factors. However, although changes within the belief-ecosystem are occurring all the time, it is not the case that each of these changes constitutes an identity crisis. Identity crises are defined in terms of the threats perceived by the individuals or the communities in question, the threats which these individuals or communities consider to be detrimental to their existing belief systems.

To borrow a rather controversial theoretical tool from Thomas Kuhn,[8] an identity crisis occurs when the adherents of a particular paradigm, or those who subscribe to a particular belief system, faced with persistent anomalies which challenge the very bases of their system of beliefs, are forced to rethink the fundamental principles of their system. Such a process of reassessment and reappraisal, which is usually quite painful and disturbing, would result in the emergence of a new paradigm, a new way of interpreting the world at large.

The Islamic belief-ecosystem has undergone various changes during its long history. However, none of these changes were regarded as constituting an identity crisis for this belief-ecosystem.

External military invasions, internal political cataclysms, environmental catastrophes, and the like, did not create a widespread sense of identity crisis amongst the inhabitants of the Islamic belief-ecosystem during its past history. This, of course, does not mean that during that long period one could not find cases of individuals or small groups of people who have experienced such a crisis. What it means is that a large scale crisis of identity cannot be discerned in the earlier parts of the development of the Islamic belief-ecosystem. It is only since the encounters of the Islamic societies with modern Western civilization, in the early nineteenth century, that the symptoms of an acute and comprehensive identity crisis in the Islamic belief-ecosystem has become evident.

As a result of this encounter, among other things, a large number of new intellectual elements were (and still are being) introduced to the traditional belief systems which, in the past, were in a state of quasi-equilibrium within the Islamic belief-ecosystem. The intrusion of these new elements has disturbed the quasi-stability of the ecosystem. It has changed both the geometry and the dynamics of the traditional belief systems within the Islamic ecosystem: the arrangements of the constituting parts of these belief systems and the ways of their interaction have undergone profound changes. In other words, the contact between Islamic societies and the West, in modern times, has put into motion a long and ongoing process of co-evolution.[9]

This ongoing process, so far, has resulted in many socio-economic and political upheavals. In Iran alone, during the twentieth century, and in the span of a few decades, two major revolutions have taken place in direct response to the flow of new elements which penetrated the traditional fabric of the Iranian society.[10] The phenomenon of change due to the interaction between new and old elements is, of course, not restricted to Iran. Throughout Islamic lands, during the past one and a half centuries, many political regimes have toppled, many new political parties and movements have appeared on the scene, countless many new institutions and new forms of life have come into being and a large spectrum of new ideas have made their debut.[11]

The so-called crisis of identity for Muslims has arisen within such an ever-changing intellectual and social matrix. A sure sign of the identity crisis is the appearance of soul-searching questions concerning the very fundamentals of the belief system. In the context of traditional Islamic societies, many questions which, prior to their encounter with the West, were simply taken for granted, gained a large degree of importance and urgency. People who used to take Islam as a perfect guide to life, were now being forced to ask difficult and painful questions such as: "Who or what is a Muslim?", "Are Muslims as the Holy Qur'an points out, really the chosen nation amongst all the other nations?",[12] "Is Islam capable of offering efficient solutions to the modern-day problems facing Islamic communities?", "Is Islam really the best religion, superior to all other systems of belief?",[13] "Is the apparent weakness of Muslim communities in comparison to Western societies a result of deep defects within the Islamic belief systems, or is it due to the defects in the approaches and attitudes of the Muslims?" and "Is there such a thing as pure Islam?" and if so "then whose version of Islam is the genuine article?"

These questions and their ilk have been recurring themes in almost all Islamic societies since the early nineteenth century. In fact one can map out the history of Islamic societies in the past one and a half centuries according to the efforts on the part of Muslims to answer these questions.

Ikhwan-al-Muslimun in Egypt, Jimmat-al-Islami in Pakistan, both the Constitutional and the Islamic revolutions in Iran, ... are all examples of relentless efforts on the part of Muslims to provide answers to these and many more serious and disturbing questions which have emerged in the Islamic ecosystem, all challenging the very foundations of this system.[14]

Despite all these efforts, which have taken different shapes and forms, in the last decade of the twentieth century and at the dawn of the third millennium, these questions have still not found satisfactory solutions. It is in this sense that we can talk of a profound identity crisis, or perhaps, of the further deepening of an already deep crisis.

However, although no satisfactory solution so far has been found, and while any claim for a quick fix should be regarded as foolhardy, it is not the case that all is doom and gloom. A closer look at the history of Islamic communities in the past one and a half centuries, would reveal that as the process of co-evolution Muslims have gone through various phases of intellectual maturation and sophistication, from disbelief and puzzlement in the early stages of their encounter with the West, to the state of suspension of disbelief, and from there to the phase of focusing on the problems and trying to get a clear understanding of the issues at hand. At present, it seems, at least in some parts of the Islamic lands, Muslims have entered the phase of critical assessment of the situation and are, at long last, proposing more or less realistic and satisfactory solutions. Those who are involved in this latest phase of activities have equipped themselves with a good level of theoretical knowledge necessary for a comprehensive appraisal of different alternatives and proposing new models.

During this latest period of change, a number of major epistemological points are gradually gaining credibility amongst ever-increasing portions of the Muslim population especially in the younger more educated generations. It is, for example, gradually being accepted that the search for final solutions, magic wands and panaceas which would resolve all the difficulties once and for all, is futile. The desire for building utopias on earth is gradually giving way to the more realistic approaches of piecemeal social engineering. Learning from one's own mistakes and from the mistakes and/or achievements of the others, Muslim or non-Muslim, is also gaining respect in many quarters in Islamic societies. Perhaps most importantly of all, people are slowly coming to terms with the fact that just one unique and absolutely valid interpretation of Islam is not within the reach of mortal souls; that rival interpretations, which may all appear to be equally valid, could be entertained by various groups or individuals, though this sort of epistemological pluralism need not result in rampant relativism.

Interestingly enough, in the course of this co-evolution, many factors which initially deemed to solely bear grave and undesirable consequences for the integrity of the Islamic belief systems, have shown also to be having beneficial effects in bringing about changes towards further enrichment of these systems. Opening of the printing houses and publication of newspapers, the introduction of modern methods of education and the appearance of political parties, were among such factors which made considerable impact on the outlook of Muslims in the past one and a half centuries. In our times, factors like globalization, advances in communication technology and information explosion are similarly exerting enormous pressures on the existing belief systems within the Islamic belief-ecosystem.

Of particular interest to the present conference, is one emergent, or rather, re-emerging factor which seems to be capable of playing a positive role in resolving, or at least damping down, the identity crisis in Muslim communities. This re-emerged factor is the discourse of "civil society" which has made a remarkable comeback, in the West, in recent years,[15] and is gradually gaining grounds in the Islamic countries.[16] In the past few years, an impressively large number of papers and books on the subject of "civil society" have been published in various Islamic countries and several conferences and seminars have also been convened by universities, research centres, or governmental bodies in these countries, to discuss different aspects of this subject.[17]

In a fashion more or less comparable to what has happened in the West, the notion of "civil society" has received a mixed reaction amongst the Muslim intellectuals and/or scholars, statesmen and political activists. In the West, there are those who ardently advocate such a society. However, there are others who would voice concern about this model. Thus, for example, whereas Ernest Gellner has praised it as an ideal whose reappearance should be heartily welcomed,[18] John Gray who used to defend such a model, has now come to the conclusion that a more pluralistic approach, with some resemblance to the pluralism propounded by Alasdair MacIntyre,[19] though not identical to it, should be developed.[20]

In the context of the Islamic belief-ecosystem, too, there are those who argue that this notion is quite incompatible with Islamic views.[21] Others are advocating an *Islamic* civil society;[22] and yet a third group are of the view that the notion of a "civil society" is ideology-natural.[23]

To adjudicate between these seemingly discordant positions, we have to impose a rather restrictive condition. The critical dialogue concerning the status of civil society within the boundaries of an Islamic ecosystem, could only be held with those interlocutors who subscribe to those interpretations of Islam which would endorse and uphold the essential right of reason in pursuing real life problems.[24] I shall call these interpretations, the "rational" ones, for the want of a better word. With regards to these interpretations, it may be asked whether civil society is realizable within an Islamic environment? And if so, whether it is desirable?

This paper argues that the "rational" approaches to Islam will benefit from some *bona fide* model of civil society, provided that they remain open to rational criticism and appraisal. It will be further argued that while there is no incompatibility between the notion of civil society and Islamic doctrines, the concept of an *Islamic* civil society, may lead to undesired consequences.

However, to begin at the beginning, we should first make it clear what we mean by a *bona fide* model of civil society? Adopting as well as adapting a working definition suggested by Cohen and Arato,[25] I would regard civil society as a sphere of social interaction between the state on the one hand and the economy on the other. This sphere, in its turn, is composed of the family, voluntary associations, social movements and forms of public communication and self-mobilisation. Civil society, in this sense, is institutionalised and generalised through laws and rights. However, in this model, civil society is not identified with all social life outside the administrative state and economic process in the narrow sense. Thus, for example, according to this working definition, political organisations, political parties and parliaments, as well as organisations of production and distribution of goods, like firms, co-operatives and partnerships are not part of civil society *perse*. The political and economic role of civil society is not directly related to the control or conquest of political and/or economic power but to the generation of influence through the life of democratic associations and unconstrained discussions in the cultural public sphere.

The argument against the incompatibility of civil society with Islam, has appeared in two distinct forms. On the one hand, there are those writers, usually Western orientalists, and occasionally their oriental companions, who, following Max Weber,[26] would claim that contrary to the Western cities, the structure of Islamic societies has not been amenable to the emergence of civil societies. B. S. Turner, in a recent study, has thus summarised the two main features of this line of argument:

> *"The first is to make a dichotomous contrast between the static history and structure of Islamic societies and the evolutionary character of occidental Christian culture ... The second ... is to provide a list of causes which explain the stationariness of Islamdom. The list typically includes the absence of private property, the general presence of slavery and the prominence of despotic government ... these features ... can be summarised by the observation that oriental social formation possessed an overdeveloped state without an equivalent 'civil society'".[27]*

However, as a number of researchers have shown, the above argument is based on an oversimplified picture of the life in Islamic societies and cities, from which many essential aspects are omitted. For example, it has been shown that in many Islamic cities, Muslim professional guilds and urban corporations had actually created embryonic civil societies. Louis Massignion, for instance, has observed that:

> *"There was not a single town ... from Central Asia to Mesapotamia, which did not have its ayyarun ... they ... seem to be more closely linked with the local bourgeoisie in support of a native prince, ... Sometimes the bourgeoisie relied on them in resisting the authorities ..., in the majority*

> *of towns which had no charta (police force),*
> *they formed an indispensable local militia,*
> *... upon whom the race of the city*
> *relied."* [28]

Bernard Lewis, in a more critical vein, having compared the similarities and the differences between the Muslim and the Western European urban grouping, has endorsed the independent nature and social function of the Islamic guilds:

> *"Unlike the European guilds, which*
> *were basically a public service, recognised,*
> *privileged and administered by public*
> *authorities, seigniorial, municipal or Royal,*
> *the Islamic guild was a spontaneous*
> *development from below, created not in*
> *response to a state need, but to the social*
> *requirements of the labouring mass*
> *themselves."* [29]

Whereas orientalists have based their argument against the compatibility of the models of civil society and Islam on the so-called "stationariness of Islamdom", quite recently, some Muslim writers have argued against the thesis of compatibility from a doctrinal point of view. According to these writers, which, by and large, advocate a traditional approach to Islam, civil society, is a product of the liberal philosophical tradition, and this tradition is inherently at odds with the Islamic ideas and ideals. S. Larijani, a lecturer in Qom seminary, is amongst the advocates of this view. In a recent paper entitled, "Religion and the Civil Society" he has spelled out the main argument of this group of writers in the following way:

> *"In a nutshell, civil society and liberalism*
> *are twin brothers, and one of the main theses*
> *of liberalism, and therefore of the civil society,*

> *is the neutrality of the state. This is not consistent with pure Islamic doctrines, unless one is so infatuated with liberalism, that one does not care about such an inconsistency, and that is another matter.*
>
> *Contrary to the views of a number of myopic intellectuals, liberalism is not only incompatible with the fundamentals of religious belief in general, and with Islamic thought in particular, but also poses grave philosophical problems for the individual. A necessary consequence of the liberal doctrine is that every immoral law, provided that it is endorsed by all and sundry, is then enactable and it is the duty of the state to pave the way for its implementation. This is because the state has no criterion for distinguishing wrong and right. Its only obligation is to safeguard the liberties. If people decided that abortion or homosexual life style should be allowed, then the state must follow suit and modify its laws to accommodate these demands...*
>
> *Such ideas are not only untenable from an Islamic point of view, because among other things, Islam does not endorse moral pluralism, but are also faced with unresolvable philosophical difficulties."*.[30]

A critical assessment of the argument of traditional Muslim writers takes us beyond the scope of the present paper. However, suffice it to say that the development of the models of civil society has not been a prerogative of the Liberal thinkers in its narrow sense. Hegel, Marx, as well as subsequent Socialist and Marxist writers have also made significant contributions to this field.[31] Moreover, to equate *laisez-aller*, or unconstrained freedom with Liberalism is to refute the actual history of ideas.

It seems the main objection of the traditional Muslim writers to the notion of civil society is that such a society would pave the way for moral and social decadence.[32] Though one can sympathise with such concerns, one should not, as some of these writers seem to have done, conflate permissiveness with moral pluralism. While the former could lead to moral impropriety, the latter basically involves divergent sub-moralities in relation to the same area of conduct.

In the past two decades, and after the demise of state-administered Socialism and the discrediting of fully-fledged free-market economy and rampant *laissez-faire*, many thinkers have striven to develop more refined models of civil society in which the rights and liberties of the individuals are reconciled with a partnership between the state and society. In such models, great emphasis has been placed on the priority of morality as a method for conducting the affairs of the state and the individual.[33]

Delicate philosophical distinctions aside, the model of civil society, alluded to above, with its strong moral component should prove to be attractive even to the traditionalist Muslim writers. In fact, the affinities between a civil society shaped according to the above approaches and the more traditional interpretations of Islam do not end here. One can think of such a society as not just built on the Hobesian kind of social contract, but as one which also benefits from a moral contract or a covenant.[34] A society built on a social contract is maintained by an external force, the monopoly within the state of the justified use of coercive power. A covenant, by contrast, is maintained by an internalised sense of identity, kinship, loyalty, obligation, responsibility and reciprocity. Parties can disengage from a contract when it is no longer to their mutual benefit to continue. A covenant binds them even - perhaps specially, in difficult times; this is because a covenant is not predicted on interests, but instead on loyalty, fidelity, holding together even when things seem to be driving apart.[35]

However, while this model of civil society might succeed in mitigating the opposition of more conservative and traditional Muslim writers, it may prompt the discontent of more critically-minded citizens of the Islamic communities. It might, for example be argued against this approach to the civil society that to endow the moral law with precedence over the law of the land could lead to dangerous and undesirable consequences. This difficulty can apparently be circumvented by adopting a solution offered by H. L. A. Hart,[36] namely, to accept that the law of the land, notwithstanding the possible sacredness of its sources, is set of fallible interpretations by mere mortals and as such is not only sacred, but may not even be moral in an ideally desired sense. However, such a law has to be made as moral as possible. This approach has of course a close parallel in the philosophy of science, namely, the thesis of verisimilitude: the view that science should be seen as an approximation to truth rather than the truth.[37]

In a civil society as proposed here, citizens can play an active role in producing a better rendering of the laws governing the conduct of the society. Critical debates and constructive discussions amongst the citizens and the authorities will pave the way for the implementation of constantly improving new laws.

Civil society in the defined sense, can also exert a decisive influence towards a satisfactory resolution of the so-called identity crisis. The identity of an individual partly takes shape in his or her society.[38] In a despotic or absolutist society, there is very limited room for manoeuvre for the individual. As a result his or her identity will not have enough opportunity to flourish and its potentials cannot be fully actualised. In a civil society strengthened with the notion of moral contract, values like freedom, equity, solidarity, democracy and basic rights can all be realised. Such a civil society can facilitate the constructive interaction between different elements of the belief systems and therefore, can assist to produce novel solutions to the so-called crisis of identity.

The argument of the compatibility between Islam and the civil society has also a third normative component apart from the historical and critical components. Human communities, Muslim societies included, are increasingly becoming pluralistic. In such societies, just one form of life cannot be imposed upon the citizens. Those who emphasise on an exclusivist reading of Islam, and would insist upon drawing rigid boundaries between the "insiders" and the "outsiders" are in danger of distorting the real message of Islam, which purports to be a universal religion - a world- view for humanity at large.

The issue of pluralism also has a bearing on the notion of an *Islamic* civil society. Traditionalists have argued that it is a superfluous or an incongruent concept i.e. we either have an Islamic society or a civil society; and since these two societies are based on two different ideologies, they cannot be reconciled.[39] However, it seems that the argument from pluralism provides a strong rebuttal of the positions of both the traditionalist and the proponents of the *Islamic* civil society. The following quotation taken from a letter recently posted on the internet, contains one such argument:

> *Islamic civil society is an oxymoron. Civil society is a secular construct which either exists or does not exist. If we accept the idea of an Islamic civil society, then in principle we should also agree to the legitimacy of Christian, Hindi, and Jewish civil societies. But that would be tantamount to celebrating the exclusions character of societies, an activist approach at best.*[40]

Indeed, civil society, like the different forms of government and the various other institutions which have evolved during the process of maturation of human civilization, is basically an instrument and therefore, ideology-neutral. It is a means to an end, and like all other means can be used properly or be misused. However, it must be emphasised that an ideology-neutral model needs not be necessarily value-free. In fact, the model of civil society, advocated here, is value-laden. Nevertheless, the values on which such a society is based are of universal character: values like rationality, freedom, equity and the like.

The thesis of an *Islamic* civil society, however, suffers from further shortcomings. Whose Islam is meant in such a society? Is there just one model of an *Islamic* civil society or many? Apparently, we are faced with a dilemma here. To opt for the first horn, of the dilemma would bring about the charges of rigidity and predetermination. To go for the second horn however, would amount to arbitrariness, if not outright contradiction in terms.

Some decades ago, Michael Polanyi, an influential philosopher of science, talking in the context of scientific views, proposed that we cannot choose a system of thought in abstract; we can choose a community, and the choice includes the dominant doctrines of the community we have chosen. His claim was that we learn to belong to a community by a lengthy process of education, and that we cannot shed or become educated overnight, at will.[41] However, this thesis, which apparently is a variation of the Wittgensteinian theme of the *form of life* does not seem to be correct. Communities do not require blind faith or pre-determined doctrines. Communities permit attempts at variations and this is effected by various activities, including the interactions of the citizens in a pluralist manner. The matter is open to different experiments within the pluralist participatory democratic system. Within the context of Islamic societies, Islamic ideals and ideas can act as regulative principles in the Kantian sense, as ideal objectives, which would inspire the citizens and towards which they would strive. These principles, contrary to Polanyi and Wittgenstein, need not and would not act as pre-imposed straitjackets, hindering the intellectual as well as material development of the people.

It was said that the model of civil society advocated in this paper, could help the "rational" interpretations of Islam to meet the challenges of identity crisis. The identity crisis, as pointed out above, is nothing but a serious threat to the very existence of the belief systems. In responding to this threat, only those belief systems which are the fittest could survive. Moreover, the fittest systems are those which have the highest capacity for adaptability and coping with the rapidly changing situations. The question which remains to be settled is that how can the "rational" interpretations of Islam increase their survival chances?

Within the context of the Islamic-ecosystem, there exists a certain type of belief system, known as mysticism, with a long history and a rich variety whose main characteristic has always been the great emphasis which it lays upon such basic values such as freedom, tolerance, equity, responsibility, love and respect for all earthly manifestations of God i.e. all creatures small and large, animate or inanimate. Although some varieties of this particular belief system have traditionally looked rather suspiciously upon the role of intellect and reason, a few highly sophisticated and well-developed versions have managed to blend in with a novel synthesis between rational and trans-rational elements like love and direct intuitive wisdom.[42]

It could be argued that in meeting the challenges facing Muslim communities in the next millennium, those rational approaches which have managed to incorporate the more sophisticated trans-rational (mystical) traditions, and have embarked on the project of implementing a model of civil society more or less similar to what briefly described here, are better placed on weather the storm which is blowing over the Islamic lands.[43]

Within the boundaries of a society which is based on such a combined approach, the ideal of siblinghood of humanity will be pursued. This is an ideal, like truth, which we can strive towards. It is of course an operative ideal, not an unrealistic utopian dream. To move towards it, we need to disseminate the notions of responsibility, freedom, equity and pluralism. Interestingly enough, all these elements, which are part and parcel of a *bona fide* model of civil society, are also indigenous ingredients of Islamic mystical belief systems.[44]

Those Muslims who intend to carry out the project of providing viable solutions to the identity crisis are aware that such solutions are unworkable without a broad-based participation, and such a participation is impossible without pluralism. Wise solutions can also be produced by those who have heeded the admonition of the Holy Qur'an and the Prophet and have dared to be wise.[45] However, to be wise, also means to be open to criticism: rationalists may seek and propose different kinds of positive proposals, but to be rationalistic they owe it to themselves to take criticism seriously.

Endnotes:

1 Nasr, S. H., 1970/1987, *Science and Civilization in Islam*, Islamic Text Society, pp. 137-8

2 "... The major lesson to learn from this aspect of Islamic astronomy is that Muslims had all the technical knowledge necessary to overthrow the Ptolemaic system, including knowledge of the heliocentric system, but they did not do so because they had not as yet become forgetful of the symbolic content of traditional astronomy nor of the fact that the best way to remind most men of the presence of God is to remind them of the limited character of the created world." Nasr, S. H. 1976, *Islamic Science: An Illustrated Guide*, World of Islamic Festival Publishing Company Ltd., p. 133.

3 Enayat, H., 1982, *Modern Islamic Political Thought*, London, Macmillan.
Hairi, A., 1977, *Shiism and Constitutionalism in Iran*, Leiden.

4 Paya, A. "The Development of Philosophical Thought in Contemporary Iran", paper delivered to the conference on "New Development in Understanding Islam and Modern International Situation", Centre for International Studies, University of Helsinki, 28 March 1994.

5 *Ibid. op. cit.* note 4. See also Shari'ati, A., 1979, *On the Sociology of Islam*, trans. H. Algar, Berekely, Calif. Mizan Press.

6 Cf. Lewis, B., 1961, *The Emergence of Modern Turkey*, London.

7 *Op.cit.*, note 3.

8 Kuhn, T., 1970, *The Structure of Scientific Revolutions*, Chicago, The University of Chicago Press.

9 For a brief account of the notion of co-evolution in biology and social sphere see, Kauffman, S., 1995, *At Home in the Universe: the Search for Laws of Complexity*, Penguin Books.

10 Koury, E., and C. MacDonald (eds.), 1987, *Revolution in Iran: A Reappraisal*, London, Routeledge.

11 H. Enayat, *op.cit.*, note 3.

12 "ye are the best of peoples, evolved for mankind, enjoining what is right, forbidding what is wrong, and believing in God ...", The Holy Qur'an 3:110

13 "The religion before God is Islam", The Holy Qur'an, 3:19
"If anyone desires a religion other than Islam, never will it be accepted of him; and in the hereafter he will be in the ranks of those who have lost.", The Holy Qur'an, 3:85

14 For a brief overview of the reformist movements in the Islamic Countries during nineteenth and the early-mid twentieth centuries see, "Islah", *The Encyclopaedia of Islam*, New Edition, vol. IV, Leden, J. Brill, 1987.
Albert Hourani's *Arabic Thought in the Liberal Age 1798-1939*, Cambridge University press, 1983, also offers useful information and analyses on a number of well-known Muslim thinkers/activists who tried to respond to the West's challenge.

15 See for example, Cohen, J. L. & A. Arato, 1992, *Civil Society and Political Theory*, The MIT Press. The authors have rightly emphasised that: "Thus we are convinced that the recent re-emergence of the 'discourse of civil society' is at the heart of a sea

change in contemporary political culture." (ibid. p.3)

16 See for example, Al-Azmeh, A., 1993, *Islam and Modernities*, London: Verso; Scwelder, J. (ed.), 1995, *Toward Civil Society in the Middle East: A primer*, London, Lymmer reinner Publisher; Norton, A. R. (ed.), 1995, *Civil Society in the Middle East*, Leiden, J. Brill.

17 For the proceedings of one such Conference see, *The Realisation of the Civil Society in the Islamic revolution of Iran: An Anthology*, The Organisation for the Cultural Documents of the Islamic Revolution, Tehran, 1997.

18 Gellner, E., 1994, Condition for Liberty: Civil Society and Its Rivals, London, Hamish Hamilton.

19 MacIntyre, A., 1985, *After Virtue*, Duckworth, 1985; MacIntyre, A., 1988, *Whose Justice? Which Rationality?*, University of Notre Dame Press.

20Gray, J., 1995, *Enlightenment's Wake : Politics and Culture at the Close of the Modern Age*, London, Routledge.

21 *Cf.* Note 32.

22 Nadri Abyaneh, F., "Civil Society and the City of the Prophet (Madinat al-Nabi)", in *The Realisation of Civil Society in the Islamic Revolution of Iran: An Anthology*, The Organisation for the Cultural Documents of the Islamic revolution, Tehran, 1997.

23 Muhammadi, M., 1996, *Civil Society as a Method*, Tehran, Nashr-e Qatreh.

24 The relation between reason and religion within the Islamic belief-ecosystem is a vexed and complicated one. Taking a cursory glance at the history of Islam, it can be seen that Muslims have adopted three different attitude towards the use of reason and the rational attitude. Some have regarded as a dangerous enemy for belief. Others have emphasised on the compatibility of reason and religion. And the third group have urged going beyond the realm of reason and into the realm of direct and immediate religious experience.

25 *op.cit.* n. 15, p. ix.

26 *Cf.* Weber, M., 1958, *The City*, The Free Press.

27 Turner, B. S., 1984, *capitalism and Class in the Middle East*, Heinemann Books Ltd., p. 68.

28 L. Massignion, "Sinf", *Encyclopaedia of Islam*, 1935, Vol. II, p. 962.

29 Lewis, B., 1937, "Islamic Guilds", in *Economic History Review*, pp. 3536.
Other researchers, emphasising the historical importance of these embryonic civil societies with the context of Islamic cities and Muslim communities, have gone further to show that while from a doctrinal point of view, there has been no restriction for the flourishing of civil society in the past Islamic communities, other historical and environmental factors have hampered their development. For one such recent defence of the notion of urban autonomy and civil society in Islamic cities, see, M. H. Ebrahim, *Islamic City: Quest for the Urban Identity in the Islamic World*, unpublished Ph.D. thesis, University of London, 1994.

30 S. Larijani, "religion and the Civil Society", in *The Realisation of the civil Society in the Islamic Revolution of Iran: An Anthology*, The Organisation for the Cultural Documents of the Islamic Revolution, Tehran, 1997, pp. 211-226.

31 *Cf.* Keane, J., 1988, *Democracy and Civil Society*, London, Verso, Ch. 2.

Hall, J. (ed.), 1995, *Civil Society: Theory, History, Comparison*, Oxford, Polity Press.

32 *Cf.* S. Larijani, *op.cit.* note 30. Similar views can be found in the works of M. H. Mesbah, a professor of philosophy at Qom seminary, who is, by far one of the most ardent proponents of this position. For a clear and concise statement of his position see his "Islam vs. Liberalism", *Iran*, Vol. IV, No. 966., p. 8

33 For a critical assessment of socialist versions of such refined models of civil society see, John Keane, *op.cit.*, note 31.
J. L. Cohen & A. Arato, *op.cit* note 15, have based their model of the views of Habermas. Karl Popper has tried to combine the aspirations of liberalism with some of the ideals of socialism, *Cf.* His *The Lesson of this Century*, Routledge, London, 1997. J. Shearmur, in his *The Political Though of Karl Popper*, Routledge, 1966, has discussed Popper's thought, and the notion of morality as a method, see, A. Paya, "Translator Note", in the Persian translation of Popper's *The Lesson of the Century*, Tehran, Tar'he-Nou, 1998. Among the modern Liberal writers, Isaiah Berlin, too has tried to develop a version of Liberalism in which, the rights and liberties of the individual and the social responsibilities of the state could be reconciled. John Gray has called Berlin's model "Agonistic Liberalism" and has discussed it in his *Post Liberalis: Studies in Political Thought*, Routledge, London, 1993, and *Berlin*, HarperCollins, 1994.

34 Kant, too was of the view that governments are obliged to keep their contract with their citizens, and this contract is moral not political. See, H. Reiss (ed.), *Kant's Political Writings*, Cambridge University Press, 1991.

35 *Cf.* Snacks, J. 1997, *The Politics of hope*, London, Jonathan Cape.

36 Hart, H. L. A., 1983, *essays in Jurisprudence and Philosophy*, Clarendon Press, Oxford, Essay two.

37 For the notion of approximation to truth see, K. Popper, *Conjectures and Refutations*, Routledge and Kegan Paul, London, 1963.

38 This of course should not be interpreted as implying a deterministic notion of identity. On the contrary, it can be argued that while external factors such as race, gender, language, geography, and history all play a role in shaping one's identity, the openness of the universe and the indeterminacy of the evolutionary process plus the role of man's free will, would render deterministic and fatalistic models of identity untenable. *Cf.* K. Popper, *The Open Universe: An Argument for Indeterminacy*, Hutchinson, London, 1982; K. Popper and J. Eccles, *The Self and Its Brain: An Argument for Interactionism*, Routledge, 1977.

39 *Cf.* S. Larinjani, *op.cit.* note 30.

40 Iftikhar Ahmad, "Islamic Civil Society",
http://www.pakistanlink.com/letters/97/Dec/19/08/html.

41 Polayni, M. 1958, *Personal Knowledge: Towards a Post-Critical Philosophy*, London, Routledge & Kegan Paul.

42 It is within the framework of such as that for example, Hafiz, the great persian Muslim mystic of the fifteenth century has emphasised the complementarity of reason and love:

"I consulted the reason, and it advised me to drink the intoxicating (spiritual) wine; therefore, Saqi, pour me wine, on the advice of such a trustworthy advisor."
Hafiz, S.G. M., *Divan* (Collection of poems), Tehran, Amir Kabir.

[43] One such argument is support of this claim can be made by analogy to the natural ecosystems. In these systems those organisms which make the best use of the very resources available within their own ecosystem stand a better chance of survival. Similarly, those belief systems which make the best use of the resources within their own belief ecosystems, i.e., their own "past traditions", will be in a better position to ward off the threats to their integrity. For a discussion of the importance of the "tradition" and the rational approach towards it see, K. Popper, "Towards a Rational Theory of Tradition", in *Conjectures and Refutations*, Routledge & Kegan Paul, London, 1972.

[44] One of the best representatives of Islamic mystical thought is Jalal al-din Rumi. Many of his views can be usefully put into practice within the large project of responding to the identity crisis. See, *The Mathnawi of Jalalu'ddin Rumi*, edited and translated by R. A. Nicholson, Vols. I-VI, Gibb Memorial Trust, 1926; *Discourse of Rumi*, translatedf by A. J. Arberry, Curzon Press, 1994; *Selected Poems From the Divani Shansi Tabriz*, translated by R. N. Nicholson, Curzon Press, 1994; *Mystical Poems of Rumi*, translated by A. J. Arberry, The University of Chicago Press, 1968.
One modern Muslim thinker who has made use of Rumi's thought in producing viable answers to identity crisis is Abdul-Karim Soroush. See for example his, *Visions and Revisions*, Oxford University Press, forthcoming.

[45] There are many verses in the Holy Qur'an, and in the tradition (sayings) of the Prophet and the (Shi'ite) Imams which lay great emphasis on the importance of the intellect and the faculty of reason and denounce those who do not make full use of it. In the Qur'an for example, we read, "And God will place defects on [the minds and souls of] those who do not use the faculty of their reason."(10:100)
And according to the Prophet: "God created the intellect (reason) ... and said by my glory and honour, I have not created anything dearer to me or more loved by me than thou. I take and give by means of thou".

Rationalization & Muslim Identity

*Muhammad Saeed Bahmanpour**

Identity, in one definition, is the way people think and behave, and the history of the behaviour and thought to which they belong. On this ground, rationality is a part of Muslim identity. According to Islamic traditions:

"nothing nobler than reason is created by God"[1]

"nothing more valuable than reason is gifted to Man"[2]

"the signs of God are comprehended only by those who apply their reason"[3]

"no opulence is greater than reason"[4]

"all blessings are obtained through reason and whoever has no reason has no religion"[5]

- "the slumber of the wise is more useful than the worship of the unenlightened ... and God has sent no prophet before making his reason perfect"[6]

"the inner guide of everyone is his reason, as their outer guides are the Prophets"[7]

"the most reasonable people are the nearest to God"[8]

If we wish to continue listing such traditions in commendation of reason and in praise of rational people, it would certainly take us into tens of pages.

Rationality is application of reason in one's decisions and behaviours, and if reason is commended in Islam to such a great extent, rationality is certainly recommended in every aspect of life.

---

* Cambridge University

The main question, however, is why amidst all these
theoretical recommendations, today, in reality, it is taken for granted
that rational life is quite separate and different from religious life; and
that rationalization is usually correlated with withdrawal from Islamic
belief and identity. To probe into this question one has to consider,
in more detail, different meanings of reason and rationality and the
importance which is attached to each of them by religion, in general,
and the religion of Islam, in particular.

Sociologists have used rationality to convey different
meanings. Max Weber, "reminds us again and again that
"rationalism" may mean very different things."⁹ Throughout its
history, rationality or rationalization has accepted different adjectives
like theoretical, practical, formal, normative or substantive,
instrumental, communicative and strategic rationalities and so on.
Consequently rationalization, from each point of view, takes different
meanings. The reason behind such a differentiation lies in different
aspects of human life upon which the emphasis for rationalization is
placed.

According to Weber, theoretical rationality is "an increasing
theoretical mastery of reality by means of increasingly precise abstract
concepts" while practical rationality is "a methodical attainment of a
definite, given, practical end by way of an increasingly precise
calculation of the adequate means."¹⁰

For practical rationality, Weber defines three components:
employment of means, setting the ends and *being oriented to values*. An action is
instrumentally rational if the application of means for given ends are
effectively planned. From the standpoint of *setting the ends*, an action
can be rational only to the degree that it is not blindly controlled by
affections or guided by sheer tradition. This is called the *rationality of
choice*. In other words, the *rationality of choice* of an action is measured
by the correctness of the calculation of ends in the light of precisely
conceived values, available means and boundry conditions.

Instrumental rationality and the *rationality of choice* taken together
make *formal rationality*, in contradistinction to normative rationality
which is a substantive evaluation of the value systems underlying
one's preferences. Actions performed in accordance with *formal
rationality* are purposive – rational (*zweckrational*) actions, and those

based on normative rationality are value-rational (*wertrational*). From the standpoint of *formal rationality*, we can demand only that the actor be aware of his preferences, and that the underlying values of his action to be consistent. But "actions are purely value-rational when the agents, regardless of foreseeable consequences, act according to their convictions of what seems to them to be required by duty, honour, beauty, a religious call, piety, or the importance of some 'cause' no matter in what it consist.

"Value-rational action is always action in accordance with "commands" or "demands" which the actor believes himself to be placed under."[11] The normative rationality of an action is measured by the unifying, systematizing power and penetration of the value standards and the principles that underlie action preferences.

These two aspects of rationality, i.e. "purposive-rational" actions and "value-rational" actions can vary independently. Advances in the dimension of purposive rationality can "take place in favour of a morally sceptical, purely purposive-rational type of action, [and] at the expense of action tied to value-rationality".[12] In fact, for Weber it was this direction - that rationalized Western culture - which seemed to be developing. The converse case is also possible, i.e. rationalization of value orientations while purposive-rational action is simultaneously impeded. This is the case, for instance, with early Buddism, which Weber considers to be a rationalized ethics "in the sense of constant, alert mastery of all natural instinctive drives,"[13] but which simultaneously leads its adherents away from getting hold of the world in a disciplined way. The complaints of Weber from Western civilization, arise from this independent development. In his view, the enhancement of *formal rationality*, in the West, has caused their life to lose meaning.

It was only in the West, according to Weber, that purposive-rational and value-rational actions combined together and started to develop side by side in the *methodical-rational conduct of life* of early Protestants. Capitalism, however, which was the product of such conduct, in the course of its development, found substantive rationality an impediment to its speedy progress forward and therefore dropped it as a nuisance. *Formal rationality* was then turned into an iron cage[14] in which lived "specialists without spirit" and "sensualists without heart" and this "nullity imagined that it had attained a level of civilization never before achieved."[15] And thus emerged Weber's criticisms on rationalization within a capitalist society. Rationalization, in his view, would show a very nice future for humanity but beneath this optimistic veneer lays nothing save hopelessness and pessimism.

It is curious that Weber envied Prophet Abraham (p.b.u.h.). In his view, Abraham died while he had attained all that life could give him. He did not expect anything else on this earth. The rationalized Man, however, is unstable up until the end of his life. He lives in doubt, in hesitation and in agony; this, moreover, is not the whole story. Weber stresses that the consequences of rationality have caused disappointment and despair. Man has lost his belief in the unseen. The reality has turned into an insipid and depressing entity which has pervaded human souls with a vacuum; a vacuum which they try to fill with unreal excitements and inhuman pleasures.[16]

Towards the end of the 19th century, the time when Weber was talking so desperately about the rationalized world, *formal rationality* had not yet released all its potential. These potentials were unfolded later on in the beginning of the 20th century through two disastrous world wars, the appearance of Fascism and the dictatorship of the media, and had caused even more melancholy and disappointment.

In the wake of these events, Max Horkiemer, Theodor Adorno, Herbert Marcuse and their followers in the Frankfurt School, came to the belief that the rationalized world has turned into a total vanity. The more the human societies rationalize, the more the relations between the people become unbenevolent and empty of affection, and lesser hopes for freedom from the yokes of capitalist society would persist.

Now, having such descriptions of *formal* and *instrumental rationalities* in mind, we might ask what kind of rationality and which aspect of it is so much respected and recommended in Islam and is regarded as an identity for Muslims. When the Qur'an advocates Man to use reason and to rationalize his life, do we know whether or not it is alluding to formal or instrumental rationality? Or, equally, could one claim that the Qur'an is advising us to follow theoretical or substantive rationality?

As for theoretical rationality, it is a rationality without commitment. The achievements of theoretical rationality could be used for good or evil with no stance taken by such rationality; and since the subject-matter of religions is to distinguish between good and evil, theoretical rationality could not be the kind of rationality which religions might talk about.

Substantive rationality, only, urges us to act according to and in line with a special commitment without saying anything about the good or evil of that commitment. As Weber puts it "actions are purely value-rational when the agents, regardless of foreseeable consequences, act according to their convictions of what seems to them to be required by duty, honour, beauty, a religious call, piety, or the importance of some "cause", no matter in what it consists."[17] Thus, the man who takes part in holy war and offers his life 'generously' to his God, the person who gives out his daily bread to the poor and sleeps hungry at night or the wrestler who lets his rival defeat him on ethical grounds, all have acted according to normative rationality; moreover, the man who offers his daughter as a sacrifice to an idol or one who kills somebody to save his friend's life or a man who ruins his power and prestige and property for the love of a woman have, also, acted according to this mode of rationality.

Indeed, which one of the above mentioned rationalities is the one recommended by religion and which has been regarded, by it, as the most valuble gift of life?

In addition to all this, Jurgen Habermas has recently proposed in this field, i.e., the communicative rationality that restricting the rationality of Man into theoretical, formal, instrumental and substantive rationalities, is based on a false theory about human beings.

He himself forwards a new theory on Man. In his view, the problem with previous sociologists was that they could not differentiate between two important elements which are, analytically, the main components of mankind, i.e. between work – work as a purposive-rational action – and social interaction – symbolic communicative action. Work or purposive-rational action is that aspect of human activity which is directed towards nature and the aim of which is the development and expansion of powers for production and for technical control of the outside world. It is a means through which Man could force nature to answer his questions.

On the other hand, interaction or communication is another aspect of the conscious activity of mankind which relates to those social institutions which are dominated by language and are controlled by social laws. In this field of activity "the actors seek to reach an understanding about the action situation and their plans of action in order to coordinate their action by way of agreement."[18]

Habermas propounds that it is the communicative action and the effort to reach understanding and agreement, and not the purposive-rational action – i.e. work – which is the most conspicuous phenomenon of the human species. It is this kind of action which forms the basis of culture and social life.

According to Habermas: "If we assume that the human species maintains itself through the socially coordinated activities of its members and that this coordination has to be established through communication and in certain central spheres through communication aimed at reaching agreement – then the reproduction of the species also requires satisfying the conditions of a rationality that is inherent in communicative action."[19]

Based on his theory, Habermas differentiates between three types of action: instrumental action, strategic action and communicative action. Instrumental and strategic actions both refer to calculated pursuit of one's interests. The only difference is that in the former it is a single actor which rationally, and by calculation, seeks the best means towards an end, while in the latter there is a common aim sought by two or more actors through coordinated rational actions. The common element in both kinds of action is the aim, which is the instrumental control of the outside world. In communicative action, however, "participants are not primarily oriented to their individual successes; they pursue their individual goals under the condition that they can harmonize their plans of action on the basis of common situation definitions."[20]

This new classification of action, according to Habermas, was the key to problems which the scholars of the Frankfurt School deemed to be unsolvable for modern society. In his view, there are three kinds of rationality correlated, and corresponding, to the three types of action i.e. instrumental, strategic and communicative rationalities. The latter rationality is the one which previous sociologists have been ignorant of, while in Habermas' view the way out of the dead-end, created by purposive-rational action, lies in the rational implementation of communicative action. A communicative action is rational when the only arbiter in it is free argument and when no external force - including power, tradition, affection etc. - could interfere during the process of reasoning. In a society dominated by rational communicative action - since claims and propositions are continuously open to criticism - it is always possible to recognize, correct and take lessons from previous mistakes. It is this rationality, Habermas hopes, that one day would overcome the *instrumental rationality* of the 19th and early 20th centuries and would set free the modern society from its iron cage. Weber, Habermas argues, "because he construed rationalization in terms of the increasing dominance of purposive rationality, did not adequately grasp the *selectivity* of capitalist rationalization or its causes. Following him in essential respects, Horkheimer and Adorno were led to deny any trace of reason in the structures and institutions of modern life."[21] This diagnosis, however, would deny the potentials of modernity which has yet to be realized. It was capitalism which chose purposive-rational action as the main pattern of action in modern society. Now, one may find and realize other kinds of action based on a different rationality – the possibility of which is provided for us by today's modern society.

Let us add this concept of rationality to our previous batch of concepts and ask again, which one of these rationalities is commended and recommended by Islam? Would the communicative rationality really bring back the meaning of life which in Weber's view was lost through *formal rationality*? And would it be the kind of rationality which the Qur'an enjoins us to follow?

From one aspect, it could be said that all kinds of rationality, discussed above - if used in their proper place within correct proportions and in a balanced way - are recommended and approved by the religion of Islam for no criterion stands higher than reason in this religion and nobody could deny the benefits of each one of these rationalities, in its place. From the other aspect, I want to claim, contrary to many contemporary Muslim thinkers, that none of these are the rationality which Islam, as a religion, recommends and admires to such a great extent.

I am elaborating disproportionately on Habermas' theory because I want to take it as the starting point for my argument. In his theory, Habermas expanded on the concept of Man and his action. He rightly claimed that human action is not restricted only to purposive – rational action and, that, their effort is not consumed, alone ,in the pursuit of their material goals. Rather, because they live together in society, the salient aspect of their activities is trying to coordinate their actions and reach agreement with each other. From a religious point of view, the concept of Man is even more diverse than this. In this view, humans not only pursue their material aims in the outside world and try to achieve it through calculated rational actions by the best means available to them, taking into account others who, like them, pursue the goals of their own lives, trying to understand and reach an agreement with each other with respect to their social activities but they, also, have other concerns beyond their individual and social lives.

Like Karl Popper, Habermas believes that Men have three different worlds: the objective world, the subjective world and the social world. He is of the view that a concept of social action should be able to explain the relation of the actor to all these three worlds and it is only the communicative concept of action which is able to do so. In this concept "the participants in communication who are seeking to come to an understanding with one another about something do not take up a relation only to the one objective world, as is suggested by the pre-communicative model dominant in empiricism. They by no means refer only to things that happen in the objective world, but to things in the social and subjective worlds as well."[22]

One cannot, however, restrict the human entity into these three worlds either. They have another world which is placed deep inside their souls and they usually take it into account when they want to carry out an action, form a reaction, judge others or do anything else related to their subjective, objective or social worlds. It is this innate world which has been the originator of all religions - during history - and which has constituted one of the most pervasive and most influential parts of human culture. It is this innate world through which so many kinds of worship for different seen and unseen things have materialized; and today, we witness that turning an ignorant eye to it has caused hundreds of psychopathic and neurotic diseases. It is the same world which has, today, caused widespread attention in the West to different kinds of meditation, Yoga, Buddhism, Hinduism, Sufism and so on.

It is because of this world that people think about their beginning and their end; that they think about how they have come into existence; who has created them? what are they living for? and why do they make any effort towards life? It is because of this world that people are concerned about their duty towards a creator who they do not know well... that they are concerned about what happens after death... that they ponder on the philosophy of life and death... and thousands of other questions which do not come under the jurisdiction of the above mentioned rationalities. And it is because of this world that people worship God without having scientific reasons for Him... that they cry before Him... supplicate to Him and sacrifice for Him or for a substitute of Him.

People have different positions before these questions and feelings. Some would think it is past history. Others might say they are useless and would deter Men from a good life. Still, others would think that they are important but are outside the limits of human reason and, should therefore be put aside and, rather, attention should be paid to more real problems. But despite all these, they are there deep within the souls of many people.

It is exactly these matters which religion, in general, and Islam, in particular, take to be the main subject for reflection and pondering; and it is human reason which has, still, to respond to such questions. This, however, could not be addressed with a rationality similar to theoretical rationality - which is good for the cognition of the world of matter and what relates to it - nor with formal and instrumental or substantive or communicative rationalities which are indispensable for all individual and social life, but with a rationality allocated to this part of human intellect which is able to apprehend and understand matters related to one's origin and one's end, to the direction of creation, to the creator and to the reason behind human life.

Reason and rationality have different aspects and manifestations or, as a tradition from our sixth Imam, Imam Ja'far al-Sadiq (p.b.u.h.) puts it, have different troops. In my view, all aspects, manifestations and troops of reason are sacred and admirable, but what religion tries to cultivate and nourish in human individuals, and would commend unconditionally and whole-heartedly, is that aspect which deals with the philosophy of life and its creator. This is the most ignored corner of our intellect and, at the same time, the noblest and most beneficial aspect of it.

This, I term religious rationality; and I think all Islamic commendations and recommendations with respect to the implementation of reason and intellect and for being rational, in fact, refer to it. This is the kind of rationality which is usually ignored and overlooked by people; hence, it is thought that the questions related to this area are out of human comprehension and, therefore, the best way to think about them is not to think about them. However, in the Qur'an and Islamic traditions, it is exactly this aspect of reason which is the essence of reason and all other aspects and manifestations of reason are small and trivial when compared to it.

Moreover, those other aspects, i.e. unreligious rationalities, so to speak, do not need any recommendation from any authority for their development. They flourish automatically due to the powerful urge of life's necessities. The best evidence with respect these rationalities is their development within major human civilizations throughout history, at the end of which stands the *instrumental rationality* of the West. Hence, it is only religious rationality which ought to be reminded and recommended.

I mentioned before that Habermas believed that it was the capitalist society which chose *instrumental rationality* for further development. He believed that the concerns and discontents expressed about modernity do not stem from the process of rationalization, "but in the failure to develop and institutionalize in a balanced way all different dimensions of reason opened up by the modern understanding of the world."[23] From our point of view, also, the most disastrous calamity of mankind lies in its incapacity to recognize and realize all dimensions and aspects and troops of reason and give to each one its deserving weight and value. From religion's point of view, of course, it is the rationality of the origin and the end which receives more attention and allocates to itself utmost value.

This view is approved by many verses of the Holy Qur'an and quite a number of traditions of the Holy Prophet and Imams. It is narrated from the Holy Prophet that he stated "woe to him who reads them and does not ponder on them"[24] when faced with the following verses towards the end of the chapter, 'Imran's Family':

> *"In the creation of Heaven and Earth and the alternation between night and daylight there are signs for prudent persons. [Those] who remember God while standing, sitting and [lying] on their sides, and meditate on the creation of Heaven and Earth [by saying]: 'Our Lord! You have not created this in vain. Glory be to you! Shield us from the torment of fire'."[25]*

Meditation and thinking are the processes of implementation of reason in order to achieve knowledge from known premises towards an unknown idea or proposition. Therefore, meditation in each field requires the efforts of that dimension of reason which relates to that field. In the above verses, those who implement their reason in arriving to some kind of understanding about the origin and the end of and the reason behind creation, are admired. It is a well known fact that meditation and thinking is commended to a great degree in the Islamic traditions to such an extent that it is narrated from Imam al-Sadiq (p.b.u.h) that "a moment of meditation is better than one year of worship."[26] As reason has different dimensions, meditation, too, possesses different subjects and manifestations. Therefore, that meditation which is better than worship should be defined and delineated. It is defined in Islamic traditions. Hasan Ibn Sayghal says: "I asked Imam al-Sadiq (p.b.u.h.): [is it true that] a moment of meditation is better than a whole night worship? He answered: Yes. The Holy Prophet said a moment of meditation is better than a whole night's worship. I asked again: How should one meditate? He answered: When you pass from a demolished house you ask: Where are the people who built you? Where are the people who lived in you?"[27]

It is this kind of meditation and this dimension of reason which is important from the religious point of view; and it is this kind of meditation which is alluded to, in the quotation from Imam al-Sadiq (p.b.u.h.) that " worship is not to perform lengthy prayers and frequent fasting, but it is meditation within the affairs of God."[28] It is quoted elsewhere from him that "Abu Dhar's most frequent worship was meditation and learning (lessons) from others' examples."[29]

In he first sermon of Nahj-al Balaghah, Ali (p.b.u.h.), the Commander of the Faithful, says: "Then Allah sent His Messengers and series of His prophets towards them to get them fulfill the pledges of His creation, to recall to them His bounties, to exhort them by preaching [and] *to unveil before them the hidden virtues of wisdom.*"[30]

Religious rationality is, exactly, that dimension of reason which is buried under piles of other rationalities and which the prophets have come to bring out for humanity as their hidden treasures and through which they could be guided and prosper.

Before explaining the components and fundamentals of this kind of rationality, I would like to cite a long quotation from Imam al-Kazim (p.b.u.h.) which is the best evidence for whatever I have tried to say about religious rationality, and through which the components of rationality and the dimensions of reason, admired by Islam, become clearer.

"Hisham ibn al-Hakam states that Abu'l-Hasan Musa ibn Ja'far (p.b.u.h.) addressed him thus:

> *"O" Hisham! Almighty God has given good news to the people of reason and understanding to this effect"* so bear thou the glad tidings unto my servants.
>
> *Those who hearken unto the word and follow the best of it; those are they whom God has guided and those they are men possessed of mind.'* (al-Zumar, 39:17 – 18)

"O' Hisham! It is through reason and understanding that God has completed evidence and proof (in respect of Himself and His religion) for mankind. ... and has declared: 'And He subjected to you the night and day and the sun and moon and the stars are subjected by His command. Surely in that are signs for a people who understand.' (al-Nahl, 16:12)

"And He has further said, 'It is He who created you of dust then of a sperm-drop, then of a blood-clot, then that you may come of age, then that you may be old men – though some of you there are who die before it – and that you may reach a stated term haply you will understand.' (al-Mu'min, 40:67)

"He has again said: 'And in the alternation of night and day, and what God sendeth down from heaven, of the provision and therewith revives the earth after its death, and the turning about of the winds there are signs for a people who meditate.' (al-Jathiya, 45:5)

"And He argued further, '...God revives the earth after it was dead, we have indeed made clear for you that haply you will use your reason.' (al-Hadid, 57:17)

"And He (God) argues still further: '...And gardens of vines, and fields sown, and palms in pairs, and palms single, watered with one water; and some of them We prefer in produce above others. Surely in that are signs for rational people.' (al-Ra'd, 13:4)

'And of His signs He shows you lightning, for fear and hope, and that He sends down out of heaven water and he revives the earth after it is dead. Surely in that are signs for a people who meditate.' (al-Rum, 30:24)

'Say: Come, I will recite what your Lord has forbidden you; that you associate not anything with Him, and to be good to your parents, and not to slay your children because of poverty; We will provide you and them; and that you approach not any indecency outward or inward, and that

*you slay not the soul God has forbidden, except by right.
That then He has charged you with; haply you will use your
reason.' (al-An'am, 6:152)*

"O' Hisham! *God has counselled the people of
reason and has drawn their attention towards the life
hereafter with the words:*

'*And the life of this word is naught but play and
vain sport; certainly the abode of the hereafter, is the best
for those who guard (themselves against evil). Do you not
then think?' (al-An'am, 6:32)*

"O' Hisham! *God has further censured those who
do not exercise their reason with the words: 'And when it
is said unto them, Follow what God has sent down. They
say: No! but will follow such things as we found our
fathers doing. What? And if their fathers had no
understanding of anything, and if they were not guided?'
(al-Baqarah, 2:170)*

"*And God has said: 'The likeness of those who
disbelieve is as the likeness of one who shouts to that which
hears nothing, save a call and a cry; deaf, dumb, blind —
they do not understand.' (al-Baqarah, 2: 171)*

"*And God has said, 'And some of them give ear to
thee; what, wilt thou make the deaf to hear, though they
not use their reason?' (Yunus, 10:42)*

"*And God has said, 'Or deemest thou that most of
them hear or understand? They are but as the cattle; nay,
they are further astray from the way.' (al-Furqan, 25:44)*

"O' Hisham! *Almighty God has mentioned about
the people of reason in high terms and has adorned them
with the finest ornaments as per his own words:*

'*He gives the Wisdom to whomsoever He will, and
whoso is given the Wisdom, has been given much good; yet
none remembers but men possessed of minds.' (al-Baqarah,
2:269)*

'*...And those firmly rooted in knowledge say: We believe in it; all is from our Lord; yet none remembers but men possessed of minds.*' (Al 'Imran, 3:7)

'*Surely, in the creation of the heavens and the earth and in the alternation of night and day, there are signs for men possessed of minds.*' (Al 'Imran, 3:190)

'*What, is he who knows what is sent down to thee from thy Lord is the truth, like him who is blind (void of knowledge)? Only men possessed of minds will remember.*' (ar-Ra'd, 13:19)

'*What (this) he who is prayerful during the hours of the night, prostrating in obedience and standing, he being afraid of the world to come and hoping for the mercy of his Lord! Say: Are they equal those who know and those who know not? Only men possessed of minds remember.*' (al-Zumar, 39:9)

'*...O' Hisham! Almighty God has said in His Book: 'Surely in that there is a reminder to him who has a heart...'*' (Qaf, 50:37) Heart means reason. And, God has further said: 'Indeed We gave Luqman wisdom' (Luqman, 31:12). Wisdom means (the capacity of) understanding and reasoning.

"*O' Hisham! God has deputed the prophets as His messengers to make the people wise and mindful of God. The more they accept and believe in these messengers the greater is their God-consciousness. The wisest among men is he who knows about Godliness most. And he who is the most perfect in his reasoning enjoys the highest status among men, in this life and the life hereafter.*

"*O' Hisham! God has given two proofs for the guidance of mankind – the explicit and the implicit. The explicit and the external proof is in the form of prophets, divine messengers and the Imams (divinely appointed guides); and, the implicit and the internal proof is reason.*

"O' Hisham! a man of reason is not only grateful to God for his lawful (means of living) nor does the (attraction of) unlawful gains wear out his patience. (A man of reason is also grateful to God for His spiritual bounties.)

"O' Hisham! one who allows a set of three things to be dominated by another set of three things has actually undone his reason. The first thing is to allow the reason to be dominated by excessive hopes and expectations. The second thing is to allow highest of wisdom to be dominated by excessive utterances. The third thing is to allow his admonition light to be extinguished (to be dominated) by carnal desires. In fact, such a person undoes his reason by his carnal desires. And one who destroys his reason (as illustrated in the three cases) also destroys both his worldly life and his faith.

"O' Hisham! how could your conduct be clean in the eyes of God when you have alienated your heart from God and His commandments and when you have been subservient to your carnal desires to the point of your reason being dominated by them (carnal desires).

"O' Hisham! to be patient in loneliness is a sign of the power of reason. One who acquires reason from God (i.e., from His Book and His prophets and their vicegerents — the Imams) has succeeded in keeping himself aloof from people of the world and from those who are lost in worldly life. Such a man turns his attention to what God holds instead of what people have. The result of all this is that God Himself becomes his solace in his discomfiture, and ally in his loneliness, wealth in his poverty, and his honour without the backing of any tribe....

"O' Hisham! limited material possessions with sound wisdom are perfectly acceptable to a man of reason. Whereas unlimited material possessions with little wisdom are not at all acceptable to him. This is why such

people have actually earned profit in the trade (of their life).

"O' Hisham! what to speak of the sinful life when the people of reason abandon even its superfluity! Forsaking its superfluity is excellence and honour while forsaking the sinful life is obligatory.

"O' Hisham! Lo! A man of reason pondered over the world and its people. He realised that he could not get the success in worldly life without hard struggle. Then he pondered over the life hereafter and again realised that the success in life hereafter would not also be secured without hard struggle. Thereupon the man of reason decided in favour of the struggle which brought eternal success, as compared with the temporary one of the worldly life....

"O' Hisham! whoever seeks contentment without wealth and desires solace free from jealousy and security for his faith, must implore God from the bottom of his heart for making his reason perfect...."[31]

It needs no mentioning that prophets and other religious authorities can speak about all dimensions of reason and commend it as they have spoken and commended. It is not surprising that we find many traditions in which *instrumental rationality*, as it is called today, is admired and in many others - those which we call normative or communicative or theoretical rationality - which are, also, recommended. This is because all aspects of reason if used in their places and in a balanced way, are necessary for the betterment of human life and, without them, the administration of life would suffer from disorder, confusion and ailment. That which should not go unnoticed is the fact that Islam, in its capacity as a guidance to eternal prosperity and to divine matters, has stressed upon a special rationality which considers it to be the main reason behind the creation of reason. It is this kind of rationality which is praised unconditionally and we are reminded in the *Qur'an* and *ahadith* that should this dimension of reason not develop within Man, other dimensions would not benefit him/her either.

FUNDAMENTALS OF RELIGIOUS RATIONALITY

In his analysis on *formal rationality*, Max Weber defined, for it, a few important components which were mainly drawn from theoretical rationality.

The most important of these components were *calculation, selectivity, prediction* and *control*. Obviously, religious rationality also has its own components without which it, itself, would be very difficult to define. These components which are mostly related to the innate world - which has been discussed before - may be classified into two major concepts: *mindfulness* and *learning lessons*, and *detachment and attachment*.

MINDFULNESS

Mindfulness is the comprehension of a concept from other concepts or events which is, in this sense, accompanied by a kind of introspection and prudence e.g. by looking at a creature, one arrives at a concept about its creator, or by noticing that he is created from an indignant drop of water, one deduces that one has to be humble before one's creator; or, by seeing how the earth becomes alive after it withers, one may conclude that it is possible for the dead to become alive again; by noticing that all existing humans on the earth are 'newcomers' and not, even, one of them was here one hundred years ago, and that none would be existing in a hundred years time, may lead one to conclude that the quality of life (on earth) is, essentially, transient and abject.

These reflections are neither deducible from philosophic reasoning nor can they be concluded by scientific methods. They refer to another part of human reason. The following examples from the Qur'an are cited as evidence to this relation:

> *"It is We Who have created you. Why will ye not admit the truth". Do ye them see the "(human seed) that ye emit; is it ye who create it, or are we the creators? We have decreed death to be your common lot, and we are not to be*

*frustrated from changing your forms and creating you (again)
in (forms) that ye know not. And ye certainly know already
the first form of creation, why then do ye not take heed?"
(56:57-62)*

 *"He has made subject to you the night and the day;
the sun and the moon. And the stars are in subjection by
His command. Verity in this are signs for men who are wise.
And the things on this earth which He has mulliphed in
varying colours (and qualities). Verily in this is a sign for
men who are mindful." (16:12-13)*

 *"Is them He who creates like one that creates not?
Will ye not receive admonition?" (16:17)*

 *"It is He who sendeth the winds like heralds of glad
tiding going before His mercy: when they have carried the
heavy-laden clouds. We drive them to a land that is dead;
make rain to descend thereon, and produce every kind of
harvest therewith; thus shall we raise up the dead perchance
ye me be" "mindful." (7:57).*

LEARNING LESSONS

 This is in fact learning from experiences which are related to
people's life and destiny. So, it could be expressed, in other words, as
receiving admonitions and taking heed of them e.g. by looking at his
neighbour's death, he reminds himself of his own death; by paying
attention to the calamities which have shrouded this life, one
concludes that that which belongs to worldly transient matters do not
deserve a whole-hearted consideration. It is quoted from Amir-al
Mu'mineen, Ali (p.b.u.h.) that "How abundant are lessons and how
rare are learners."[32] Qur'anic verses are manifold in this respect e.g.:

 *"And we did not send before thee (as Messengers) any
but men, whom we did inspire. (Men) from the people of the
towns. Do they not travel through the earth and see what was
the end of those before them? But the home of hearafter is best*

for those who do right. Will ye not them ponder? Until when the messenger gave up hope (of their people) and (come to) think that they were treated as liars, there reached them our help and those whom we wished were delivered into safety. But never will be warded off our punishment from those who are in sin. There is, in their stories lessons for men endued with reason. It is not a tale invented, but a confirmation of the Books before it and a detailed exposition of all things, and a mercy to any such as believe." (12:109-111)

Amir-al Mu'mineen, Ali, (p.b.u.h.) has a very interesting address in Nahj-al Balaghah in this respect:

"The responsibility for what I say is guaranteed and I am responsible for it. He to whom experiences have clearly shown the past exemplary punishments (given by Allah to peoples) is prevented by piety from falling into doubts."[33]

He (p.b.u.h.) says elsewhere:

"This world is a place of destruction, tribulation, changes and lessons. As for destruction. the time has its bow pressed (to readiness) and its dart does not go amiss; its wounds does not heal; it afflicts the living with death, the healthy with ailment and the safe with distress. It is an eater who is not satisfied and a drinker whose thirst is never quenched. As for tribulation, a man collects what he does not eat and builds what he does not live. Then he goes out to Allah without carrying the wealth or shifting the building. As for its changes, you see a pitiable man becoming enviable and an enviable man becoming pitiable. This is because the wealth has gone and misfortune has come to him. As for its lessons, a man reaches near (realisation of) his desire when (suddenly) the approach of his death cuts them, then neither the desire is achieved nor the disirer spared. Glory to Allah!

*how deceitful are its pleasures how thirst-rousing its
quenching and how sunny its shade. That which approaches
(i.e. death) cannot be sent back, he who goes away does not
return. Glory to Allah! how near is the living to the dead
because he will meet him soon and how far is the dead from
the living because he has gone away from him."*[34]

This kind of meditation and this type of rationality is a special
manifestation of reason which is not enlightened but in a minority of
people.

That is why it is, repeatedly, stated in the Qur'an that most
people do not use their reason.

DETACHMENT AND ATTACHMENT

Mindfulness and learning from admonitions bring about a
kind of mentality in which Man could detach oneself from worldly
bounds and meditate about the other world. This kind of meditation
and absorption onto the world of supernatural or eternal world is
another category of religious rationality. It is stated in a tradition
from Imam Ali (p.b.u.h.) that "the definition of reason is detachment
from the temporal and attachment to the perpetual".[35] Also, it is
narrated from Imam Zayn-al Abideen (p.b.u.h.) that "standing up
from the deceitful nature and attention to the everlasting world is a
sign of rationality".[36]

Finally, I could not help, myself, mentioning one point. In
other kinds of rationality, there exist potentials and capacities which
may have not been unfolded, as yet; and, as it is said by Condorcet,
the capacity of human being for learning and development is
indefinite. However, in religious rationality, it is thought that some
people like prophets have grasped all of it and nothing would be
added until they would have been made aware of it. These are the
people who become perpetual, in this field.

When these components reach completion, in a person, then
different manifestations of religious rationality materialize within
him. In a tradition from Imam al-Sadiq (p.b.u.h.) quoted, in Al-Kafi,

the following manifestations are expressed as troops of reason. I
would like to conclude this paper by quoting this long tradition in
which all aspects of religious rationality - and some other dimensions
of reason - are mentioned:

'The Almighty God bestowed upon reason seventy-
five kinds of troops:
Good which has been appointed as the wazir
(vizier) of Reason is the opposite of Evil which, in its turn,
is the wazir of Ignorance; Faith and Belief, opposite of
which is Disbelief; Confirmation, the opposite of which is
Repudiation; Hope, the opposite of which is Frustration;
Justice, the opposite of which is Oppression; Divine
Pleasure, the opposite of which is (divine) displeasure;
Gratitude, the opposite of which is Ingratitude; Optimism
(in respect of all good in this life and the life hereafter), the
opposite of which is Pessimism; Complete Reliance on God,
the opposite of which is Lust and greed (which is the result
of distrust in God); Kind heartedness, the opposite of which
is the Hard heartedness; Mercifulness, the opposite of
which is Indignation; Knowledge, the opposite of which is
Ignorance; Wisdom, the opposite of which is stupidity;
Chastity, the opposite of which is Shamelessness;
Renunciation (from what God has declared to be
unlawful), the opposite of which is Temptation;
Friendliness and Sociability, the opposite of which is
Stupidity and Awkwardness (which doesn't enable a man
to adjust himself to the society); Divine Fear, the opposite
of which is Audacity; Humility, the opposite of which is
Conceit; Ease, the opposite of which is Hastiness;
Forbearance, the opposite of which is Insolence and
shallowness of mind; Silence, the opposite of which is
Garrulity; Resignation to God, the opposite of which is
Conceit and defiance; Acceptance, the opposite of which is
Scepticism. Patience, the opposite of which is Impatience

and restlessness; Forgiveness, the opposite of which is Vengeance; Contentment, the opposite of which is Neediness; Remembrance (of God and the life hereafter), the opposite of which is Forgetfullness and indifference; Keeping (in mind), the opposite of which is Forgetfullness and oblivion; Sympathy (with others), the opposite of which is Estrangement and alienation; Contentment, the opposite of which is Greed; Consolation, the opposite of which is Forbidance; Amity, the opposite of which is Enmity; Fidelity, the opposite of which is Treachery; Obedience (to God and His prophets), the opposite of which is Defiance and disobedience (to them); Submission, the opposite of which is Domination; Safety and Security, the opposite of which is Calamity and peril; Love, the opposite of which is Hatred and detestation; Truthfulness, the opposite of which is Falsehood; Right, the opposite of which is Wrong; Discharge of Trust, the opposite of which is Defalcation Sincerity (purity of motives), the opposite of which is Hypocrisy (mixed motives); Gallantry, the opposite of which is Cowardices; (Understanding, the opposite of which is Stupidity; Knowledge [of God and His religion], the opposite of which is [their] denial).

Affability and Toleration (which leads to the keeping of secrets of others), the opposite of which is Exposure and Betrayal; Soundness and, good faith for others behind their back, the opposite of which is Cunning and Double-talk. Covering the secrets (of others), the opposite of which is their exposure; observance of prayers, the opposite of which is the neglect of prayers; Observance of Fast, the opposite of which is Gluttony; Struggle (in propagating truth), the opposite of which is the withdrawal from it. Performance of Pilgrimage at Mecca, which means the observance of pledge made to God before creation (i.e. not to worship any one except Allah), the opposite of which is Violation of the Pledge; Concealing the

*tales of others, the opposite of which is tale-bearing; Doing
good to Parents, the opposite of which is disobeying and
disregarding their rights; Reality as against display; Good as
against being bad; Self-concealment and Self-restraint (in
respect of one's capabilities) as against self-adornment and
self-aggrandisement; Guarding the secret of religion from the
enemies to save life as a measure of strategy as against its
senseless disclosure involving loss of prestige and life; Doing
justice as against partiality; Organisation in human society
(i.e. cordiality of social relations) as against iniquity and
injustice; Purity and refinement as against impurity and
coarseness; Modesty as against immodesty; Moderation as
against extravagance; Cheerfulness and freshness of heart as
against fatigue and depression; Facility as against adversity;
Blessing and enrichment as against wretchedness and
eradication; [Safety and Good Health as against calamity
and affliction;] Steadfastness as against garrulity; Wisdom
as against worldly possessions;*

*Prestige and reverence as against lowness and
lightness; Happiness and felicity as against unhappiness and
misery; Repentance and penitence as against persistance, in
sinful life; Repentance (i.e. asking God for forgiveness) as
against deception and guile over one's sins; Preservation (of
one's capabilities and possessions) as against negligence and
carelessness; Prayerfulness to God as against turning away
from Him; Liveliness with briskness as against dullness
with sloth; Delightfulness as against sadness; Friendship,
intimacy and union against separation and disunion;
Generosity as against miserliness.*

*All the said high qualities which serve as a powerful
army of Reason are never concentrated in any single
individual except in a Prophet, his vicegerent and a believer
whose faith has duly been tried and tested by the Almighty
God. And there is no friend of ours (divinely appointed*

Imam) who does not possess any of these qualities but also possess at the same time some of the disabilities allotted to ignorance until he develops his Reason to perfection and eradicates the disability accruing from ignorance. It is at this stage that he is installed in the high ranks at par with the prophet and his vicegerents. This higher status is achieved through the recognition of Reason and its formidable army and after keeping aloof from ignorance and its allies. May God grant us the ability to obey God and earn His pleasures.[37]

This is Muslim identity: not in defiance with any aspect of rationalization; rather, it is, in itself, a special kind of rationalization of life which has always been recommended by God's prophets and has been regarded, by them, as the noblest quality in mankind.

Endnotes:

[1] Muhammad Muhammadi Reyshahri, Mizan al-Hikmah, Qum, 1404 A.H., Vol. 6, p. 399.

[2] Ibid., p. 398.

[3] Qur'an on many occasions has alluded to this fact. See for example 2/164, 10/42, 13/4, 16/12.

[4] Nahj al-Balaghah, trans. Seyyed Ali Reza, Ahlul Bayt Assembly, U.S.A., 1977, p. 3.

[5] Mizan al-Hikmah, Vol. 6, p. 401.

[6] Ibid., p. 398

[7] M.M. Fayz Kashani, Al-Mahajjat al-Baydha, Qum, Daftare Entesharat Islami, Vol. 1, p. 171.

[8] Mizan al-Hikmah, Vol. 6, p. 423.

[9] Jurgen Habermas, "The Theory of Communicative Action", Vol. 1, trans. T. McCarthy, Beacon Press, 1984, p. 168.

[10] Max Weber, "The Social Psychology of the World Religions.", in Gerth & Mill, eds., "From Max Weber", p. 293.

[11] Max Weber, *Economy and Society* G. Roth & C. Wittich, eds. Berkeley 1978, p. 25.

[12] Ibid., p. 30.

[13] Ibid, p. 627.

[14] Max Weber, The Protestant Ethics and the Spirit of Capitalism, New York, 1958, p. 181.

[15] Ibid., p. 182.

[16] J. Frund, Sociologie de Max Weber, Farsi translation, Tehran, 1368, p. 28.

[17] Economy and Society, p. 25.

[18] The Theory of Communicative Action, p. 86.

[19] Ibid., p. 397.

[20] Ibid., p. 286.

[21] Ibid., p. xxxvi

[22] Ibid., p. 84.

[23] Thomas McCarthy, Reflections on Rationalization Theory of Communicative Action, in *The Frankfurt School.* Eds. Joy Bernstein, Routledge, 1994, Vol. 6, p. 190.

[24] Al Mahajjat al-Baydha, Vol. 8, p. 194

[25] Chapter 3, Verses 190-191.

[26] Mizan al-Hikmah, Vol. 7, p. 543.

[27] Shaykh Abbas Qummi, Safinat al Bihar, Dar al-Uswah, Tehran, 1414 A.H., Vol. 7, p. 144.

[28] Ibid., p. 143.

[29] Mizan al-Hikmah, Vol. 7, p. 542.

[30] Nahja al-Balaghah, tras. Seyyed Ali Reza, Ahlul Bayt Assembly, U.S.A. 1997, p. 3.

[31] Al-Kulayni, Al-Kafi, Trans. Sayyid M.H. Rizvi, W.O.F.I.S. Vol. 1, pp. 31-45.

[32] Mizan al-Hikmah, Vol. 6, p. 37.

[33] Nahj al-Balaghah, Address no. 16.

[34] Ibid., address no. 114

[35] Mizan al-Hikmah, Vol. 6, p. 433.

[36] Ibid., p. 430.

[37] Al Kafi, pp. 51-55.

Cultural Globalization and Muslim Identity

*S. R. Ameli**

INTRODUCTION

In this paper, I begin by making a brief reference to the early formation of Islamic identity, and then look at the general differences that exist between religious identities within traditional, modern and post-modern cultural environments. This critical look is especially relevant to Islamic identity. I continue with an analytical examination of the meaning of globalization and its relevant concepts, including Islamic identity in this context. I shall also briefly consider the different groupings created in response to the international pressure generated from cultural globalization.

To clarify the scope of the discussion, I feel it necessary to point out that when the issue of Muslim identity is debated, I do not intend to analyze the identity issue from philosophical or jurisprudential (*Fiqhi*) points of view. Neither do I wish to look at this issue from an ethical perspective or from within any religious discipline.

For the purposes of the present paper it is necessary to make a distinction between Islamic and Muslim identities. Muslim identity, as such, becomes a relevant topic for sociology, anthropology, psychology, political science or even the philosophy of social sciences

* Institute of Islamic Studies, Islamic Centre England - London

- where the interaction between religion and society is studied - while Islamic identity, as a topic, becomes the subject of analysis within the domain of philosophy, divinity, theology and related areas. One must bear in mind that there is a close relationship between the two identities and certainly one can not analyze Muslim identity without paying attention to the important issue of Islamic religion.

ORIGIN AND DEVELOPMENT OF ISLAMIC IDENTITY

The issues of selfhood, or identity, and globalization are two of the most important issues of the second millennium. Religious identity is the by-product of the interaction between religion and society. It is through this interaction that religious ethos and principles manifest themselves in different forms of action.

Religious identity is a collection of symbols and indicators that are fused together and used by individuals to measure the strength of their own religious identity and it will accordingly have a social manifestation. The formation of Islamic identity exhibited itself in the shape of religious struggle within the context of Islamic Jihad and in the form of unyielding resistance when subjected to torture by those who rejected the divine message.

This Islamic character also shows itself in many other norms, conducts, costumes and values that collectively differentiate Muslims from non-Muslims. Accordingly identity becomes a kind of lining up and a closing of ranks as well as an independent and detached way of thinking that differentiates Muslim societies from non-Muslim societies living around them. It is natural to believe that due to the force of circumstances imposed on the early Muslims, their Islamic identity manifested itself primarily in the shape of resistance to the external pressure. Although this is a unique characteristic of the early days of Islam, we find that at the end of the second millennium, Muslims are again having to express their Islamic identity in the form of religious resistance. The religious uprising of Muslim communities within the midst of European and North American societies, the uprising of black Muslims under the banner of the Nation of Islam and other similar movements are only different modes of this same religious resistance.

Over the years, Islamic selfhood has undergone numerous and diverse changes. Primarily, these changes have been due to differing cultures, political structures, histories and social systems, as well as geographical distance. These differing factors in different parts of the world resulted in diverse models being used to express the notion of Islamic identity. Personal interpretation and perceptions have had a noticeable effect on the emergence of diverging methods of expressing Islamic identity. It is clear that despite the existence of a high degree of communality between all Muslims, the mode of expression used by each nation to show their Islamic identity is different. One only needs to look at the manifestation of this identity in Pakistani, Turkish, Albanian, Indonesian, Iranian or Iraqi Muslims.

TRANSITION FROM A TRADITIONAL SOCIETY TO A MODERN AND POST-MODERN SOCIETY

A further structural change within the concept of Muslims' identity, as well as all the other collective religious identities that have come to the forefront, is the transformation within the social structure that has taken place and the transition from a traditional society to a modern one. This transition has brought with it a new culture known as the post-modern culture. As fast and efficient engine-driven transportation facilities and mass communication systems were not available in the traditional society, communities tended to be isolated and removed from other societies and cultures. An agricultural-based economy and non-delegatory social responsibilities over large extended families in a predominantly rural society created a very simple society within which the pace of change of religious identity was extremely slow. The slowness of the change created an illusion of permanence of religious identity, such that this identity was seen as being passed from one generation to another with hardly any change taken place within each generation. A very strong and powerful religious norm was in control of all the religious activities that took place within a society and any attempt to make changes within the domain of religions thinking or action would have faced strong social resistance. Based on these factors, one could safely assume that "integration", "continuity" and "solidarity" were part of the religious characteristic of a traditional society. As the technological revolution brought about mass communication and a quantum leap within the development of media, societies became part of an environment that was totally different from that prevailing within a traditional society.

At this juncture in time, religious identity went through unique changes. Firstly, a religious society suddenly found itself facing institutions that were totally detached from religious belief and offered new sciences that were devoid of all religious inclinations. Secondly, if we were to define post-modernity as the unique cultural by-product of the institutionalization of modern phenomena (more professional film-making in cinema, global satellite television, international news houses and agencies, science acquiring an international language, multinational economic cartels becoming more powerful, the reliance of society on networking, increased importance placed on leisure, excitement, fashion, and change) then it is possible, to a degree, to distinguish and differentiate between modern and post-modern society. Despite this distinction, one must be aware that using such a definition does not enable a clear separation to be made between modern and post-modern society, as it is not possible to fix a historical time that marks the end modernity and the beginning of post-modernity.

The fragmentation of religious identities, the relativization of religious belief and the pluralization of religious understanding are only few of the distinct characteristics of a post-modern society. It is within such a cultural environment, particularly from the 1960s to the present, that one sees claims being made to the effect that religion should be regarded as a private affair and that the significance and relevance of religion is diminishing daily. Advocates of this view are primarily concerned with the Christian world and/or socialist societies and their conclusions are drawn from events taking place in these societies. The works of three eminent sociologists who researched and theorized about the role of religion in society, that is Durkheim (1976), Marx (1963), and Weber (1963), show that all of them are of the opinion that religion has no role to play and should be marginalized even further. However, of the three aforementioned sociologists, only Weber considered Islam to be an exception to this general rule. He believes that due to the inherent social potential that exists in Islam, it will remain an effective and a potent force within society. Giddens (1989) on the other hand, while supporting Weber in his point of view, claims that at a time when other religions are seen to be totally irrelevant to the development of societies, the appearance of a religious revolution in Iran, means that we must accept that religion as a social phenomenon has a very important role to play.

The development and use of professional and sophisticated technology in global communications has been one of the most explicit and powerful markers of this period. This communication technology has created cultural, economical and political globalization. The extent of this globalization has forced religious identity into crises. Religious identity has had to react and rise to the challenge and the response has manifested itself externally in many different ways. I shall attempt to shed some light on these different manifestations but before doing so I want to consider the concepts of globalization and religious identity in more detail.

THE CONCEPT OF GLOBALIZATION AND ITS IMPACT ON MUSLIM IDENTITY

The Concept of Globalization

Sociologists have defined globalization in many different ways. Robertson (1992) defines globalization as the process by which the world becomes a single place, where events in one part of the world have significant consequences for action in another part of the world. For Giddens, (1989: 520) globalization is the general term for the increasing interdependence of world society. For him, it would be a mistake to think of globalization simply as a process of the growth of world unity. He argues that the globalizing of social relations should be understood, primarily, as the reordering of time and distance in our lives. In this way, activities and events happening well away from the social contexts in which we carry on our day-to-day activities have an increasing influence on our lives. Waters (1995: 3) defines globalization as a social process in which the constraints of geography on social and cultural arrangements recede, and in which people become increasingly aware that they are receding. He believes that globalization is the direct consequence of the expansion of European culture across the planet, via settlement, colonization and cultural mimesis.

What is common between and supported by all these definitions is the belief that communication technology from transportation, telecommunication, mass media and global television and radio, to cinema, Internet, newspapers and news agencies has linked the cultural relations of all societies and has in effect created what McLuhan (1964) called the "Global Village" but on a grand scale (Gurveitch, 1991: 178). If in the past neighbourhood referred to the locality of the same avenue, or even small town, today neighbourhood has a much wider social scope. Sociologists like Waters, Beyer (1990, 1994 and 1998) and Featherstone (1995) have defined globalization to be, in effect, global Westernization, irrespective of whether this definition holds true in all cases or not. One must admit that the spirit of Western culture is manifesting itself in many non-Western cultures. McDonalds, Coca-Cola, jeans, rock music and many other aspects of American culture can be seen in the midst of societies that are separated from American culture by thousands of miles. The commercial products, cultural phenomena and international politics of a particular system claiming to be a global power enables the creation of an artificial culture that follows its own way of life. Featherstone, (1995) crystallizes this point by pointing out that the McDonalds snack or the Coca-Cola drink are not only consumed physically as material substances, but are consumed culturally as an icon of a particular way of life.

Let me end this section by pointing out, as Waters had done, that globalization primarily works in three major areas: politics, economic and culture. While they are independent, there is a close link between them and each one influences and is influenced by the other. It is simply impossible to look at the globalization of culture without paying attention to the domain of politics and economics.

Therefore, the globalization of culture is a phenomenon that influences and is influenced by economic and political factors.

Characteristics of Globalization

What is the culture of globalization? A brief look at the changes that have taken place within the structure of societies that have gone through this transition, would show that there are three distinct religious-cultural effects within the sphere of religious thinking, beliefs and actions. One is the speed of change within cultural phenomena, in total contrast to the slow pace of change within traditional societies that created an illusion of permanence. The second effect is that ethical and religious values lost their absoluteness and turned into relative concepts, this in turn led to a pluralistic attitude towards religion. And finally, the third effect is the extreme conflicts between religion and various by-products of cultural globalization.

Rapid change is a feature of a globalizing society. It raises the probability of perceived anomie at the personal and group level when too much changes over too short a period of time. On a deeper and more important level, however, speed is less an issue than the direction of change and the issue of who controls the change. In broad terms, the problem is one of power, not just meaning. The accelerated change that societies are struggling with is essentially due to environmental factors. Television, radio, the huge, well- organized and professional film making industries, advertising and the appearance of various models of thinking are coming into contact with other cultures in the world through diverse media and publications. What has been created is a huge networking society. An inherent part of its characteristics is its ability to change the concepts of entertainment, fashion and beauty. This is a society that continually changes and the speed of change within its cultural and artistic domains has not allowed any time for thinking and reflection. The ceaseless pace of change has not left any time for globalization to mix with any culture or for selfhood and identity to assert itself. In a constantly changing environment, it is very difficult to shape one's identity.

Globalization brings with it the relativization of particularistic identities along with the relativization of religion as mode of social communication (Beyer, 1994: 4). The speed of change within the present world has made Man incapable of making decisions and denies him the time needed for reflection. Consequently, religious and cultural values have lost their absolute character and have been turned into relative issues. In such an environment, one's mind is constantly moving from one issue to the next and from one picture to another. The closeness and proximity of the cultures and the religious thinking have made the process of decision-making more difficult.

Plurality within the domain of culture, religious thinking and beliefs has been a further by-product of the relativism that has been generated by globalization. This mode of thinking denies the absolute nature of any values and rejects the idea that any one particular kind of thinking has a monopoly on truth.

Significant conflict between spiritual identity and globalization

Disregarding the social and political dimensions, spirituality, holiness and beliefs in the hereafter are essential constituents of all divine religions, especially Islam. In contrast to these beliefs, globalization is making every effort to institutionalize materialism and selfishness. It is also endeavouring to negate and neutralize spirituality and holiness. Within the post-modern world, this aim is entrenched in the language of economics and cultural products.

Muslim Identity.

What is the Muslim identity? Before we define Islamic identity, we need to clearly define identity itself. Once we have a clear definition of identity in general, religion and Muslim identities can be defined.

The concept of identity, initially, emerged from psychology and was then developed into a sociological concept. From a psychological point of view, identity means the sense of self that develops as the child differentiates itself from parents and family and takes a place in society. In other words, identity refers to a sense of personal distinctiveness together with personal continuity and personal autonomy. In sociology and social psychology, the more common conceptions of identity tend to stress the fact that a sense of identity is formed from the dialectic between the individual and society. To Eriksen, (1991) the term identity connotes both a persistent sameness within oneself (self-sameness) and a persistent sharing of some kind of essential character with others (cited by Mol, 1976: 57). Berger and Luckmann (1967: 174) defined identity as a phenomenon that emerges from the dialectic between individual and society. Religious identity is the outcome of a religious personality, where the religious dimension manifest itself in one's thoughts, behaviour, words and actions. Accordingly, religious identities enjoy a particular name, a relatively clear history and a clearly established system of rules and regulation. Deep-rooted history, myths, legends, role models, rituals and regulations support this identity.

As for defining Muslim identity, it is difficult to arrive at a single definition due to the diversity of culture and character of those following Islam. It is possible, however, to use qualitative characteristics to define Muslim identity. In another words, the use of different and varied criteria, such as the type of nationalistic or secularistic characteristics, intellectual approach and conformity to tradition, can be used to define a particular group. Each of these characteristics is unique in itself and cannot be described in general terms, in this paper.

Fragility of Muslim Identity

Returning to globalization and its effect on religious identities, especially that of Muslim identity, it must be admitted that globalizational processes have created a slippery surface for those actively and dynamically intent on conforming to, maintaining and perpetuating a religious identity. Globalization has driven the effect of religion out of the social domain and into a personal environment, consequently changing the way of thinking of human societies. Beyer (1990:373-395) supports this point. His thesis, proposes that the globalization of society, while structurally favouring privatization in religion, also provides fertile ground for the renewed public influence of religion. By public influence, Beyer means that one or more religions can become the source of a collective obligation, such that deviation from specific religious norms will bring, in its wake, negative consequences for adherents and non-adherents alike.

Therefore, collective action in the name of these norms becomes legitimate.

Of course, what has been said should not be taken to mean a general decline in religious tendencies but it does mean that there has been a reduction within the sphere of religious influence. For example, a brief look at the collective conscience of societies would show that not only is there no decline in the belief in God in Western societies, especially in North America, but also that there is a marked increase in religious studies. There is, however, a marked decline in the preservation of religion as an ideology with its own way of thinking, social structure and system of education. The change within religious motivation does not stem from changes within deep-rooted ideological perception, like dialectic materialism replacing metaphysics, or from a profound shift in people's disposition towards the reality of living and life. The change is primarily due to people being busy with the colourful and ever-changing picture of daily living and the very real power it has to attract them.

Turner has also cited this point. Turner, (1994) believes that religion is not undermined by matters of cognition but by the whole structure and style of the globalization processes that commodify everyday life. He suggests that the main threat to the Islamicization of knowledge is not cognitive. The main threat to religious faith is in fact the commodification of everyday life. People do not adopt or reject belief systems simply on the rationalistic grounds that they are not intellectually coherent. Beliefs are adopted or rejected because they are relevant or not relevant to everyday needs and concerns. What makes religious faith or religious commitment problematic in a globalized post-modern society is that everyday life has become part of a global system of exchange of commodities, which are not easily influenced by political leaders, intellectuals or religious leaders. The corruption of protein faith is going to be brought about by Tina Turner and Coca-Cola and not by rational arguments and rational inspection of presuppositions and the understanding of Western secularism. This is what is wrong fundamentally with Gellner's book Postmodernism, Reason and Religion (1992) and Ahmed's book on Post-modern and Islam (1992). They are both talking about intellectual cognitive problems of religious leaders and intellectuals, not the problems of everyday life. What they both fail to emphasise is that the Ford motor car did more damage to Christianity than any type of argumentation (Turner, 1994: 10).

As we have pointed out, a further reason for the break-up of religious identities is that identity and selfhood are, essentially, like a building that has a clear and strong foundation. While the trend of globalization is not dissimilar to a whirlpool that first breaks down all the historical ties and because of the inherent complexity and ambiguity within its nature, and within the values created in this period, it impacts on religious identity, and even on nationalistic selfhood, and generates the same ambiguity and vagueness in them. Consequently, religious identities are turned into myths and this metamorphosis takes the shape of a new way of thinking for this period. Kellner, (1995: 233) suggests this point from the post-modern perspective. For Kellner, as the pace, extension and complexity of modern societies accelerate, identity becomes more and more unstable, more and more fragile.

Within this situation, the discourses of post-modernity problematize the very notion of identity, claiming that it is a myth and an illusion. Post-modern theorists claim that subjects have imploded into masses (Baudrillard 1983), and that a fragmented, disjointed, and discontinuous mode of experience is a fundamental characteristic of post-modern culture, in terms of both its subjective experiences and its texts (cited by Kellner, 233). Many of the post-modern theories privilege media culture as the site of the implosion of identity and the fragmentation of the subject, yet there have been few in-depth studies of media texts and their effect from this perspective (Kellner, 1995: 234). The phenomena of nostalgia and self-alienation that were debated by Baudrillard (1983) and Robertson (1992), has become the major problem that religious identity has to face. These phenomena turn into a kind of descent and widespread sickness that leads to breakdown and decay within the notion of religious identity. According to Baudrillard (1983:12), 'when the real is no longer what it used to be, nostalgia assumes its full meaning'. Baudrillard has claimed that post-modern culture distinguishes neither between reality and unreality, nor between true or false representation. For Robertson (1992:159), in the late twentieth-century nostalgia is intimately bound up with the globalized body, which is embodied in consumerism. He describes the almost globally institutionalized nostalgia that is a product of contemporary processes (Robertson, 1990:55).

The pace of change is so speedy that people do not posses any permanent values in their lives. As a matter of fact, there seems to be a complete breakdown in all social relations. This in turn lends to one not having an anchor in one's life and all one's attachments being short-lived. In addition, the reality of this period leads to a distancing between the physical Man and his true spirit, which in religious teaching is expressed as the *Fitrah* (true nature) of Man. These teachings tell us that Man can only find serenity and peace when he discovers his true spirit and that a distancing between the physical Man and his true nature leads to self alienation, loneliness and nostalgia. Of course, this kind of interpretation is beyond the scope of sociology.

MUSLIM RESPONSE TO THE GLOBALIZATION PROCESS

What has been cited so far would lead us to conclude that the issue of identity selfhood and globalization are among two of the most important cultural issues of the second millennium. There is no doubt that the environment created by globalization differs totally from our entire past history. The new cultural environment, as Waters puts it, has created a geopolitical-quake across diverse societies and has influenced their entire social structures. For Robertson, globalization is the process by which, due to the compression of the world, collectivises and forces individuals to interact at new levels of intensity, and therefore to re-formulate their identities with respect to one another. This involves the alteration, retrenchment or invention of new social identities and the transformation of symbolic boundaries. Giddens, (1991: 32) claims that, "Transformations in self-identity and globalization are the two poise of the dialectic of the local and the global in conditions of high modernity".

There is no doubt that Muslims' response to the pressure

generated by the globalization of culture is not the same from one society to another. Therefore it is not possible to take a uniform approach or response to this matter. There is a structural difference between the response of the older generation and that of the new. The fundamental difference between men and women's reactions to the phenomenon in the latter part of second millennium is also very interesting.

What emerges from the research carried out and arguments put forward by different scholars is that, in response to the compelling influence of globalization, there are four different types of selfhood and identity emerging:

- Resistance identity
- Legitimizing identity
- Mix hybrid identity
- Drifting vagrant identity

When Muslims find themselves in a minority, whether religious or cultural, in terms of their response to Western culture, they either respond negatively towards the prevailing environment, or they become assimilated and absorbed into the environment. Sometimes they find themselves in an intermediate state between the two cultures. They absorb a certain amount of both cultures and can lose their sense of direction and drift aimlessly during routine daily life - together with its special characteristics, and more permanent relationships.

Resistance Identity

Resistance identity is generated by those who are in positions/conditions that are devalued and/or stigmatized by the logic of domination, thus building trenches of resistance and survival on the basis of principles different from, or opposed to, those permeating the institutions of society (Castells, 1997). As we have pointed out earlier, this kind of identity is similar to the sense of identity felt by Muslims in the early period of Islamic history. The reason for this similarity, could be the common perceptions and feelings that are shared by both periods: the sense of danger, the sense of scorn and humiliation, the sense of losing all value (religious and humanistic) and the sense of being deprived of peace and tranquillity. The desire to resist social trends that generate these feelings is of course a natural part of the human character.

Resistance identity in essence originates from the insecurity and danger that is felt by Muslims when faced with Western culture. These feelings force individuals to return to the perceived security and safety of tradition. This type of identity is clearly visible within Islamic societies, especially those living as minorities in Western countries. The religious uprising of Muslims around the world, the formations of very serious and strongly traditional religious movements within the European and North American society and the black Muslim up-rising under the banner of the Nation of Islam are nothing but examples of this type of identity. They are a strong reaction in response to the profanities that are directed against everything sacred in religion. One could cite the Salman Rushdie affair, the strong Muslim objection to the use of the word Mecca for bingo halls and the derogatory films that have been made about Islam as classical examples and manifestations of this type of identity.

One must remember that objecting to profanity and resisting attacks on religious values are not exclusively Muslim characteristics. Such resistance is also found in the Christian world, although it may be manifested in different ways. The demand for a return to a purist Christian society, the inclination towards Gnosticism and the spiritual schisms that ensue, are nothing but examples of this trend within Christian societies. Parekh, (1990) suggests a similar point when he says that in the face of an advancing global culture, many societies display an understandable tendency to return to the security of the traditional way of life and to romanticize a past age. Robertson (1985) is also opposed to the general direction of secularization arguments in the sociology of religion. He hints that globalization might involve the resacralization of the world (world in the sense of that which is secular or profane). In order to make sense of our lives in this new, global context, many groups are re-enchanting the world using old or new religious symbols. Robertson says he would be surprised if there was not a resurgence of religion in response to globalization.

The globalization process, therefore, is not without resistance.

Resistance may take the form of an opposition to the world as a single whole (which Robertson calls anti-modernity), or an opposition to the conception of the world as a series of equivalent, relativized, ways of life (which he calls anti-postmodernity). Within Turner's framework, Islamic fundamentalism is seen as a reaction against cultural and social differentiation and fragmentation. More specifically, fundamentalism is an attempt at de-differentiation (Turner, 1994:77).

There are numerous similarities between the religious resistance of early Islam and that of the post-modern period. In the early part of Islamic history, Muslims found themselves trapped between two different kinds of treatment. From one side, the most appalling humiliation was inflicted on them and from the other side, the highest honour and reverence awaited them. The depth of their conviction and their commitment to their cause led them to persist with their slogans and to resist any pressure to deviate from them. In their endeavour to achieve reverence they were even prepared to give up their lives and become martyrs. These beliefs constituted the basic foundation of Islamic identity. Presently, the entire religious uprising has the nature of resistance, because Muslims have found themselves facing a similar environment. They have found themselves in an environment where their religion and cultural inheritance are subjected to ridicule and all their historical values endangered. With the advent of the 21st century, this feeling is shared by many sections of the society.

Legitimizing Identity

Legitimizing identity is that which is introduced by the dominant institutions of society in order to extend and rationalize their domination vis-à-vis social actors, a theme that is at the heart of Sennett's theory of authority and domination, but also fits with various theories of nationalism. Such identities are the result of conformity between selfhood and the social institutions of a society. In other words, this identity is the by-product of an acceptance of the institutionalized norms of a society.

The Muslim minorities that live in the West are surrounded by many social institutions that are non-Islamic in nature and character.

Across the entire political infrastructure and in all areas of education, entertainment and leisure (schools, television, radio, cinema, newspapers and other literature) the environment and general culture of the West are alien to the Muslim mode of thinking. Hence, it is natural to believe, as Castells (1997) has indicated, that legitimizing identity can only take shape in a civil society as such identities follow the general condition, norms and legal and social order of a society.

Hybrid Identity

Mixed identities are, in essence, identities that have been influenced equally by two major factors. From one side, they are affected by a deep-rooted attachment to everything that has been passed from one generation to the next throughout history. This dimension of identity is shaped and moulded within the environments of home, school, mosque and the general cultural domains that were important to the person.

In reality, one's religious personality is the outcome of these factors. The other dimension of identity is shaped by the newly created general environment that one lives in, and struggles with on a daily basis. This kind of identity can be seen within immigrant communities whereby the new generation, primarily made up of young people, have a mixed culture arising from a metamorphosis of the starting culture and the end culture.

The contemporary society is also an amalgam of a traditional identity and a modern identity. This blend of two identities, forces one to have two completely different pictures of the same situation, just like a person that masters two different languages and is familiar with two different cultures. Such a person is continuously faced with two roots, two beliefs and two ways of thinking. He finds himself, ceaselessly, swayed by two opposing waves, and torn between two forces that are at variance with each other. Such a mix in one's character could be due to one's dual motives or due to the effect of the two major external sources that influence a person. In a recent study, Jessica Jacobson, (1998) has shown that the majority of second generation Muslims in the West suffer such a paradox.

Vagrant Identity

This type of identity is exclusively for the youth, especially that of modern youth. The sense of hopelessness that one feels, when one is subjected to change on a huge scale, as well as monotonous daily activities and conflicting and contradicting role models, leads one towards a dual personality. Social disillusionment and association with groups of weak characters, are two more factors which generate a vagrant identity within individuals.

When one lives within a society that has no clear aims, each community searches for its own goals and agenda. The ambiguity which arises in such an environment, together with severance of deep-rooted historical ties, leads to despondency and ultimately to a vagrant identity. The decentralization of the importance of values, religious activities and conduct, also add a further strain on one's search for identity, leading to further confusion and uncertainty. Within traditional societies, the factors that influenced people's identity were very limited and few. In contrast, within contemporary societies, there is multiplicity of factors and sources each having a direct or indirect influence on an individual's search for identity. The consequences of such a condition are the feelings of hopelessness and nostalgia as well as loneliness. Once one is subjected to such an environment it would be extremely difficult, if not impossible, for one to maintain any particular belief or to follow one specific path. One finds one's determination and resolve weakened when faced with such an overwhelming pressure.

Global Religion

Just as new technology has created the right environment for the globalization of Western cultures, or to be more precise, the culture of Western commercial multinational institutions, it has also created the right environment for the globalization of other cultures. If, for the most part of human history, these cultures existed in parallel but totally isolated from Western culture, then the present technological development prepared the way for these cultures to come together and, by working together, to transform into a global entity. One only needs to look at the thousands of international religious or non-religious organizations and associations that are active around the world. The available technologies have made it possible for a small community to have the news of its activities turned into news headlines in a very short time.

Globalization has made it possible for one to access all corners of the earth. Religious activities and beliefs are not an exception to this phenomenon. After the late Imam Khomeini's fatwa, when Salman Rushdie was asked by the Channel Four correspondent as how he reacted to the fatwa, Rushdie replied "Initially I thought that it would be a short lived affair, fatwa has been issued in another parts of the world, its effect will be local, however within twenty four hours, I realized that the fatwa has turned into an international symbol and the whole world became unsafe for me".

Globalization within the domain of religion, especially due to Islam's belief in the universality of its calls and messages, make it possible for Islamic issues to turn into international issues. This is also the case with other divine religions.

CONCLUSION

The conclusion that I draw from this discussion is that cultural globalization is closely linked to political and economic globalization. They cannot be separated from one another. The effects of the globalizational trend on Muslim identities is not uniform and the consequences of globalization do not necessarily lead to the assimilation of Islamic identity or to Islamic conformity to this culture. In numerous cases, Islamic identity takes the defensive route and resists the prevailing universal culture. A direct correlation between the two issues can be identified. The more the pressure, humiliation and contempt are directed against the Islamic identity, then the stronger and more powerful its spirit of resistance can become. As for hybrid identities, the internal conflict within individuals to which this gives rise could lead them to crises of identity, resulting in further self alienation and nostalgia.

Finally, my discussion in the paper might be considered theoretical and could possibly be further developed by sociological research and analysis.

Bibliography:

Ahmed, A. (1992) *Postmodernsim and Islam*, London & New York, Routledge.

Baudrillard, (1983) *Simulation.* Translated by Paul Foss, Paul Patton, and Philip Beitchman. New York: Semiotext(e).

Berger, P. and Luckmann, T., (1967) *The Social Construction of Reality*, London, Allen Lane the Penguin Press.

Beyer, P. (1990) *'Privatization and the public influence of religion in global society'* in M. Featherstone (ed.) Global Culture, London, SAGE.

Beyer, P. (1994) *Religion and Globalization*, London, SAGE.

Beyer, P. (1998) *'Globalizing System, Global Culture, Models and Religion(s),'* in *International sociology*, March 1998: vol. 13(1):79-94, London, Thousand Oaks, CA and New Delhi, SAGE.

Castells, M., (1997) *The Information Age: Economy, Society and Culture Volume II: The Power of Identity*, Blackwell, Great Britain.

Durkheim, E. (1976)*The Elementary Forms of the Religious Life* (London: Allen and Unwin. First Publish: 1912).

Eriksen, T. H. (1991) *The Cultural Contexts of ethnic Differences, Man* 26, (1) page 127-44.

Featherstone, M. (1990) *'Global Culture: an introduction'*, in M. Featherstone (ed) Global Culture. London: SAGE.

Featherstone, M. (1995) *Undoing Culture: Globalization, Postmodernism and Identity*, London, Thousan Oaks & New Delhi, SAGE.

Gellner, E. (1992) *Postmodernism, Reason and Religion*, London & New York, Routledge.

Giddens, A. (1991) *Modernity and Self-Identity: Self and Society in the Late Modern Age.* Stanford University Press.

Jacobson, J. (1998) *Islam in Transition: Religion and Identity Among British Pakistani Youth*, London & New York, Routledge.

McLuhan, M. (1964) *Understanding Media*, London, Routledge.

Kellner, D., (1995) *Media Culture, Cultural Studies, Identity and Politics between Modern and Post-modern*, London and New York, Routledge.

Marx, K. (1963) *'Economic and Philosophical Manuscripts'* in T. B. Bottomore (ed), *Karl Marx: Early Writings*, Harmondosworth, Penguin.

Mol, H., (1976) *Identity and The Sacred: A Sketch for a New Social-Scientific Theory of Religion*, Great Britain, Basil Blackwell . Oxford.

Parekh, B. (1990) *Britain and the social logic of pluralism in Britain: a Plural Society*, London: Commission for Racial Equality.

Parker, D., (1995) *Through Different Eyes: The Cultural Identities of Young Chinese People in Britain*, Hong Kong, Singapore and Sydney, Avebury.

Robertson, R. and Chirico, J. (1985) *Humanity, Globalization and WorldWide Religious Resurgence: a Theoretical Exploration*, Sociological Analysis: 46 (3).

Robertson, R., (1990) *After Nostalgia? Wilful Nostalgia and the phases of globalization* in B. S. Turner (ed.) *Theories of Modernity and Post-Modernity*, London, Sage.

Robertson, R.,(1992) *Globalization: Social Theory and Global culture*, London, Sage.

Turner, B. S. (1994) *Orientalism, Postmodernism & Globalism*, London & New York, Routledge.

Waters, M. (1995) *Globalization*, London & New York, Routledge.

Weber, M. (1963) *The Sociology of Religion*, Boston, Mass Beacon.

The Future of Young Workers under Islamic versus Western Economic Systems

Karen Pfeifer*

ABSTRACT

Given the relative stagnation and high unemployment rates of the countries of the Middle East, what positive contributions might the Islamic business sector make to improve the future outlook of young workers? In a small, non-random sample of 15 firms in Egypt, it was found that the 8 non-Islamic firms, as a group, had a significantly higher rate of profit, but that the 7 Islamic firms that paid significantly higher wages, had a lower profit/wage ratio and were more likely to share profits with workers. The Islamic business sector can make a contribution to economic growth by improving its innovativeness and productivity performance, raising profitability to fund greater investment in the future. At the same time, it should not sacrifice its superior equity performance in a false "trade-off of equity for efficiency," but use the profit-sharing system to include workers in investment for growth and new employment.

* Smith College, Northampton MA 01063, USA

INTRODUCTION

Slow economic growth, high unemployment and stagnant living standards nettle the countries of the Middle East. Even those countries in the Arab World designated as successful economic reformers by the International Monetary Fund, after years of "structural adjustment," face high rates of unemployment. In 1995, according to the IMF's own estimates, Egypt's rate was between 10% and 22%, Jordan's 14%, Tunisia's 15% and Morocco's 23%.[1] Morocco experienced two rounds of what began as peaceful political protest by unemployed school graduates in Rabat in November of 1998 - the second one broken up by riot police wielding clubs. The massive crisis of bankruptcies and disemployment induced by the Asia financial crisis in model developers Indonesia and Malaysia, also Islamic countries, has further undermined the credibility of the path promoted by the IMF. A developing country in crisis cannot rely on foreign capital alone for investment, employment and income growth.

If "structural adjustment" does not generate the development necessary to produce growth of new employment, then how else might it come about? No other single source seems adequate. The exhaustion of the state-led route to development, with the contradictions entailed in its reliance on import-substitution industrialization, implies that governments are, today, ill-equipped to foster sufficient investment for sustainable economic growth. The domestic private sector in developing countries is, in general, bifurcated between a formal sector dominated by a few large, well-connected and influential private companies or corporate groups and an informal sector, in which microenterprises are related to each other, their market and the rest of the economy in anarchic and, often, obscure ways. Further, while a growing informal sector might generate new employment due to its labor-intensive working methods, microenterprises cannot provide better than substandard wages, benefits or working conditions.While the remains of the public sector, the foreign capital sector and the formal and informal domestic capital sectors might together invest sufficiently to create additional new jobs, the fact is that, they have not yet done so - at least in the four Arab countries named above. Indonesia and Malaysia show that, even if it is done, it can become undone, especially in a globalized economy where investors freely move their capital across borders.

What role, if any, might the Islamic business sector play in this developmental scenario, specifically in providing new employment with decent wages, benefits and working conditions? If Islamic firms behave and perform differently from non-Islamic firms, in the face of a common set of competitive pressures and a common institutional and legal environment, the Islamic sector might be another important source of investment and, simultaneously, set a new standard for growth with equity.

THE ISLAMIC ECONOMIC ETHOS

Islamic economics can most fruitfully be understood from a socio-economic (or institutionalist) perspective.[2] An economic system is not absolute and universal, but embedded in a socio-cultural context. People's economic behaviour is based on shared cultural understandings. Even the "pursuit of self-interest" by the rational individualist is learned, and this form of behaviour coexists with other forms based on social or altruistic motives such as "teamwork" on the job or charitable giving for purposes other than tax deductions.

Islamic economics' critique of Western economic values devolves out of this same logic. "Homo economicus," who pursues self-interest, usually in the form of profit maximization, to the exclusion of all else voids life of meaning and robs human beings of their souls. Welfare systems for the poor are variable and undependable because no-one is defined as being responsible for the poor. Capitalist firms milk their workers as hard as they can with callous disregard for their humanity, leading to exploitation and class conflict. The payment of interest to idle money balances severs the link between production and remuneration and contributes to widening income inequalities.

These critiques lead Islamic economists to call for the development of economies based on more humane precepts. Instead of "Homo economicus," "Homo Islamicus" pursues profits subject to moral and religious constraints and social supervision. Instead of a "welfare state," now being deconstructed by structural adjustment anyway, the systematic institution of *zakah* (annual wealth tax of 2.5%) makes all property owners responsible for the welfare of the poor in a predictable way. Islamic welfare organizations have replaced the ineffective state in several countries (especially Egypt and the West Bank and Gaza) in providing support for healthcare, education and social services for the poor.

Income redistribution, as well as poverty, is also addressed by *zakah* (one has to give away part of one's income-producing wealth each year) and by inheritance rules such as the prohibition of primogeniture and the protection of a female heir's right to a share equal to half that of the male. By these rules, it is difficult for property ownership to become concentrated in a few hands.

Islamic employers can reduce exploitation and class conflict by cultivating harmony in the workplace, showing workers respect and setting a good example in religious and social practices.[3] They can provide better remuneration, both in the absolute level of salaries paid and in shallower top-to-bottom salary ratios. They can keep employment steady even when demand for their product falls. They can engage in profit-sharing to reduce inequality between owners and workers and also to motivate workers to raise productivity. Exploitation and class conflict can be reduced by the substitution of interest-free banking, the profit-and-loss-sharing system (PLS), in place of the Western style banking at interest.

METHOD OF THE RESEARCH

The research undertaken[4] asked whether Islamic business firms might meet these expectations in an economic environment shared with non-Islamic firms in a country like Egypt. Egypt was chosen because it has the largest and most diverse economy in the Arab World, including a growing private sector and a well-established Islamic business sub-sector.[5]

The inquiry was conducted using the case study method, based on interviews in 1993 and 1994 with the owners or general managers of 15 non-financial companies operating in agriculture, industry and the service sector. Banks and financial firms *per se* were deliberately excluded from the sample. The non-random sample of firms was obtained through the network of contacts the researcher was able to build over a one-year period. Each interview lasted about 2 hours.[6] Additional information was gleaned from trips to industrial centers and a farm outside of Cairo where tours of production facilities were provided to the researcher.

The subject firms were separated into two groups, Islamic (IFs) and non-Islamic (NIFs), based on their methods of finance. As shown in Table 1, these two groups were then loosely matched into pairs by type of industry: plastics manufacturing, automotive manufacturing, textiles and clothing, meatprocessing and poultry production, publishing and printing, prepared food and tourist services, household appliances and carpets, with one non-Islamic firm left over in the production of household chemicals.

Because it was not feasible for the sample to be randomly drawn or for checks on reliability of accounting data to be obtained, the results are not definitive. However, they do suggest important similarities and differences between the two types of firms.

FINANCE AND PROFIT DISTRIBUTION

The methods of finance used by our firms can be summarized as follows:

- family or partners savings   6 IFs   6 NIFs
- never borrow at interest   7 IFs   --
- commercial bank loans or
  development funds   --   8 NIFs
- Islamic banks or groups   4 IFs   --

- retained earnings   1 IF   3 NIFs
- stock market   1 IF   --

The two groups are about equal in terms of the predominant importance of personal savings to the firm, understandable given the small size of most private sector firms in Egypt. What most clearly distinguishes the two groups is that the owner/managers of all IFs indicated that their firm never borrows (or lends) at interest. In contrast, the eight NIFs all take loans or place deposits at interest. Another difference is that three NIFs rely on retained earnings while only one IF does so. Only one firm, an IF, raises capital on the stock market.

Four IFs have strong connections to Islamic banks or investment groups using *musharakah* or *murabahah*. This arrangement provides the Islamic firm with the benefit of the bank's technical advice and market information as well as finance. However, it also forces the firm to share managerial control with the bank, and, if only Islamic methods of finance are available, this may alter the firm's decision-making process.[7]

All fifteen firms stated that net profits are shared in proportion to equity held by the investors. This seems to be a rock-hard principle of both capitalist and Islamic business. Four Islamic firms (Clothing-IF, Meatprocessing-IF, Publishing-IF and Appliances-IF) and three non-Islamic firms (Poultry-NIF, Publishing-NIF and Tourism services-NIF) indicated (often elsewhere in the interview) that the owner-manager took a salary before net profits were distributed. The rationale for this practice is that the owner-manager is contributing his time and expertise as well as his capital to the enterprise.

Bank lending or bank investment aside, then, the two sets of firms are rather similar in other methods of finance and do not differ at all in methods of profit-distribution.

ASSETS AND PROFITS

Text Tables 1 through 6 draw from the accounting data base in Appendix B. Following El-Ashker's method,[8] profits are calculated as total revenues minus total costs for 1993, and fixed assets are determined by replacement value at the end of 1992. Our rate of profit, then, is profits relative to fixed assets (we do not have enough data to calculate net profit).

Table 1 presents the values for fixed assets and loans outstanding. The NIFs all have greater assets than their matched IFs. Meatprocessing-IF is a possible exception, with another 60 mn LE worth of capacity expected to come into operation by the end of the year of the interview (1994). The mean value of fixed assets of the six IFs for which we have data is 27.63 mn, while the mean value of fixed assets of the six NIFs for which we have data is 107.78 mn, the latter about four times as large as the former. However, five of those six NIFs are also carrying significant debt loads, Automotive-NIF having an impressive debt:asset ratio of 90%.

Table 2 presents profit volumes and rates of profit for the five IFs and six NIFs for which we have sufficient data to cite or estimate a rate of profit. The numerator, profit, equals total revenues minus total costs for 1993 after deducting for interest and fee payments. It does not take account of taxation, *zakah* donations or profit distribution. The denominator of the rate of profit is total fixed assets at end-1992. The preferred variable for the denominator would be stockholders' equity, but we have insufficient data to use it.

The mean rate of profit of the five IFs for which we have information is 18.0%. Rates of profit of the NIFs are higher than those of the IFs in three out of four pairs. Furthermore, the mean rate of profit is 52.3% for the six NIFs, almost three times greater than that of the five IFs. An Independent Samples Test of the difference between these two means indicated that this difference is significant at less than the 10% confidence level (see Table 6 for the specific statistical test results).[9]

QUALITATIVE COMPARISONS OF BEHAVIOUR

The pairs, and the two groups as a whole, were compared along a number of behavioural dimensions. These include choice of product, form of ownership, location, founding date, market structure and competition, imports and exports, technology and the labor process, and labor relations (details in Appendix Tables, C1-C5). In brief, there seem to be small differences in choice of product and some differences in location and founding date. Perhaps more interesting is the greater role for foreign capital in ownership of NIFs versus the greater role for Islamic banks or investment groups in IFs, with product choice, location and date of founding influenced by these roles.

The differences in market structure and competitive (or rather non-competitive!) behaviour were negligible, and all firms in the sample are similarly dependent on imports of raw materials and capital goods, as is typical of developing countries. However, 6/8 of the NIFs export part of their product, as compared to 4/7 IFs, and the NIFs have a tendency to export a higher proportion of their output. All of the firms expressed concern about the impact of structural adjustment, mainly that it induced a deep recession, and about the threat, from imports, that liberalization entails. However, most of the NIFs also expected to benefit from it, while IFs tended to be ambivalent or negative. This fits with the latter's lesser tendency to export.

Choice of technology is typically embodied in capital goods (mostly the imported ones). Computerization has become crucial for all firms at this time. However, a possibly important difference was that the NIFs were more apt to invent or tinker with their technology or work process when they got a chance. Four NIFs described these kinds of projects, and the impact on productivity, whereas no IFs did so.

Employment policies, such as education and skill requirements, are driven mainly by the nature of the industry and are rather similar among firms. Furthermore, the firms share common paternalistic attitudes and behaviours toward their "family" of employees. Six firms (2 IFs and 4 NIFs) mentioned the moral (as well as the legal) barriers to firing workers. The proportion of female employees varies widely among firms within each group. However, while all the non-Islamic firms employ some women, four of the seven Islamic firms have a policy of not employing women at all, two on principle (women should be at home taking care of the family) and two on practical grounds (women cannot handle heavy machinery or work late at night).

SALARIES AND PROFIT DISTRIBUTION

There appears to be a difference between the two groups of firms with regard to salary. Table 3 indicates that average monthly salaries of employees in the Islamic group are higher, and that the average for the group as a whole, LE 450, is startlingly higher than the average for the non-Islamic group, LE 256. An Independent Samples Test of the difference between these two means indicated that it was significant at less than the 5% level (see Table 6).[10]

Table 4 shows the salary range and the ratio of highest to lowest salaries. The breadth of the range is greater in the non-Islamic than the Islamic group, 53:1 versus 27:1. Both the average monthly salary and the salary range data suggest that Islamic firms have greater distributional equity.

Table 5 presents another measure of relative equity i.e. the ratio of profits to the wage-and-salary bill. This ratio indicates the distribution between the owners and the workers of the net product (or value added) produced by the firm. The lower the ratio, the more equitable is the distribution. The ratio is lower, on average, for the Islamic group than for the non-Islamic group: for every pound paid out to employees as wages and salaries, the Islamic owners take just LE 1.15 in profit, while the non-Islamic owners take LE 13.14. An Independent Samples Test of the difference between the means of the two groups indicated that this value was significant at less than the 5% level (see Table 6). Like the findings on salaries above, this suggests that there is a more egalitarian distribution, on average, among Islamic firms than non-Islamic.

Table 6 presents the results of the "comparison of means" statistical tests done on the key variables. These results give credence to the suggestion that Islamic and non-Islamic firms are different in basic measures of performance (rates of profit) and behaviour (average salaries and profit/wage ratios).

Table 7 suggests that there are few differences between the Islamic and non-Islamic firms in provision of most benefits, including healthcare, retirement program, paid vacations, sick leave, bonuses and a miscellaneous category of services to employees. The fact that the first three are legally mandated - at least for industry - assures their uniformity, although a few firms do more than the minimum required. Beyond that, the one benefit in which there appears to be an important difference is profit sharing: while just one of the seven non-Islamic firms for which we have information shares profits with workers, profits are shared with workers by four out of six Islamic firms.

It was still the case in 1994 that profit sharing was required by Egyptian law for joint-stock firms in the private sector with more than 50 employees.[11] The four IFs and one NIF who share profits with workers are all joint stock companies and said that profit-sharing is "required by law;" the other firms, although they employ more than 50 workers and operate on a comparable (often greater) scale, are legally "partnerships" and do not have to share profits. It appears that more Islamic than non-Islamic firms defined themselves as joint stock companies, presumably with the knowledge that they would have to share profits. It is tempting to see this feature of the Islamic group as parallel to the more egalitarian final distribution of net income for which we saw evidence above. However, this feature may have more to do with the legal origins of the firms (Islamic banks or investment groups, U.S. corporate structure) than with any conscious or deliberate benevolence toward workers.[12]

INTERPRETATION

The Islamic and non-Islamic firms in our sample have many important traits in common. No meaningful differences appeared between the two groups of firms in how they relate to their customers, for example, or in the capital goods they import. Furthermore, all firms seem equally driven by the force of market competition, equally terrified by the prospect of the more open competition with imports expected from liberalization, and equally willing to contemplate joining together with other firms in the industry to set prices and output at more profitable levels. They are also similar in their paternalistic attitude toward employees and in their employment policies, although a majority of IFs explicitly prefer not to employ women.

The Islamic firms in our sample are as well distributed across the spectrum of economic activities and industries as the non-Islamic firms. This may be the outcome of a deliberate policy on the part of Islamic banks and investment groups, an illustration of their efforts at channeling capital to targeted industries.[13] If so, it gives credence to the idea that Islamic financial institutions engage in a kind of indicative planning, a practice reminiscent of the Japanese and Korean models of development. However the outcome so far appears not to differ from the non-Islamic, and presumably unplanned, dispersion of private firms across sectors.

There were significant differences between our two sets of firms in terms of fixed assets and profit rates. There are several possible factors at work that may help explain these disparities:

(1) a positive correlation of profit with asset size, i.e., economies of scale,[14]

(2) advantages to the NIFs from an earlier starting date or some heritage from a firm which started as far back as the pre-Nasser era;

(3) Islamic banks and investment companies may not invest sufficiently in productive Islamic firms to help them build their asset bases and profit potential because the profit-and-loss-sharing system is too risky;[15]

(4) NIFs may be more efficient on average, perhaps due to their greater tendency to innovate and export.

Both the IFs and the NIFs in our sample claim to pursue social objectives which constrain profit-maximization, as indicated by firms' responses to the "other benefits" questions: deliberating for two months over whether to fire someone, facilitating personal loans for workers, and attending employees' family weddings and funerals are but a few examples. Clothing-NIF even kept on a whole factory's worth of non-working employees for six months while a burned-down facility was replaced. Yet the NIFs appear to have higher profit rates.

On the other hand, Islamic firms as a group pay higher salaries, present more equity in salary distribution and have more balance between the profit and wage shares of output. They are also more likely to share profits with workers. However, only one firm director, that of Filters-IF, expressed explicit desiderata for an Islamic economy in which distributional equity is administered through the wage system and price and quantity are determined by social utility.[16] None of the respondents in the sample expressed awareness of any actual profit rate, salary or profit/wage ratio differentials between the IFs and the NIFs, so it is not clear that the observed behavioural and performance differences are intentional.

The different behaviour and performance might reflect different internalized norms or a different type of decision-making apparatus between the two sets of firms. It is also possible that the Islamic and non-Islamic firms operate in two distinct, albeit overlapping, economic environments in which different behaviours are expected and rewarded, rather than a single uniform environment. An important theoretical implication here is that the social and moral institutions that surround economic activity are important and that markets do not stand alone.

What can the Islamic economic sector contribute to improving growth performance and generating employment with equity in the Muslim world? If the Islamic firms described in this study are representative, then the Islamic sector can serve as a bright example of how to distribute equitably the net product with workers, via higher wages and profit sharing, and how to treat workers in a humane, familial way. However, it is essential that Islamic firms more actively seek out appropriate technological change and introduce their own innovations, in order to raise productivity (output per worker) and profitability. Otherwise it will become harder and harder for them to stay in business.

This process of innovating and raising productivity is not a matter of simple individual profit-maximization for its own sake, but an essential ingredient in building an accumulation fund for new investment and the creation of new jobs. There is no reason to sacrifice the high equity standards observed here to a false "trade-off of equity for efficiency." Some part of the workers' share of profits, for example, could be voluntarily deposited into the firm's investment fund, buoying the economies of scale effect. In this way, employees as well as employers and banks can participate in new investment, and have the satisfaction of helping to create new jobs for others as well as obtaining higher returns in the long run as economic growth takes off. With such a scenario, the future would be significantly brighter for young workers in an Islamic economic system, or even in a mixed system as in Egypt, than it is at present.

GLOSSARY

Murabahah. A lease-to-own or mortgage-like arrangement, in which the bank purchases a durable good for a consumer or a capital good for a firm. The consumer or firm then pays the bank back on an installment plan, with the final pay-back price higher than the original price by some pre-arranged amount. Firms can also provide credits to each other using this method (e.g., a supplier provides credit to a customer) and Islamic trading firms use it for international transactions.

Musharakah. A partnership arrangement, in which two or more parties contribute capital to an enterprise or a single project and then share profits (or losses) in proportion to equity.

T Test or Test of Means. A standardized statistical technique for measuring whether the means (arithmetic averages) of two samples are significantly different, that is, measuring the likelihood that the difference could have been obtained simply by chance.

TABLE 1:
FIXED ASSETS, 12/31/92, and OUTSTANDING DEBT, mid-1993, LE mn

Islamic Firms			Non-Islamic Firms		
	fixed assets	loans		fixed assets	loans
Plastics-IF	40.0	0	Plastics-NIF	70.0	0
Filters-IF	14.0	2.7	Automotive-NIF	99.2	89.6
Clothing-IF	NA	NA	Clothing-NIF	56.4	16.0
Meatproc-IF	50.0	0	Poultry-NIF	60.0	12.0
Publishing-IF	1.5	0	Publishing-NIF	29.0	12.0
Food serv-IF	50.3	0	Tour serv-NIF	142.0	18.0
Appliances-IF	10.0	0	Carpets-NIF	400.0	NA
			Chemicals-NIF	5.0	NA
Mean Assets of 6 IFs: 27.6			Mean Assets of 8 NIFs: 107.7		

TABLE 2:
PROFITS AND RATE OF PROFIT, 1993

Islamic Firms			Non-Islamic Firms		
	Profits LE mn	Rate of Profit (%)		Profits LE mn	Rate of Profit (%)
Plastics-IF	7.8	19.5	Plastics-NIF	57.5	82.1
Filters-IF	0.73	5.2	Automotive-NIF	67.5	68.0
Clothing-IF	NA	NA	Clothing-NIF	13.9	24.6
Meatprocessing-IF	NA	NA	Poultry-NIF	8.7	14.5
Publishing-IF	0.75	50.0	Publishing-NIF	10.5	36.3
Food service-IF	-0.09	-0.2	Tour serv-NIF	93.5	65.8
Appliances-IF	1.54	15.4	Carpets-NIF	NA	NA
			Chemicals-NIF	NA	NA
Mean profit rate, 5 IFs: 18.0			Mean profit rate, 6 NIFs: 48.6		

TABLE 3:
AVERAGE MONTHLY SALARY[17], LE, 1993

Islamic Firms		Non-Islamic Firms	
Plastics-IF	417	Plastics-NIF	191
Filters-IF	500	Automotive-NIF	432
Clothing-IF	NA	Clothing-NIF	167
Meatprocessing-IF	606	Poultry-NIF	300
Publishing-IF	NA	Publishing	195
Food services-IF	273	Tourist services-NIF	455
Appliances-IF	528	Carpets-NIF	NA
		Chemicals-NIF	NA
AVERAGE OF 5 IFs	465	AVERAGE OF 6 NIFs	290

TABLE 4:
SALARY RANGE AND RATIO, LE per month, 1993

Islamic Firms	Salary range	Ratio top to bottom	Non-Islamic Firms	Salary Range	Ratio top to bottom
Plastics-IF	4000/200	20:1	Plastics-NIF	2500/100	25:1
Filters-IF	4000/100	40:1	Automotive-NIF		NA
Clothing-IF	NA		Clothing-NIF		6:1[18]
Meatprcsing-IF	15000/500	30:1	Poultry-NIF	2000/225	9:1[19]
Publishing-IF	NA		Publishing-NIF	8333/150	56:1[20]
Food serv-IF	3000/120	25:1	Tour serv-NIF	15000/230	65:1
Appliances-IF	2500/120	21:1	Carpets-NIF	NA	6:1[21]
			Chemicals-NIF	NA	NA
MEAN RATIO OF 5 IFS		27:1	MEAN RATIO OF 6 NIFS		28:1
			MEAN RATIO OF 3 NIFS[22]		49:1

TABLE 5:
RATIO OF PROFITS TO WAGE AND SALARY BILL, LE mn, 1993

Islamic Firms			Non-Islamic Firms		
	Profit/ Wages	ratio value		Profit/ Wages	ratio value
Plastics-IF	7.8/5.0	1.56	Plastics-NIF	57.5/2.5	22.80
Filters-IF	0.73/0.6	1.22	Automotive-NIF	67.5/3.1	21.77
Clothing-IF	NA		Clothing-NIF	13.9/3.0	4.62
Meatpking-IF	NA		Poultry-NIF	8.7/1.8	4.83
Publishing-IF	NA		Publishing-NIF	10.5/0.9	11.70
Food serv-IF	-.086/1.29	-.07	Tour serv-NIF	93.5/6.0	15.58
Appliances-IF	1.54/1.9	0.81	Carpets-NIF	NA	
			Chemicals-NIF	NA	
MEAN RATIO OF 4 IFS		0.88	MEAN RATIO OF 6 NIFS		13.55
Range of these 4 IFs		-.07 - 1.56	Range of these 6 NIFs		4.62 - 22.8
Ratio top to bottom		1.49	Ratio top to bottom		4.94

TABLE 6:
RESULTS OF INDEPENDENT SAMPLES TEST OF MEANS

	N = no. of observations	degrees of freedom	T-test value, absolute	significance level
Rate of Profit	5,6	8.9	2.166	.059
Average Monthly Salary	5,6	8.7	2.271	.050
Profit/Wage Ratio	4,6	5.1	3.878	.011

TABLE 7:
PROVISION OF BENEFITS TO EMPLOYEES

	Islamic Firms	Non-Islamic Firms
Healthcare as mandated by government	5 yes 2 yes and more 0 no	6 yes 2 yes and more 0 no
Retirement as mandated by government	6 yes 1 yes and more 0 no	7 yes 1 yes and more 0 no
Paid vacations as mandated by government	4 yes 2 yes and more 1 no (service sector)	6 yes 1 yes and more 1 NA
Sick leave	4 yes 2 NA 1 no (employer decides) 0 no	6 yes 2 NA
Profit sharing	4 yes 1 NA 2 no	1 yes 1 NA 6 no
Bonuses [seen by firms as alternative to profit-sharing]	2 yes	3 yes
Misc: Transport, housing, meals, personal loans	5 yes 2 NA 0 no	5 yes 3 NA

Bibliography:

Aziz, A., 1993. "Firm Level Decisions and Human Resource Development in an Islamic Economy," in Ehsan Ahmed, ed., *Economic Growth and Human Resource Development in Islamic Perspective*, Herndon VA: The International Institute of Islamic Thought: 50-55.

Choudhury, M.A., 1992. "The Islamic Profit Sharing System in Comparative Perspective," *The Middle East Business and Economic Review*, 4 (2): 14-18.

El-Ashker, A.A., 1987. *The Islamic Business Enterprise*, London: Croon Helm.

Handy, H. and IMF Staff Team, 1998. *Egypt: Beyond Stabilization, Toward a Dynamic Market Economy*, Washington DC: International Monetary Fund.

Kuran, T., 1995. "Further Reflections on the Behavioral Norms of Islamic Economics," *Journal of Economic Behavior and Organization*, 27: 159-163.

Kuran, T., 1983. "Behavioral Norms in the Islamic Doctrine of Economics, A Critique," *Journal of Economic Behavior and Organization*, 4: 353-379.

Oweiss, I.M., 1990. "Egypt's Economy: the Pressing Issues," in Ibrahim M. Oweiss, ed., *The Political Economy of Contemporary Egypt*, Washington DC: Center for Contemporary Arab Studies, 1990: 3-49.

Pfeifer, K.A. 1997. "Is There an Islamic Economics?" in Joel Beinin and Joe Stork, eds., *Political Islam, Essays from Middle East Report*, Berkeley CA: University of California Press: 154-165.

Posusney, M.P., 1997. *Labor and the State in Egypt: Workers, Unions, and Economic Restructuring*, N.Y.: Columbia University Press.

Posusney, M.P. and K.A. Pfeifer, 1997. "Islam, Islamists and Labor Law," in Sohrab Behdad and Farhad Nomani, eds., *The Foundations of Public Policy in Islam*, in the annual series, *International Review of Comparative Public Policy*, Nicholas Mercuro, series ed., Stamford CT: JAI Press Inc.: 195-223.

Said, H.M., 1972. *The Employer and the Employee -- Islamic Concept*, Karachi, Pakistan: The Times Press.

Siddiqi, M.N., 1979. *The Economic Enterprise in Islam*, Lahore, Pakistan: Islamic Publications Ltd.

Ul Haque, N. and A. Mirakhor, 1987. "Optimal Profit-Sharing Contracts and Investment in an Interest-Free Economy," in M.S. Khan and A. Mirakhor, eds., *Theoretical Studies in Islamic Banking and Finance*, Houston TX: The Institute for Research and Islamic Studies, chapter 7.

Endnotes:

1   Handy 1998: 43, Table 17. The figures for unemployment are estimates made by the IMF staff.

2   This approach to understanding Islamic economics and its application to labor relations in particular are developed in Pfeifer 1997 and Posusney and Pfeifer 1997.

3   Siddiqi 1979: 110-114, 139-141; El-Ashker 1987: 202, 209-213; Aziz 1993: 50-55; Said 1972, chapters 4-7; Choudhury 1992: 14-18. Kuran 1983 and 1995 provides balanced and telling critiques of both the Islamic economics literature and the behavior of Islamic institutions.

4   This research was assisted by a grant from the Joint Committee on the Near and Middle East of the Social Science Research Council and the American Council of Learned Societies, with funds provided by the National Endowment for the Humanities and the Ford Foundation.

5   El-Ashker 1987: 101-102, uses this rationale for his investigation of Islamic firms in both the financial and real sectors of the Egyptian economy. Oweiss 1990 provides estimates of the size of the hidden economy, partly based on holdings in Islamic financial institutions.

6   A copy of the detailed "Framework Form," Appendix A, used to guide these interviews can be obtained from the author upon request, as can Appendices B and C1-C5 mentioned below.

7   El-Ashker 1987: 54, 82-84, 100.

8   El-Ashker 1987: 198-202.

9   This significance level means that there is a 5.6% probability of obtaining by chance the means difference generated by our data, or, put the other way round, that there is a 94.4% probability that the difference found is not due to chance.

10 The test results indicate that there is a 1.6% probability that these results could have been obtained by chance, or, put the other way round, that there is a 98.4% probability that the results were not due to chance.

11 Posusney, 1997: 176, 201. The labor law was under reconstruction in 1994 and 1995 to accommodate liberalization and profit-sharing was one of the benefits under study for revision or elimination.

12 The managing director of Automotive-NIF, made it clear that he was not happy about the profit-sharing requirement. The IF directors did not complain; however, the director of Plastics-IF indicated that the firm had shared profits in the past but dropped the practice in favor of bonuses at the management's discretion.

13 Suggested by Mr. Khairy El-Rabbat, general manager, Della Misr, interview, August 9, 1994, in describing the development of Della Baraka (a Saudi-based, family-held consortium of Islamic companies). Similarly, Mr. Adil Gazzareen, chair, Federation of Egyptian Industrialists, who has investments in both the Islamic and non-Islamic sectors, argues that Egypt's industrial development needs to have guidelines to channel investment, some sort of indicative planning, interview, August 8, 1994.

14 "Economies of scale" means that costs per unit of output go down as quantity is increased (because fewer inputs are used in making each unit), thus profits per unit go up.

15 This problem might be overcome with development of the institutions necessary to support the PLS system, for example better constructed contracts and a legal system to enforce them. These arguments are developed at length by Ul Haque and Mirakhor 1987.

16 The manager argued that *zakah* is insufficient to meet social welfare needs and that a strong Islamic state is essential to ensure that these needs are met.

17 Calculated by (wage-and-salary bill) / number of employees / 12 months.

18 This scale is compressed because the owners take monthly income from profits, not salaries, which brings down the top of the scale, while production workers earn piece rates as well as wages, which brings up the bottom of the scale.

19 Owner-managers take salary in dollars, $1800-2000 per month, which is not included in salary scale.

20 This figure includes profit shares to top managers.

21 Employer said only that firm "pays wages up to six times the minimum wage." The ratio does not include managers' salaries.

22 Excludes Clothing-NIF, Poultry-NIF and Carpets-NIF from the calculation, all of which leave managerial salaries out of the reported range, thus lowering the ratio.

Human Rights and Muslim Identity

*Dr. Azzam Tamimi**

Identity has been defined as oneness: that which endures as a self-regulating unity throughout change; or as sameness: that which can be identified as being the same from among a diversity or plurality of things. It has also been defined as self-identification. An institution is said to have an identity when the members are able not only to distinguish it from other institutions, but also to convey its distinctive character in words, gestures and practice, so as to reassure themselves that it should exist and that they have reason to belong to it. The phrase Islamic identity may, thus, be understood to refer to those criteria that are not only common to Muslims but which also distinguish them from non-Muslims. In view of the fact that a high degree of plurality exists among Muslims, the set of criteria that define Muslim identity would have to be minimal. In my opinion, these criteria would have to include the belief in God as the only deity worthy of worship and total obedience, and the acceptance of Muhammad, peace be upon him, as the messenger of God through whom revelation was communicated to humanity. For Muslims, divine revelation is the frame of reference in all matters pertaining to Man's relations with his Creator as well as to Man's relations with his fellow humans, Muslim or otherwise. This basic tenet of Islamic faith, upon which all other fundamentals are based or from which they may be derived, is the common denominator among all Muslims

* The Institute of Islamic Political Thought, London

irrespective of their sect or race. There are at least three ways in which one may relate Muslim identity to the issue of human rights. The first would be to discuss how this identity can be reinforced by means of defending and safeguarding human rights.

The concept of human rights, in Islam, is rooted in the concept of divinity. Muslims believe that Man was created by a transcendental God who favours no human over another except in terms of piety and good conduct. In a bid to defend Islam or to promote it, several contemporary Islamic scholars and thinkers have sought to show that Islam has, from the outset, laid the foundations for human rights by asserting the supremacy of the value of justice and of the principle of human dignity. Some of the efforts made in this regard has been aimed at developing an Islamic, as compared to secular, discourse on human rights. Both in the Qur'an and the Sunnah, the value of justice is considered as the highest of all values. It is derived from one of God's main attributes i.e. The Just. Hence the emphasis on 'equity' rather than equality in Islamic thought. This is one of the areas where the Islamic conception of human rights differs from its secular counterpart. The principle of human dignity derives from the belief that *al-insan* (the human being) is the vicegerent of Allah, on earth. *Al-insan*, who is honoured and preferred to all other creatures, is expected to lead a life guided by Allah's law, or the Shari'ah. This is another area where disagreement exists. The word *al-insan*, in Islamic terminology, refers to the human being irrespective of gender, colour or race. Three Qur'anic verses, which are crucial in determining a Muslim's identity, summarize the concept of human dignity:

1- Behold, thy Lord said to the angels: "I will create a vicegerent on earth." (2: 30)
2- We have honoured the children of Adam; provided them with transport on land and sea; given them for sustenance things good and pure; and conferred on them special favours, above a great part of Our Creation. (17:70)
3- O mankind! We created you from a male and a female, and made you into nations and tribes, that you may know each other.

Verily the most honoured of you in the sight of Allah is the most righteous of you. (49:13)

The second approach would be to talk about the violations of basic human Rights - whether in Muslim countries or where Muslims are a minority - that have brought about adverse effects on Muslim identity and which threaten its essential features. One would talk about modes of repression and persecution that go back to the colonial era, or that persist under secularist national rule in the modern territorial state that inherited power from the colonial authorities. Ataturk's Turkey, Pahlavi's Iran and Bourguiba's Tunisia are excellent examples illustrating how the post-independence territorial state has sought to obliterate Muslim identity i.e. not through a simple process of secularization that had separated church from state, but, rather, through a systematic process of Westernisation. This process has ranged from the destruction of a traditional civil society to, actually, forcing people to change the way they dressed, spoke, wrote (their languages), brought up their children and the way they conducted their public, as well as most private, affairs. The Muslim world is one of the very few remaining regions in the world where local culture is being systematically eroded through the persistent violation of fundamental human rights. Mosques have been placed under direct government control, freedom of the press is non-existent, opponents are silenced or liquidated, women are punished for choosing to be modest, Men are persecuted for choosing to follow the sunnah (way of the Prophet) and prisons host more prisoners of conscience than criminals. In the absence of the rule of law - and in the courts of military 'justice' - thousands have lost their lives without being able to defend themselves or appeal against their convictions. Even in countries where some form of democracy was experimented with, when it became apparent that democratisation did not serve the interests of minority ruling elite, the process was immediately interrupted or even reversed. Though not the only one, the Algerian case may be the best example.

The third approach would be to address the threat to Muslim identity posed by the very same people who claim to defend human rights. This threat emanates from the fact that some of the values promoted, defended and universalized by the Western-led international human rights movement clash with some of the characteristic features of Muslim identity.

The secularist discourse on Human Rights undermines Muslim identity by negating, in the name of universalism, the right of Muslims to any cultural specificity. To prove their respect for human rights, Muslims are told they must board the boat of modernity. The price they are expected to pay for this ride is to re-think their religious convictions or re-interpret their sacred texts so as to conform to international standards and universal values. It is not surprising, thus, that some Muslims regard the human rights movement a post-colonial tool of cultural imperialism. Regrettably, such a radical view amounts to a denial of the role played by numerous organizations around the globe in defending human rights and in exposing the violations and violators. The contribution of the international human rights movement is indispensable and should be greatly appreciated. What is also greatly appreciated, and should in all fairness be recognized, is that the Western human rights tradition, whose roots are founded in the European Enlightenment, has enhanced both the dignity of the human being and the value of human civilization. Four major contributions are accredited to this tradition. Firstly, it has endowed the individual with certain basic rights such as the right of free speech, the right of association, the right to a fair trial and so on. Secondly, it has strengthened the position of ordinary citizens against the arbitrariness of power. Thirdly, it has expanded the space and scope of individual participation in public decision-making; and fourthly, it has forced the State and authority in general to be accountable to the public. However, in spite of the positive contributions, there exists serious misgivings. Some of these misgivings relate to the attitude of the West, past and present, towards the issue of human rights. Historically, the 'human' to whom Europeans referred to, when they spoke of human rights was no other than their own citizen i.e. the French human, the English human or the Western human, in general. This probably explains why Europe - a 'fruit' of the renaissance - was engaged in the process of building the edifice of the individual *within* its own borders whilst destroying the human person *without* (i.e.

external to its borders). While human rights expanded among 'whites', European empires inflicted horrendous human wrongs upon the 'coloured' inhabitants of the planet. Native populations in the Americas and Australia were eliminated and millions of Africans were enslaved. Millions of humans throughout the world were suppressed. Western colonialism in Asia, Australia, Africa and Latin America represented the most massive systematic violation of human rights ever known throughout history. Much of these violations involved undermining other people's cultural and religious identities. Although formal colonial rule has ended, Western domination and control continues to have an impact upon the human rights of the vast majority of the people of the non-Western world in ways which are more subtle and sophisticated but no less destructive and devastating. On the one hand, the colonial ruling elite has been replaced, in many cases, by Westernised local elite - very often authoritarian and corrupt - who serve their Western masters and help to perpetuate this unequal and unjust relationship. On the other hand, the dominant West controls global politics through the United Nations Security Council. If the Western powers so desire, they can get the Security Council to starve a million people to death and force them to submit to their will. The dominant West controls global economics through the IMF, the World Bank, GATT and the G7 or the G8. The dominant West also controls global news and information and it possesses powerful means to dictate, to the rest of the world, styles of life through music, cinema, fashions etc. Some misgivings concern the way human rights organizations conduct their business. The overwhelming majority of human rights organizations have a radical secularist vision of Man and the world. For the secularists, human rights are based on the idea of natural rights. This means that God is left little or no place in Man's life. While this pre-supposes that nothing sacred remains, in reality, the divine sacred is replaced by a secular sacred. Inevitably, some of what Muslims may hold to be unquestionable, or immutable, may be considered a violation of human rights. Questions such as the roles of men and women in family life, the Islamic law of inheritance, the Islamic code of penalties and the Islamic code of moral conduct are some of the issues constantly targeted by the secularist human rights movement.

I have, over the past few years, participated in debates over these issues with representatives of international as well as regional human rights organizations. Insisting on the universality of their vision, the secularist human rights defenders refuse to entertain the mere suggestion that a common ground can be reached i.e. not by re-interpreting Muslim sacred texts, but rather by revising, re-examining, rethinking or re-writing the Universal Declaration of Human Rights. After all, this declaration, whose articles I would say are acceptable save for a few exceptions, was born out of the global conditions that prevailed in the aftermath of the Second World War. I would like to share with you some of the experiences I have had for, I believe, they illustrate the magnitude of the problem. One of these experiences was in the form of a live TV debate between me and the assistant to the secretary general of Amnesty International. The Amnesty official insisted that the Universal Declaration was binding upon all and that it was Islam which needed to be re-interpreted in a manner conducive to reconciling it with the declaration. It could clearly be seen throughout the debate that the spokesman for Amnesty found it more outrageous to cast doubt on the universality of the Universal Declaration than to cast doubt on the validity of divine revelation.The second experience took place in two symposia organized by the New York-based Lawyers Committee for Human Rights over two successive years to discuss Islam and Human Rights. During both meetings (held in 1996 and 1997), the Muslim participants, who insisted that it was beyond anyone's power to alter or omit a categorical Qur'anic text, were accused by some secularist participants of fundamentalism and inflexibility. Fahmi Huwaidi, who attended the second of these symposia, was confronted by a non-Muslim participant who told him that she was told that this group of Islamists was among the enlightened and moderate. She was at a loss because she could not understand how a person could be enlightened and moderate and at the same time oppose the amendment of a text from the Qur'an. Among the Qur'anic verses that the secularists thought should be modified or re-interpreted were those dealing with family relations, especially with regard to marriage and divorce, as well as those dealing with inheritance and corporal punishment. It was not convincing enough for the secularists to be told that while no-one who believed in Allah and His Book could change or tamper with certain absolute areas, Muslims were encouraged to exercise *ijtihad* to provide safeguards that might prevent abuse of the legal order. This *ijtihad*, it was stressed, would have to come from within the House of Islam and in response to real needs and not in acquiescence to pressure from outside or in order to appease the power to be. Several Muslim participants expressed concern that the whole purpose of the project was not to initiate dialogue with the aim of reaching a common ground, but rather to impose the Western perspective of human rights as well as the secularist view of the world, upon the Muslims.

The third experience occurred last May when I was invited to participate in a symposium organized in Helsinki by yet another American foundation called "Search for Common Ground". On the eve of the first session, which was supposed to be exclusively for the Arab participants to discuss the promotion of human rights in the Arab region, delegates were invited to have dinner in a nearby Chinese restaurant. As part of the informal discussion over dinner, a Palestinian secularist colleague, of Christian origin, expressed the opinion that only secularization could bring about an improvement to the standard of human rights within the Arab region. Together with an Islamist colleague from Lebanon, I argued against the secularist thesis and sought to prove that, contrary to the claim made, secularization has, in fact, been accompanied by a marked deterioration in the respect for human rights within the Arab region. The discussion shifted to an analysis of international standards and the universal declaration of human rights and as to whether cultural specificity should be taken into consideration. The following morning, as I headed for breakfast, the organizer's secretary whispered into my ear that the organizer wished to speak to me. I waited for her and we had breakfast together. She said that she was told I had a very interesting discussion the previous night. I thought she was impressed! I briefed her on the main points raised in the discussion and reiterated that if common ground is indeed what we are searching for, we need to assert the right to cultural specificity and to question the assumption that the universal declaration of human rights was universal. She turned to me and said: "Azzam, I don't know how to say this to you, but I would like you not to speak at today's session." She explained to me that my ideas would disrupt the harmony of the series of meetings her institution had held so far. In other words, it was not recommended at this stage to question what had already become an absolute. I understood from her - and later on, from other key persons involved in the organization of the function, and who were put in charge of steering the discussions - that this forum had a well-defined, previously agreed on, agenda and that it would not be acceptable to throw in new proposals. This experience confirmed my suspicion that the whole project was designed to bolster the peace process in the Middle East through the enforcement of secular notions of human rights. One of the ways of doing this is to assert universality and deny specificity; to come up with ideas as to how to change the perceptions of people in the Middle East in order to make Israel appear more acceptable to them. The assumption was that the values that make Israel unacceptable are those derived from Islam, and for this reason Islam had to be re-questioned. One of the main objectives of this project was to suggest plans aimed at effecting changes in school curricula. It was suggested, for instance, that values that are not conducive to respecting the human rights of the Israelis or to the establishment of peace in the region should be removed from teaching curricula. The Islamic value of *jihad* was a prime target. This is one of the many ways in which human rights activists have embroiled themselves, or have allowed themselves to be exploited, in a campaign to undermine Muslim identity. This embroilment has been detrimental to the credibility of the human rights movement within Muslim quarters. Another way was illustrated by the position adopted by the Western human rights movement in support of Salman Rushdie and later on in support of Taslima Nisreen. It is not support for Salman against the fatwa, which concerns me. In my assessment, the fatwa was issued for purely political reasons and had benefited the author of Satanic Verses - whom it brought fame and prosperity - more than it benefited Islam and the Muslims. What is of concern is the support for Salman's, and later on Taslima's, alleged right to free expression without any consideration for the fact that their writings insulted the entire Muslim community that constitutes no less than one fifth of the world's population. While secular human rights activists talk about freedom of expression as a very important civil liberty, they forget that there is also a right to honour and to dignity for whole communities. It has been suggested that the Western civilization, by virtue of the way it has developed, seems unable to empathize with the notion of the sacred, which is very important in other societies. What about the rights of the people who consider the sacred and the transcendent as important values? Should they not be entitled to be respected? Should not their right to honour be observed? It has also been suggested, as Richard Webster once remarked, that the unconditional Western support for writers Rushdie and Nisreen is not a support for the freedom of thought, but for the European secular tradition of blasphemy. It is worth noting that although Islamic values show a high regard for human dignity and great respect for the fundamental rights of Man, the secularist discourse within the human rights movement seeks to show the exact opposite. It is not surprising that the human rights movement in the West gives credence to certain individuals of Muslim origin whose main concern has been to cast doubt on the validity of the Islamic sacred text. In Western human rights circles, the followers of Mahmud Taha, such as Abdullahi An-Na'im, are regarded an authority on Islam although in the eyes of most Muslims, they would just be regarded apostates. The reason such people are favoured by the Western human rights movement is that they call for repealing more than half of the Qur'anic text for allegedly contravening universally accepted values, including those related to human rights. An-Na'im is highly regarded within these circles for his role in propagating the idea of his mentor that Medinite revelation, which deals primarily with laws and codes intended to guide individuals and communities in all affairs, is a hindrance to Muslim progress. Ask any Muslim what he or she thinks will remain of Islam once Medinite Qur'an is omitted and you will hear but one word: 'nothing'.

In conclusion, I would like to stress that there is a need today for the establishment of an Islamic human rights movement to defend human rights without conceding Muslim identity. One of the objectives of such a movement would be to bolster Muslim identity through the defence and promotion of human rights. At the same time, the movement would be expected to search for a common ground on which all the defendants of human rights, irrespective of their ideological convictions, may stand. The value of Human Rights is indeed a universal value and the cause of defending these rights is a universal cause. For both the value and the cause to remain universal and in order to prevent their monopoly by one particular culture, cultural specificity has to be recognized and respected. In fact, cultural specificity is an indispensable feature of universality.

Activists in the secular camp of the human rights movement need to understand that it will do the human rights cause no good to undermine Muslim identity in the name of defending the universality of human rights.

Paper presented to the International Conference on 'Muslim Identity in the 21st Century: Challenges of Modernity', London, 31 October 1998.

1. Peter A. Angeles, The Harper Collins Dictionary of Philosophy, 1992 Edition.
2. Roger Scruton, A Dictionary of Political Thought, Pan Books, 1983
3. Dr. Chandra Muzaffar: From Human Rights to Human Dignity, p.1,International Conference on Human Rights 6-7 December 1994, Kuala Lumpur, Malaysia.
4. Ibid.
5. Dr. Chandra Muzaffar, see ref. above.
6. Ibid
7. Hj. S. M. Hohd. Idris, International Conference on Human Rights 6-7 December 1994, Kuala Lumpur, Malaysia.
8. Fahmi Huwaidi, Hiwar At-Turshan (Dialogue with the Deaf), Al-Ahram, Cairo 11 Nov. 1997.
9. Chandra Muzaffar, from a talk at the Islam and Equality Symposium, organized by the Lawyers Committee for Human Rights, London 14-16 October 1997.
   10. Richard Webster, Paper entitled: Free Speech, History and the Christian Tradition of Blasphemy, The Collapse of Secularism Symposium, Centre for the Study of Democracy, London June 10, 1995.

Chapter 3

The Impact of Education and Communication Technology on Muslim Identity

Education, Sacred Authority, and the Religious Imagination in Contemporary Muslim Societies

*Dale F. Eickleman**

ABSTRACT

This chapter explores the relationship between the massive expansion of higher education in the Muslim world since the 1950s and its implications for ideas of religious knowledge and authority. The new "ways of knowing" and the emerging networks for communication and action created by expanded contemporary opportunities for higher education and various "new" communications media offer insight into the changing interplay of religion, politics and national identity.

In April 1997, in Istanbul, at the invitation of the Mayor's office, I gave a lecture in their "From East, From West" series. I contrasted the top-down religious transformations of earlier eras with the current reconstructions – I emphasize the plural – of religious thought, the impetus for which emanates from outside the ranks of established elite. My point of departure was the famous series of lectures given in Lahore by the Indian intellectual, Muhammad Iqbal (1877-1938), *The Reconstruction of Religious Thought in Islam* (Iqbal 1934); I also had in mind sociologist Karl Mannheim (1883-1947), who initiated a book series called the "International Library of Sociology

* Dartmouth College (Hanover NH)

and Social Reconstruction." Mannheim's reference to "reconstruction" reflected his view that the basis for civil society in Europe had collapsed by the late 1930s and had to be built up again. Iqbal's primary concern was the voices of a Muslim intellectual elite. Mannheim saw an equivalent role for secular intellectuals. Both thinkers implicitly shared a "top-down" approach to how major social transformations are carried out, assuming that articulate intellectuals drawn from established élites had a decisive influence on all others in their respective societies.

My approach differs from that of Iqbal and Mannheim in two respects. I suggest that the major impetus for change in religious and political values in the late twentieth century comes from "below". It is not just changes in explicit ideologies that matter – those formulated by established intellectuals – but also the implicit, background understandings against which the beliefs and practices in any given society are formulated. These implicit understandings are what the philosopher Charles Taylor calls the "social imaginary" (Taylor 1993: 218-19). With the importance of these background understandings in mind, an Iranian political scientist, Fariba Adelkhan, recently argued that the major transformations of the Iranian revolution did not occur in 1978-79. Instead, it took place in the last decade, with the coming of age of a new generation of Iranians who were not even born at the time of the Revolution and who therefore had a significantly different interpretation of social context than that of the preceding generation. Adelkhan argues that a "religious public sphere" (*escape public confessionel*) has emerged in Iran in which politics and religion are subtly interwined, and not always in ways anticipated by Iran's established leaders. The other transformation that she notes is the emergence of a greater sense of personal autonomy for both women and men (Adelkhan 1998: 152-247).

Mass higher education and mass communications are intimately linked to those new senses of religious and political authority. Even when they are used to sustain old patterns of belief and authority, their very structure engenders new "authoritative" ways of thinking about self, religion and politics. Understanding these transformations requires a recognition of the spectrum of religious politics that now play a significant role in the popular understanding of politics and moral authority in many Muslim majority societies. Unfortunately, buzzwords such as "fundamentalism," and catchy phrases such as Samuel Huntington's (1993) rhyming "West versus Rest" and Daniel Lerner's (1964: 405) alliterative "Mecca or mechanization" are of little use in understanding these new understandings. They obscure, or even distort, the immense spiritual and intellectual ferment that is taking place today among the world's nearly one billion Muslims, reducing this innovation, in most cases, to a fanatical rejection of everything modern, liberal or progressive. Fanaticism, for sure, plays a part in what is happening - dramatically and violently - but this is far from the whole story; and exclusive focus on this point confuses issues, blocks understanding and deflects attention away from the vigour of internal debate among Muslims who advocate an Islamic politics. In Western societies, a constant theme since the Reformation has been an essential tension between fanaticism and civil society (Colas 1997). Today there is a similar essential tension in many Muslim-majority societies. An uncompromising elitist secularism - not limited to Western observers but also prevalent in many Muslim-majority societies - prefers to ignore this spectrum of debate because it entails listening to new political voices and taking them into account. The result is to deflect attention from conceptual innovations, open-ended debates, an awareness of developing religious practices and understandings, and emerging networks for communication and action that encompass virtually all Muslims and profoundly shape the direction of contemporary Muslim thought.

MASS HIGHER EDUCATION AND MASS COMMUNICATION

The most important element of these contemporary transformations is the unprecedented access that ordinary people now have to sources of information and knowledge about religion and other aspects of their society. What distinguishes the present era from prior ones is the large numbers of believers engaged in the "re-construction" of religion, community and society.

Mass education and mass communication are important in all contemporary world religions. However, the full effects of mass education, especially higher education, only began to be felt in much of the Muslim world since mid-century and in many countries, considerably later. Morocco, for instance, committed itself to universal schooling after gaining independence from France in 1956. Though in 1957, only 13,000 secondary school degrees were awarded, and university enrollments remained low; by 1965, there were more than 200,000 students in secondary schools, and some 20,000 in universities. By 1992, secondary school enrollment topped 1.5 million, and university students numbered 240,000 (Eickelman 1992: 645-46). While illiteracy rates in the general populace remain high – 43 percent for men and 69 percent for women – there is now a critical mass of educated people who are able to read and think for themselves without relying on state and religious authorities (World Bank 1996: 200).

The situation in Oman, one of the oil-rich Gulf states, is more dramatic because the transformation has taken place in a much shorter period. In 1975-76, a mere 22 students graduated from secondary school. Little more than a decade later, in 1987-88, 13,500 were enrolled in secondary education. In 1996-97, 76,500 were enrolled; and there were more than 7,000 post-secondary institutions, including the national university, which had opened in 1986 (Sultanate of Oman 1997: 574-87).

In other Muslim-majority countries the story is much the same, though the starting dates and levels of achievements differ. In Turkey, Indonesia and Malaysia, mass education has reached every city, town and village. In Turkey, for instance, adult illiteracy rates as of 1995 were 8 percent for males and 28 percent for females, down from 65 percent and 85 percent, respectively, four decades earlier. Secondary schools are now ubiquitous, and both private and public universities have proliferated. In Indonesia, university enrolment, only 50,000 in 1960, reached 1.9 million in 1990 (World Bank 1996: 201). Iran, also, has seen a significant expansion in education opportunities at all levels. In all these places, the number of people able to talk back to religious and political authorities, and not just listen to them, has increased dramatically.

Both mass education and mass communications, particularly the proliferation of media and the means by which people communicate, have had a profound effect on how people think about religion and politics throughout the Muslim world. These multiple means of communication have eroded the frontier between "authorized" and illicit communications, making the control of information and opinion much more difficult than it was in prior eras and fostering, albeit inadvertently, a civil society of dissent. We are still in the early stages of understanding how different media – including print, television, radio, cassette and music – influence groups and individuals, encouraging unity in some contexts and fragmentation in others, but a few salient features may be sketched (see Eickelman and Anderson 1997).

At the "high" end of this transformation is the rise to significance of books such as *al-Kitab wa-l-Qur'an* [The Book and the Qur'an](1992), written by the Syrian civil engineer Muhammad Shahrur. It has sold tens of thousands of copies throughout the Arab world in spite of the fact that its circulation has been banned or discouraged in many places. One legal scholar, Wael Hallaq (1997: 253) regards Shahrur's book as the "most convincing" of contemporary attempts to reformulate Islamic legal theory. The success of Shahrur's first book – two others have subsequently appeared and a fourth is in preparation – could not have been imagined before there were large numbers of people able to read it, understand its advocacy to the need to reinterpret ideas of religious authority and tradition, and apply these reinterpreted Islamic precepts to contemporary society.

Shahrur (1992) draws an analogy between the Copernican revolution and Qur'anic interpretation, which he says has been shackled by the conventions of medieval jurists:

> *People believed for a long time that the sun revolved around the earth, but they were unable to explain some phenomena derived from this assumption until one person, human like themselves, said, 'The opposite is true: The earth revolves around the sun.'*

> *. . . After a quarter of a century of study and reflection, it dawned on me that we Muslims are shackled by prejudices (musallimat), some of which are completely opposite the [correct perspective] (1992: 29).*

On issues ranging from the role of women in society to rekindling a "creative interaction" with non-Muslim philosophies, Shahrur argues that Muslims should re-interpret sacred texts anew and apply them to contemporary social and moral issues. He writes, "If Islam is sound [*salih*] for all times and places," then we must not neglect historical developments and the interaction of different generations. We must act as if "the Prophet just . . . informed us of this Book" (Shahrur 1992: 44; see also Shahrur 1994).

Shahrur is not alone in attacking both conventional religious wisdom and the intolerant certainties of religious radicals. Other thinkers also advocate constant and open re-interpretation of how sacred texts apply to social and political life. Another Syrian thinker, the secularist Sadiq Jalal al-ʿAzm, for instance, does the same. A debate between al-ʿAzm and Shaykh Yusif al-Qaradawi, a conservative religious intellectual, was broadcast on al-Jazira Satellite TV (Qatar) on 27 May 1997 in the program "al-Ittijah al-Mu'akis" [The Opposite Direction], moderated by Faysal al-Qasim. For the first time in the memory of many viewers, the religious conservative came across as the weaker, more defensive voice. That program is unlikely to be rebroadcasted on state-controlled television in most Arab nations, where programming on religious and political themes is generally cautious. Nevertheless, satellite technology and videotape render traditional censorship ineffective. Tapes of the broadcast are circulating from hand to hand in Morocco, Oman, Syria, Egypt, and elsewhere.

Voices elsewhere also advocate the reform and rethinking of tradition. Turkey's Ali Bulaç, a university-based theologian, has captured the imagination of the educated young with the call for authenticity and a reinterpretation of the first years of the Prophet's rule, applying Muhammad's precepts and practices to current controversies about pluralism and civil society (Göle 1996: 27). Fethullah Gülen, Turkey's answer to media-savvy American evangelist Billy Graham, appeals to a mass audience. In televised chat shows, interviews and occasional sermons, Gülen speaks about Islam and science, democracy, modernity, religious and ideological tolerance, the importance of education, and current events. Because he regards Turkish nationalism as compatible with Islam, Gülen has the pulse of a wide spectrum of religiously minted Turks (Eickelman 1998: Aras 1998).

For a pan-Arab audience, Morocco's Sa'id Binsa'id (1993) argues that a proper understanding of Islam enjoins dialogue, a willingness to understand the opinions of others, adaptation and a disposition toward good relations within a framework of civility. Indonesian and Malaysian moderates make similar arguments. So does Iran's Abdelkarim Soroush, who, to the annoyance of some conservative clerics, has captured the religious imagination of Persian readers (Vakili 1996). His work, in translation, also reaches Turks and others in the Muslim world. In Pakistan, a recent book making an argument similar to Shahrur's, *Qur'anic and Non-Qur'anic Islam* (1997), by Nazir Ahmad, a retired military officer, quickly went into a second printing.

Not all religious books are aimed at highbrows. Mass schooling has created a wide audience of people who read but are not literary sophisticates, and there has been an explosive growth in what a French colleague of mine, Yves Gonzalez-Quijano (1998: 171), calls generic "Islamic books" – inexpensive, attractively printed texts intended for such readers. Many address practical questions of how to live as a Muslim in the modern world and the perils of neglecting Islamic obligations, and not all appeal to reason and moderation. Many of these books have bold, eye-catching covers and sensational titles such as *The Terrors of the Grave*, or *What Follows Death* (Tahtawi 1987), while other, more subdued works offer advice to young women on how to live as Muslims today. Often based on the sermons of popular preachers, Islamic books are written in a breezy, colloquial style rather than the cadences of traditional literary Arabic, and are sold on sidewalks and outside mosques rather than in bookshops. While Egyptian Nobel Laureate Naguib Mahfouz is considered successful if he sells 5,000 copies of one of his novels in a year in his own country, Islamic books often have sales in six figures.

Like modern mass communications and travel, mass higher education and publishing inculcate pervasive "habits of thought" (Bourdiue 1988, 1989). They do so by transforming religious beliefs into a conscious system, broadening the scope of religious authority and redrawing the boundaries of political community. Religious beliefs and practices are increasingly seen as systems (*minhaj*), to be distinguished from non-religious ones. It is not sufficient simply to "be" Muslim and to follow Muslim practices. One must reflect upon Islam and articulate it. When activists declare that they are engaged in the "Islamization" of their society, the sense of thinking of religious beliefs as a system becomes explicit.

Another aspect of modern Islamic thought and practice is direct and broad access to the printed, broadcast and taped word: More and more Muslims take it upon themselves to interpret the textual sources – classical or modern – of Islam. Much has been made of the "opening up" (*infitah*) of the economies of many Muslim countries, allowing "market forces" to reshape economies, no matter how painful the consequences in the short run. In a similar way, market forces support some forms of religious innovation and activity over others. Thus, in Egypt, when Nasser sought to undermine al-Azhar in 1961 by eliminating the formal difference between religious and secular students, religious students were pushed towards *da'wa*, the propagation of the faith (Zghal 1996). Soon, some of these preachers acquired greater prestige and followings than many of the traditionally trained scholars. Unlike government-supported mosques, many of the popularly supported ones have clinics and social centres attached to them, thus blurring the line between religion and community. In dramatic contrast with conventional practices, members of some religious groups in Cairo, such as al-Sunniyin, perform "outreach" on city busses, preaching and engaging in a religious give-and-take with passengers (Ghannam 1997). In Bangladesh, teenage romance novels, once a popular speciality distributed in secular bookstores, now have Islamic counterparts which are distributed through Islamic bookstores (Huq in press). The result is a collapse of earlier, hierarchical notions of religious authority based on claims to the mastery of fixed bodies of religious texts.

THE EMERGING PUBLIC SPHERE

Without fanfare, the notion of Islam as dialogue and civil debate is gaining ground. Like the Copernican revolution, the current break in religious authority in the Muslim world is likely to be seen as significant only in retrospect, and it is not without resistance. In general, however, a new sense of public is emerging throughout Muslim-majority states and Muslim communities elsewhere. It is shaped by increasingly open contests over the use of the symbolic language of Islam. New and accessible modes of communication have made these contests increasingly global, so that even local issues take on transnational dimensions. Muslims, of course, act not just as Muslims but according to class interests, out of a sense of nationalism, on behalf of tribal or family networks and from all the diverse motives which characterize human endeavour. Increasingly, however, large numbers of Muslims explain their goals in terms of the normative language of Islam. Muslim identity issues are not unitary or identical. However, claims of such shared identity have become a significant force in both Muslim-majority states and those in which Muslims form only a minority of the population. It is in this sense that one can speak of an emerging Muslim public sphere.

This distinctly public sphere exists at the intersection of religious, political and social life and contributes to the creation of civil society. Contemporary Muslims have access to contemporary forms of communication that range from the press and broadcast media to the Internet. Muslims, like Christians, Hindus, Jews, Sikhs, and protagonists of Asian and African values, now have more rapid and flexible ways of building and sustaining contact with constituencies than was available in earlier decades. The asymmetries of the earlier mass media revolution, which favoured "top-down" communications, are being reversed by new media in new hands.

This combination of new media and contributors to religious and political debates fosters awareness on the part of all actors of the diverse ways in which Islam and Islamic values can be treated. It feeds into new senses of a public space that is discursive, performative, and participative, not one confined to formal institutions recognized by state authorities.

Just as there is general scholarly recognition that there are multiple paths to modernity (Eisenstadt 1996: 396-426), there is a practical awareness of multiple claims to the task of staging virtue (Salvatore 1998), including a public engagment in the name of religion. In this respect, Muslim activists, at least in public discourse, come close to what Michael Warner (1990: 42-43; see also Salvatore 1997: 55-56) has called the republican virtues of colonial America. Print - and, today, other media - direct consciousness to and craft and certain models of civility, membership within a community, and citizenship within a nation, all resting on more or less mutual understandings of commitments and expectations.

Publicity-shared ideas of community, identity and leadership take new shapes in such engagements, even as many communities and authorities claim an unchanged continuity with the past. Mass education, so important in the development of nationalism in an earlier era (Gellner 1983: 28-29), remains important. The proliferation of media and means of communication are equally significant because they have multiplied the possibilities for creating communities and networks among them, dissolving prior barriers of space and distance and opening new grounds for interaction and mutual recognition.

References:

Aras, Bülent (1998) "Turkish Islam's Moderate Face," *Middle East Quarterly* 5, no. 3 (September): 23-30

Adelkhan, Fariba (1998) *Être moderne en Iran*. Paris: Karthala.

Bannani-Chraïbi, Mouniya (1994) Soumis et rebelles: Les Jeunes au Maroc. Paris: CNRS Éditions.

Binsa'id, Sa'id (1993) "al-hiwar wa-l-fahm la l-qat'iyya wa-ljahl" [Dialogue and Understanding, Not Alienation and Ignorance], *al-Sharq al-Awsat* (London), July 7, p. 10.

Bloch, Marc (1964 [orig. 1939]) *Feudal Society*. Chicago: University of Chicago Press.

Bourdieu, Pierre (1988) *Homo Academicus*, translated by Peter Collier. Stanford: Stanford University Press.

_____, (1989) La noblesse d'état. Paris: Les Éditions de Minuit.

Colas, Dominique (1997) *Civil Society and Fanaticism: Conjoined Histories*, translated by Amy Jacobs. Stanford: Stanford University Press.

Eickelman, Dale F. (1992) "Mass Higher Education and the Religious Imagination in Contemporary Arab Societies," American Ethnologist 19, no. 4 (November): 643-55.

_____, (1998) "Inside the Islamic Reformation," Wilson Quarterly 22, no. 1 (Winter): 80-89.

_____, and Jon W. Anderson (1997) "Print, Islam, and the Prospects for Civic Pluralism: New Religious Writings and Their Audiences," *Journal of Islamic Studies* 8, no. 1 (January): 43-62

_____, and James Piscatori (1996) *Muslim Politics*. Princeton and London: Princeton University Press.

Eisenstadt, S. N. (1996) *Japanese Civilization: A Comparative View*. Chicago: Chicago University Press.

Eisenstein, Elizabeth L. (1983) *The Printing Revolution in Early Modern Europe*. Cambridge: Cambridge University Press.

Gellnner, Ernest (1983) *Nations and Nationalism*. Ithaca: Cornell University Press.

Ghannam, Farha (1997) "Public Space, Structures of Feeling, and the Islamization of Everyday Life in Urban Egypt," unpublished paper. Cited with permission.

Göle, Nilüfer (1996) "Authoritarian Secularism and Islamist Politics: The Case of Turkey," in *Civil Society in the Middle East*, Vol. 2, edited Augustus Richard Norton. Leiden: E. J. Brill, pp. 17-43.

Gonzalez-Quijano, Yves (1994) *Les Gans du Livre. Édition et champ intellectuel dans l'Égypte republicaine*. Paris: CNRS Éditions.

Hallaq, wael B. (1997) *A History of Islamic Legal Theories*. Cambridge: Cambridge University Press.

Huntington, Samuel (1993) "The Clash of Civilizations?" *Foreign Affairs* 72, no. 3 (Summer): 22-49.

Huq, Maimuna (in press) "From Piety to Romance: Islam-Oriented Texts in Bagladesh," in *New Media and the Muslim World: The Emerging Public Sphere*, ed. Dale Eickelman and Jon Anderson. Bloomington: Indiana University Press.

Iqbal, Muhammad (1934) *The Reconstruction of Religious Thought in Islam*. London: oxford University Press.

Lerner, Daniel (1964 [1958]) *The Passing of Traditional Society: Modernizing the Middle East*. New York: Free Press.

Salvatore, Armando (1997) *Islam and the Political Discourse of Modernity*. Reading: Ithaca Press.

———, (1998) "Staging Virtue: The Disembodiment of Self-Correctness and the Making of Islam as a Public Norm," *Yearbook of the Sociology of Islam* 1: 87-120.

Shahrur, Muhammad (1992) al-Kitab wa-l-Qur'an: Qari'a Mu'asira [The Book and the Qur'an: A Contemporary Reading]. Beirut: Sharikat al-Matbu'at li-l-Tawzi' wa-l-Nashr.

———, (1994) Dirasat Islamiya al-Mu'asira fi-l-dawla wa-l-mujtama'a [Contemporary Islamic Studies on State and Society]. Damascus: al-Ahli li-l-Taba'a wa-l-Nashr.

Sultanate of Oman, Ministry of development (1997) *1996 Statistical Yearbook*. Muscat: Ministry of Development .

Taylor, Charles (1993) "Modernity and the Rise of the Public Sphere," *The Tanner Lecture on Human Values* 14: 203-60.

Warner, Michael (1990) *The Letters of the Republic.* Cambridge: Harvard University Press.

World Bank (1996) *World Development Report 1996.* New York: Oxford University Press.

Valkili, Valla (1996) *Debating Religion and Politics in Iran: The Political Thought of Abdolkarim Soroush.* New York: Council on Foreign Relations.

Zghal, Malika (1996) Gardiens de l'Islam: les oulémas s'Al Azhar dans l'Égypte Contemporaine. Paris: Presses de Sciences-Po.

Cybermuslim and the Internet: Searching for Spiritual Harmony in a digital world

*Bahman Baktiari**

In the 1990s, followers of the Prophet are building a "virtual Muslim community" in cyberspace. Across the world, thousands of well-educated, computer-literate Muslims are going on-line, looking for news, political activism, and discussion of their faith. A simple search function under the heading of Islam produces over 463,470 items, and under the heading of Muslim, 317,420. In one site, an individual has linked over 1000 Islamic sites to his web page (http://www.islamworld.net/#mov). On these sites, Muslims have postings about meetings, fund-raising, and needs of mosques in far-flung places, and they offer news of interest that is not published in the mainstream press.

The Muslim Internet Community, which did not exist 10 years ago, is currently made up largely of Muslim college students and professionals who are leading a cyberspace political debate unprecedented in the Islamic world made up of one billion people in total. More than 40 countries are predominantly Islamic, Arabs being less than 20% of the total Muslim population. [The largest number of Muslims, 150 million, are Indonesians]. Then there are 20 million Chinese, 55 million Russians, 100 million Indians, 95 million Pakistanis, and 90 million Bangladeshis. [And millions upon millions

---

* University of Maine

Africans who live in Nigeria, Mali, Sudan, Algeria, and Morocco].
Islam is a global phenomenon, embracing in its fold over 400 ethnic
groups. It is estimated that by the year 2000, Muslims will constitute
27 percent of the world population. The 56 states which are
predominantly Islamic will constitute one third of the membership of
the United Nations.[1]

Young Muslims around the world are becoming familiar with
each other in a way not possible even a decade ago. A Muslim in
Hong Kong can find out what is happening to fellow Muslims in
Texas, and a Muslim youth in California can find out what is
happening to fellow Muslims in Britain. Muslim cyberspace
discussions now include everything from what constitutes a proper
Islamic upbringing to contrasting the Holy Qur'an and Einstein's
Theory of Relativity. Even the Moslem Brotherhood organization
has produced an impressive web page. (http://www.ummah.org.uk/
ikhwan/index.html).

In a world of global flows of wealth, images, and power, the
search for identity [collective or individual, ascribed or constructed]
becomes a fundamental source of meaning. [The Muslim Students
Association (MSA), which has subscribers on nearly every campus in
the United States and Canada, generates about 150 pages of
discussion a day on Islamic issues on their numerous web sites]. As
Manuel Castells has eloquently put it, computer-mediated
communication is helping to dismantle the very vision of the world
that in the past it fostered. By the year 2000, 80 percent of the world
population will be online. A new website is being launched every
minute worldwide. This raises several important questions. Will the
changes brought about by information technology produce a
qualitatively different definition of what it means to be a Muslim? In
a world characterized by simultaneous globalization and
fragmentation, can Muslims acquire a sense of identity that increases
their capacity to relate to other identities, or will it bring about a
greater separateness from others?[2]

These are important questions that need to be answered as we
examine the impact of information technology on the Muslim world.
In this paper, I will examine the impact of Internet on Muslim
identity in the 21ˢᵗ Century. Let me say what I mean by identity.

By identity, I mean the process by which a social actor recognizes itself and constructs meaning primarily on the basis of a set of attributes, But as James Piscatori and Dale Eickelman (Muslim Politics, Princeton, 1996) Have pointed out, we need to be aware of the diverse social beses and expressions of these searches for meaning, which take the form of re-intellectualizations of Islam that seek to relate it to perceptions of current conditions and respond to the range and in the forms of those conditions.

My finding is that when it comes to the impact of Internet there are many reasons to doubt the populist and community-building theories. The conditions that would be required for the populist transformation of Muslim identity fly in the face of fundamental facts about other sources of influence on Muslim identity. The central theoretical problem for the populist claim is the absence of a clear link between increases on information about Islam on the Net and consolidation and growth of Islam. Instead of the populist picture, what is happening with the Net is a sort of accelerated pluralism in the Islamic community. Above all else, the Net is accelerating the process of information availability without any clear direction as to the impact of this on the believers.

INFORMATION REVOLUTION & THE INTERNET

The Internet network is the backbone of global computer-mediated communication today. It was developed in the late 1960s at the initiative if the U.S. Department of Defence. Its intent was to enable scientists and engineers working on military contracts to share computers, resources, and ideas, the latter through "e-mails". The popularity of Internet spread slowly throughout the academic world, which in the mid-1980s was its principal user. [Two innovations revolutionized the ease with which we can use Internet today. One was Swiss software engineers Tim Bernerslee's invention of the World Wide Web and the "hypertext" to link documents with one another. The other was a software program known as Mosaic, written primarily by Marc Andereesen, an undergraduate student at the University of Illinois].

Use of the Internet has grown from less than 100,000 internet hosts in 1988 to 15 million in 1997.[3] In the 1990s, the Internet comprised more than 70,000 computer networks connecting an estimated 50 million users around 130 countries. [More than 9,000 newsgroups containing discussions or picture databases are accessible through the Internet]. In the United States, the number of people using has grown at a rate of 50% to 75% for several years, putting on a path into American life like the that taversed by radio in the 1920s and 1930s and television in the 1950s and 1960s. We know that those technologies have had profound implications nut just for America, but also for the Muslim world in general. It is reasonable to assume that the Net will have equally strong implications. Experts believe that Internet can one day link 600 million computer networks, compared to 1973 when 25 computer networks were linked.

The United Arab Emirates (UAE) has the largest number of corporate web sites, around 500 web sites, followed by Lebanon with 400 and Egypt with 350. The total number of web sites in the Middle East is around 3,000, according to the Middle East Internet Directory 1999 to be released in January by Dubai-based web design company Cyber Gear. However, all the Middle East countries put together account for just 0.25 percent of the total Internet users the world wide. The average growth rate in the Middle East is 10 percent per month.

(By the year 2000, the number of Internet users is expected to reach 142 million). Interestingly, about 47 percent of Internet users are aged between 36 and 59, while 37 percent are aged between 21 and 35. Just about 13 percent are above 60. According to the directory E-mail is the most popular application on the web, and 90 percent of Internet subscribers us it regularly. Finland is the most wired country in the world, with an Internet for every 25 citizens. The US is the next with a link for every 50 citizens. By the year 2000, 46.5 percent of the online population will be women. (http://www.middleeastdirectory.com).

Those who believe that the Net will restructure societies in a populist direction have articulated their claims in various ways. Amitai Etzoini sees in the Internet the possibility of an advancement of the state of public affairs through "teledemocracy".[4] Lawrence

Grossman argues that a third great epoch of democracy is arriving by the hand of technology.[5] Sociologist Manuel Castells talks about a "revolution" in information technology, and eleborately outlines its implications in a book called The Rise of Network Society.[6] The grandest claim yet may be that of Nicholas Negroponte, who expects "the nation-state to evaporate" under their influence of new technologies. For him, we live in a world that has become digital.[7]

The peaceful coexistence of various interests and cultures in the Net creates a flexible network of networks where institutions, governments, business associations, and individuals create their own "sites". The nature of the Internet is such that anyone can publically advance his view freely and claim to be anything. One researcher states the central claim held by supporters of computer-mediated communication: "Community" is created when people interact with one another on the Net sufficiently long that they develop lasting relationships, and the Net frees this process of community-building from the limitations of physical proximity.[8]

These claims are important not because they address a fashionable topic, but because they entail more fundamental claims about the impact of this information technology revolution on Muslim identity. An examination of the "Muslim" sites on the Internet makes quite clear three consequences: 1) Reducing geographical limitations; instant availability of information from all parts of the world. 2) Challenging traditional methods of Islamic Learning and Education. 3) Accelerated pluralism in Islamic political activity.

Impact of the Net on Muslim Identity: Geography will matter less.

The Net has already overrun geographic borders, making possible the creation of virtual communities of Muslims who live as far apart in Indonesia and Iceland.

The most important impact of the Net on Muslims is the removal of geographical limitations. Creators of a web site called Online Islamic Propagation Team (http://members.aol.com /Islam Team/) as an online community of Muslims that are aimed at spreading Islam via web pages, email chat, message boards, and news groups. These arc the main forms of cyber communication, millions

224 Muslim Identity in the 21st Century

of people use daily. Muslims should be active in spreading Islam among the users of the cyber world, the Online Islamic Propagation Team makes sure Islam's voice is heard in such means communication. Visitors to the Alaqsa Mosque Website, (http://www.ramadhan.org/) can get a copy of the Friday speech from Alaqsa Mosque in occupied Muslim Land every week.

A monthly called Islamic Voice provides news under the heading "Community News," has items about various events, such as the state of Qatar will soon establish a museum of Islamic Art in the Capital, Doha, as well as the news that "Tokyo University has decided to create a cemter for Islamic Studies." (http://www.islamicvoice.com/).

The most ambitious attempt is by a group of Muslim professionals to collect proposals for the creation of a project called Masjed Net (http://www.masjid.net/). Recognizing the potential of Internet for "uniting and strengthening Muslims around the world," founders of Masjed.net want to transform the Internet into "an effective tool for obtaining Islamic information and services." Another project called The World Islamic Network (http://www.islamic.org.uk.WIN/) lists its primary goals of "fostering greater cooperation and unity amongst Muslim, as well as identifying the shared aims and goals of Islamic Internet content providers so as to develop and present an ever more effective vision of the aims and goals of the Ummah."

Finally, the Web site of Islamic Connection (http://pw2.netcom.com/~benalio/sahail.html) opens up with the statement of "if you are interested in becoming a Muslim please e-mail me at this address," The Web site of Sister Net (http://www.msa-natl.org/SISTERS/), created in 1992, seeks to provide the opportunity to discuss issues that some of us, as Muslimaat, would feel uncomfortable in discussing with other male counterparts (e.g. birth control, polygamy, etc.), as well as a "forum through which we can focus on the specific issues and needs which concern Sisters in a comfortable and supportive environment, Insha Allah. As Sisters who are seeking higher education/working/etc. we face different challenges/dilemmas than our Brothers in the same situation."[9]

Another group of Muslims have created an e-mail service just for Muslims. (http://www.muslimsonline.com/webmail.html). This way Muslims can identify themselves as a Muslim on the Internet, and pick the username that they want to use.

As it can be seen from the examples above, the Net has certainly changed the information environment of Muslim individuals, making it possible for everyone to obtain information about developments in most of the Islamic world. What is not clear is how this breakdown in geographical barriers is altering the Muslim individual's ability to related to his or her own culture. Are young cyber Muslims who are surfing the Net becoming more sophisticated about their faith, or more confused? The most significant and interesting changes may be that the Net is affecting processes of identity formation, showing less coherence and less correspondence with established institutionalized sources of information in the community.

EDUCATION & LEARNING

Just as the Net is gradually eliminating geographical limitations, it is also providing alternative sources of learning and education. One of Turkey's Islamic organizations will soon embark upon a project for the service of Islam and the various Islamic issues via the Internet. The project will be implemented in conjunction with the Islamic Encyclopedia Foundation in Turkey so that it is able to impart accurate facts and figures on Islam and Muslims. The organization that has undertaken the project has created a special working group to oversee the work and has selected a number of expert advisors on various topics. They will advise on various issues and will answer questions from those interested in knowing more about Islam and the various issues concerning it.

The School of Islamic and Social Sciences in the United Kingdom (SISS) http://www.siss.edu/ is one of the first Islamic educational centers to capitalize on the information revolution and offer a Master's degree for Imams. The M. P. I. Degree emphasizes the contemporary North American context in all of its studies, and seeks to build an awareness and sensitivity in its students for the real needs and aspirations of Muslims, whether native or immigrant, residing in North America. The difference is that students do not have to be "present" in the class. They will be connected to the class via an audio or audio-video conference system. Even the oral exam, called "a course completion interview," will be arranged within driving distance of your location!

Also, the SISS offers an annual one month leadership and educational intensive program "designed to educate, instruct and train a select group of 40 students from across North America and from araound the world in Tafseer, Tajweed, Fiqh, Shariah, Hadith, Seerah, Islamic History and issues pertaining to Muslims living in the West." It is managed by an Iraqi teacher who came to the United States in 1984. In this one month program, the school offers the opportunity for participants "to develop a strong Muslim personality and to inculcate an Islamic identity through social, personal and group interaction with the scholars." All of this for a tuition of $1000.00!! Interested people can apply on-line. So if you have been studying Tafseer for the past 20 years, maybe you should have taken a one-month program.

Another site called *Fatwa Page* aims to provide responses to anyone's questions about Islam, whether it be for a Muslim or a non-Muslim, and to help solve general and personal social problems. Responses are composed by Sheikh Muhammed Salih Al-Munajjid, a known Islamic lecturer and author. Questions about any topics are welcomed, such as theology, worship, human and business relations, or social and personal issues.

Creators of a *Shia* Internet site called *Al-Islam* http://www.al-islam.org/ have put together what they call the Ahlul Bayt Digital Islamic Library Project (DILP). Their objectives are to digitilize and present on the Internet "quality Islamic resources, related to the history, law, practice, and society of the Islamic religion and the Muslim peoples with particular emphasis on Twelver Shia Islamic school of thought.... Our purpose is to facilitate dissemination of knowledge through this new medium to locations where such resources are not commonly or easily accessible. In addition, we aim to encourage research and enquiry with the use of computer

facilities." There is also a Shia on-line Islamic reference page where people can read Islamic texts on-line.
http://members.aol.com/IIKweb/Reference.html

One thing is clear: A student from the School of Islamic and Social Sciences can be an Imam in a mosque without having completed the traditional programs, and without having spent any time in a classroom. Nevertheless, traditional centers of Islamic education have also joined the Net, setting up websites and advertizing their programs. As stated by Manuel Castells, what is remarkable in this Network Society is not just the fact that developments of new technologies are changing the way we interact with each other, but also the fact that the old society is also trying to use this technology to retool itself by using the power of technology to serve the technology of power.[10]

ACCELERATING PLURALISM: ISLAMIC POLITICS & INTERNET

Politics is also a growing area of utilization of the Net by Muslims. On the one hand one can say that the Net is enhancing local democracy by creating a kind of electronic participation, through which Muslims of various background can post their opinions on the Web. As Mark Bonchek has observed, the Net decreases the transaction costs involved in identifying potential sources for support, mobilizing them, and coordinating their efforts.[11]

Beyond this idea of electronic participation is the intensification of pluralism. Pluralism is a familiar idea in social and political theory. Pluralism usually designates the constitution of society and politics through the recognition of a plurality of diverse social and cultural groups, often thought of as competing interest groups. More broadly, pluralism implies multiple group differences, whether they be ethnic, racial, economic, nationa, religious, gender, sexual, original, or ideological in nature.[12]

A number of Islamic parties have set up websites describing their ideology, program, and plublicizing their list of publications.

Moslem Brotherhood in Egypt, the Jamaat-e Eslami in Pakistan, Iran Freedom Movement, and the Islamic Movement in Palestine Hamas, http://www.palestine-info.org/hamas/rightframs.html have all joined the Internet, posting their everything from news to history. The Hizbollah in Lebanon has gone on the Net, describing themselves as a "an Islamic freedom fighting movement founded due to the Israeli military seizure of Lebanon in 1982, which resulted in an immediate formation of the Islamic resistance units for the liberation of the occupied territories and for the ejection of the aggressive Israelis forces…. We don't seek the application if Islam by force or violence but by peaceful political performance, which gives the opportunity for the majority in any society to adopt or reject it. If Islam becomes the choice of the majority then we will apply it, if not, we will continue to coexist and discussion till we reach to correct beliefs." http://www.hizbollah.org/hizb/english.html.

In 1996, anti-Muslim reaction after the Oklahoma City bombing in April 1995 caused two Muslim professionals to create DERVISH, first-of-its-kind Web site for Muslim professionals. Founded and financed by two staff members of the World Bank in Washington, Kemal Ahmed and Adnan Hassan, the Web site provides educational materials and is open to the public, a kind of virtual Rotary Club with a Muslim twist. The new Web site for Muslim professionals is named "DERVISH", after the universal ideals advocated by the Sufi Muslim tradition.

Governments have also joined the Net. The Islamic Republic of Iran provides the best example. There is website for the Supreme Leader Ali Khamenei, http://www.islam-pure.de/imaminfo.htm. Moreover, some followers of the Iranian Supreme Leader have constructed several elaborate sites devoted to writings of Ayatollah Khamenei. http://members.ail.com/SEYYAD42/index.html calling their site, the Velayat Page, they have set up a system for questions to be asked via the Internet. You can direct your questions to any of the following: Ayatollah Khamenei, the late Ayatollah Khomeini, or Ayatollah Sistani. After you ask your question, you have to also tell the site what you think of the web page!

President Khatami has also his own website. http://www.khatami.com/. You can send an e-mail to

president@khatami.com. In his first visit to the United Nations in
September 1998, President Khatami was connected via Internet to
Iranian community in the United States who sent questions and
comments to the President. The president answered questions live on
the Internet, and participants from all of the United States could hear
his answers. Internet allowed President Khatami to touch base with
Iranians without leaving New York.

The power of Internet has also attracted the government of
Turkey. They have set up an elaborate page asserting that "the
Republic of Turkey is a democratic, secular and social State governed
by the rule and law; bearing in mind the concepts of public peace,
national solidarity and justice; respecting human rights and loyal to
the nationalism of Ataturk." http://turkey.org/turkey/ An
opposition group on another website states: "The citizens of Turkey
cannot freely use their rights to participate in governing themselves.
The real party in power is the MGK (National Security Council),
made up mostly of military individuals, who with the 1982
constitution have had their responsibilities and authority broadened."
http://www.mazlumder.org.tr/mazlum2en.htm
Even the Taliban have set up an elaborate web site, Listing
everything from the latest sermon by Molla Omar, as well as
'investment' opportunities in Afghanistan. http://www.taleban
.com/.

Powerful institutions of higher learning, such as the Al Azhar
University, http://www.alazhar.org/index8.htm have joined the
Internet in the hope of maintaining the stature and prestige of Islam.
In early June 1998, the commercial network American Online was
bombarded with protest letters regarding religiously offensive
materials on the website of a subscriber. The protest brought in the
president of the Al Azhar University, Ahmed Omar Hashem. We
warned the AOL that his university might sue them for allowing the
Web site to sit to sit on its computers. He said "this is aggression on
the human heritage and sacred values not only of Moslems, but of all
humanity. The ideas on the site are frivolous but a legal action against
this company may be necessary to stop such distortions." In a
posting they state: "By the way, Al Azhar University was instrumental
in shutting down an AOL website in the United States because they

considered it to be blasphemy. Be careful what you say, be careful
what you write, or this great institute "radiating learning and
knowledge to all parts of the world" will threaten to sue you."
http://byrden.com/miracle/AlAzhar.shtml.

One Muslim started the Internet Islamic Lobby,
http://geocities.com/Athens/Troy/8147/aboutus.htm, stating that
"We want to show the world that Islam is the religion of truth. Our
mission is to project a strong Islamic voice through the net, refute
the sites that wrongly insult Islam, the Koran and our Prophet. We
want to provide comprehensive answers." Another lobby group, the
Council of American Islamic Relations, CAIR, uses its Internet site to
post Action Alerts on issues on concerns to Muslims.
http://www.cair-net.org/. The group actively monitors anti-Islamic
activities in the United States and the Net has made it easier to spread
information faster. In the United States, the Net has certainly
contributed to a greater presence for Muslims. Most of the political
websites seek to integrate Muslims into the American political system
by connect their American citizenship to their faith. Since of the
estimated 64 million Internet users worldwide, 41 million are in the
United States, this provides Muslims with unlimited opportunities to
influence the political process. The American Muslim Council opens
its web page with the following, "Democracy only works for those
who participate. To make a difference, you must vote and make your
voice heard by letting your elected representatives know where you
stand." http://www.amermuslim.org/. Their site includes an On-line
Activist Guide, providing a complete selection of all the available
politics-related internet sites which can help Muslims understand the
structures of the US political system.

CONCLUSION

As Muslims see it, technological change plays little role in the
corruption of society. Indeed, they have accepted advanced
technologies like Internet and have readily adapted them for their
purposes. One can regard Internet as a major corrupting force, like

the Saudi government, but only because of the content of the programs, not because of the medium itself.

Nevertheless, it remains to be seen whether the virtual communities Muslims are creating on the Net will ultimately replace all other forms of social interaction. There is no doubt that the Net is changing the face of Islam, as well as the lifestyles of young Muslims who "surf" the Net today. But are they more knowledgeable about Islam today? Does participation in on-line communities created by Muslims increase or decrease their feelings of power? Nearly a century ago before computers had become part of our lives, William James asked this question: "Under what circumstances do we think things are real?"[13]

One major consequence of the Net for Muslim identity will be a crisis of authenticity as they struggle to connect what they see on the Net with what they experience in their own societies. It is the beginning of a new age. Learning how to set up web pages is as important as reading the holy book Quran. Even religious fundamentalists do not reject technology, but rather, they want to put it at the service of God's Law. While the Net will certainly change the informational environment of Muslim individuals, it will likely not alter their overall cultural identity. As Manuel Castell puts in his third volume, in 'The Information Age', the twenty-first century will not be a dark age. Neither will it deliver to most people the bounties promised by most extraordinary technological revolution in history. Rather, it may be characterized by informed bewilderment. The last word on the Net will not be written for some time to come.

SELECTED ISLAMIC WEB-SITES

Masjed Net
http://www.masjid.net

Islam on the Web
http://www.geocities.com/Athens/Oracle/5118/

On-line resources in America
http://islam.org/port/default.asp

On-line resources in Europe
http://islam.org/port/europe/default.asp

On-line resources in Asia
http://islam.org/port/Asia/default.asp

A comprehensive educational web-site
http://islam.org/

Islamic Organizations On-line
http://www.colostate.edu/Orgs/MSA/islamnet/orgs.html

Islamic Organizations On-line: Country by Country site
http://islam.org/World

The University Institute of Islamic Education
http://www.habbak.com/islam/

Al_QALAM The Muslim Youth Movement of South Africa
http://786.co.za/al_qalam/Default.htm

The American Muslim Council (AMC)
http://amermuslim.org/

A Shia Organization
http://iiny.org/iaiep/iaiep_def.htm

Muslim Women's League
http://www.win.net/mwl/

Articles posted on the web
http://www.usc.edu/dept/MSA/humanrelations/womeninislam/

Fatwa Systems On-Line
http://www.cais.com:80/islamic/fat_sys.html#formsu

Iranian Parliament On-line
http://www.iranmajlis.org

Ayatollah Ali Khamenei, Iran's Supreme Leader
http://members.aol.com/SEYYAD42/index.html

Taleban of Afghanistan
http://www.taleban.com/

Hizbollah of Lebanon
http://www.hizbollah.org/hizb/english.html

The Islamic Movement in Palestine Hamas
http://www.palestine-info.org/hamas/rightframe.html

Alaqsa Mosque Web-site
http://www.ramadhan.org/

Al-Nisa': An online newsletter for Muslim women
http://www.freeyellow.com/members3/alnisa/

The Middle East Internet Directory
http://www.middleeastdirectory.com

Further Readings:

Louis Brenner, <u>Muslim identity and social change in sub-Saharan Africa</u>, London: Hurst, 1993

Anthony Appiah, (edited) <u>Identities</u>, Chicago: University of Chicago Press, 1995

The essays in this volume originally appeared in the journal Critical Inquiry

Chapters of Interest: 3, 9, 13 and 19.

1) "British Cannibals": contemplation of an event in the death and resurrection of James Cook, explorer/Gananath Obeyesekere
2) Race into culture: a critical genealogy of cultural identity/walter benn michaels
3) Occidentalism as counterdiscourse: "He Shang" in post-Mao China/Xiaomei Chen
4) Fashion and the homospectatorial look/Diana Fuss
5) Policing the black women's body in an urban context/Hazel V. Carby
6) Woman skin deep: feminism and the postcolonial condition/Sara Suleri
7) Acting bit: identity talk/Gayatri Chakravorty Spivak
8) The empire renarrated: Season of migration to the north and the reinvention of the present/Saree S. Maksisi
9) What is a Muslim: fundamental commitment and cultural identity/Akeel Bilgrami
10) Nationalism and social division in black arts poetry of the 1960's/Philip Brian Harper
11) Black   writing,   white   reading: race   and   politics   of   feminist interpretation/Elizabeth Abel
12) The erotics of irishness/Cheryl Herr
13) Diaspora: generation and the ground of Jewish identity/Daniel Boyarin
14) The time of the Gypsies: a "people without history" in the narratives of the West/Katie Trumpener
15) White philosophy/Avery Gordon and Christopher Newfield
16) The no-drop rule/Walter Benn Michaels
17) Fashionable theory and fashionable women: returning Fuss's homospectatorial look/Molly Anne, Rothenberg and Joseph Valente
18) Look who's talking, or if looks could kill/Diana Fuss
19) Response to Identities/Michael Gorra
20) Collected and fractured: response to Identities/Judith Butler

Endnotes:

1   Jack Shaheed, <u>Arab and Muslim Stereotyping in American Popular Culture</u>, Washington: Georgetown University Center for Muslim-Christian Understanding, 1997.

2   For example, Muslim women have created their own web pages, (http://www.albany.edu/~ha4934/sisters.html), supporters of Louis Farakhan have their own web sites appealing to African-American community.

3   <u>Time</u>, May 19, 1997, p. 69

4   Amitai Etzoini, *The Spirit of Community: Rights, Responsibilities, and the Communication Agenda*, New York: Crown Publishers, 1993.

5   Lawrence Grossman, The Electronic Republic: Reshaping Democracy in America, New York: Viking Press, 1995.

6   Manuel Castells, the Rise of the Network Society, Oxford: Blackwell Publishers, 1996.

7   Nicholas Negroponte, *Being Digital*, New York: Vintage, 1995, p. 165

8   H. Rheingold, "A Slice of Life in My Virtual Community," in L.M. Harasim, edited, *Global Networks*, Cambridge: 1993, p. 61. Under IT 2000 plan, the government of Singapore is planning the most ambitious Internet community plan. It plans that all 750,000 households on the island will be connected to a comprehensive computer network by the year 2000 with the compulsory installment of broadband coaxial and optical fiber networks. Households, businesses, schools, libraries, government departments, and statutory authorities will be electronically inter-linked to facilitate shopping and other commercial and official transactions, as well as provide cable and interactive television services and Internet. A wireless communications network will also afford mobile computer access to information services throughout Singapore. So extensive is the plan that even public space is likely to be wired. It is proposed that television cameras be fitted at corridors, lifts, public parks, car parks and neighborhood centers for monitoring purposes. See Gary Rodan, "The Internet and Political Control in Singapore," <u>Political Science Quarterly</u>, vol. 113, no. 1, 1997.

9   There is also an on-line newsletter for Muslim women called Al-Nisa'. (http://www.freeyellow .com/members3/alnisa/)

10 Network Society, op.cit. p. 52

11 Mark Bonchek, "Grassroots in Cyberspace: Using Computer Networks to Facilitate Political Participation," presented at the 53rd Annual Midwest Political Science Association, Chicago, April 6, 1995. Url: http://www.ai.mit.edu/projects/ppp/home.htm

12 Robert Dunn, *Identity Crisis; A Social Critique of Postmodernity*, Minneapolis: University of Minnesota Press, 1998, p. 143.

13 William James, *Principles of Psychology*, Volume 2, New York: Dover Publishers, 1950, p. 283

Covering Islam:
Media and its Impact on Muslim
Identity

*Hamid Mowlana**

ABSTRACT

International Conference on "Muslim Identity in the 21st Century: Challenges of Modernity", School of Oriental and African Studies, University of London, October 31-November 1, 1998.

When the process of secularism was completed in Europe and capitalism had engendered a measure of personal freedom, the nation-state replaced communitarian and feudal systems in the West. In the Islamic world, the process was quite different since the concepts of the state and the community were in sharp contrast to those developed in the West. The nation-state system was never accepted by large segments of the Muslim world in the first place, and this continues to be the major source of crisis in Islamic countries. Today, as the nation-state fails to deliver the required sense of security of citizens, a feeling of anchorlessness develops within the individuals, and thus people turn to local identity, shifting their loyalty to their own immediate groups for protection. Unlike in the West, it is not the changing or shifting role of the nation-state but the very existence of it that is responsible for fragmentation and

* School of International Service, American University, Washington D.C.

disunity as well as the ongoing crisis in the Islamic world.

The crisis of political legitimacy was further enhanced by a number of conceptual as well as policy developments during the post-World War II period. With the triumph of romanticism and secularism after the French Revolution, naturalism came to occupy and dominate the world-views of the West. In the Islamic view of the natural and transcendent orders, the latter governs the flow of the former. A large part of Islamic law deals with social order and Muslims, today, are concerned not with the state of modernization but the state of transformation and identity. Under the slogans of modernization, economic development, and technological progress, the Islamic countries were deprived of the right to recognize a unique and distinct civilization and culture of their own.

The crisis of identity in the Muslim world, in general, and in a number of Islamic countries, in particular, was further exacerbated by the two forces of modern media and information technologies. On the national level, the media, as a pillar of secular force, reinforced a notion of the modern nation-state system with all its political, economic and cultural ramifications. On the global level, specifically since World War II, the mainstream world media portrayed Islam and the Muslim world in a negative and often misleading and inaccurate way, thus contributing to the contradictory images of identity arising within the national system.

In the closing decades of the twentieth century, three important developments have had the most profound impact on the nature and content of information in the Islamic world and the quest for a self-identity. The Islamic Revolution in Iran and subsequent political movements in other Islamic countries set the tone for the islamization of the media and created a new ecology of communication in a number of regions. The disintegration of the Soviet Union and the emergence of newly independent states in Islamic regions such as Central Asia contributed to the potential expansion of a greater Islamic communications network. Finally, the growth of national and international telecommunications has the potential to affect the integration of the Islamic regions and the political and economic development there. The Islamic world is developing its communications media with a new awareness of global change and, at the same time, a profound sense of history and Islamic identity.

HISTORICAL SETTING

The crisis of Muslim identity has been influenced by the two forces of modern media and information technologies. On the national level, the media, as a pillar of secular force has often reinforced a notion of the modern nation-state system with all its political, economic, and cultural ramifications contributing to the rise of a national identity. On the international level, in particular since World War II, the mainstream media of the world has portrayed Islam and the Muslim world often in negative and misleading terms, thus contributing to the erosion of an Islamic identity. Therefore, contradictory images of national, ethnic, racial and sectarian identities portrayed in the media not only have been the major obstacles to the formation of a cohesive Islamic identity both on national and regional levels but have also had a deteriorating impact in the mobilization and assimilation of the population in the developmental process.

The discourse on the nation-state in the Western industrialized world deals almost exclusively with the evolution of a particular kind of state that had its origin and development in Western Europe over the past 200 years, in predominantly Christian and capitalist countries. In Islamic countries, the conception of the state, however, historically offered a radically different version of the relationship of governing bodies to society. Over the last fourteen centuries, the notion of the state in an Islamic context has undergone the process of articulating its unique identity in the contemporary world. The division of different geographical, linguistic and national groupings, in this part of the world, into the modern nation-state system since the turn of the twentieth century has created an ongoing crisis of identity, which requires close scrutiny. As I shall attempt to demonstrate here, unlike the West, it is not the changing or shifting role of the nation-state but the very existence of it, perpetuated by the media, that is responsible for fragmentation, disunity and the ongoing crisis of identity in the Islamic world. It is precisely for this reason that the crises of the modern nation-state system in the Islamic world must be analyzed in its cultural context, since the process of 'nation-building' has been incompatible with the cultural settings of these societies.

The crisis of identity in the Muslim world was and continues to be ignored by many writers and analysts because of the emphasis they put on the analysis of formal political institutions such as the state, political parties, bureaucratic institutions and modern parliamentary and governmental infrastructures. Yet, the traditional Islamic political and social institutions, the informal political channels through which interest articulation and political demands are expressed, the deep Muslim feelings and reservations about the nation-state system that persist beneath a modernizing culture in the last two decades, and the crucial role of the media in propagating the existence of a nation state, all, have altered the balance of political forces nationally and regionally.

Today, the Islamic nations face one of the most severe dilemmas of their contemporary existence; yet, how they will deal with this crisis of identity remains largely problematic because the very political structure of the nation-state (upon which they have been erected) is in part the cause of their underlying instability. How is it that this inherently unsound situation arose? The blame lies in part with the West and in part with those national elites who wield power in their countries. While the West developed those concepts which today torment the Islamic world and imparted them to the Muslim region during the colonial era, the import of Western ideology is something which has not ceased with the end of colonial occupation.

It is within this context that the role of the media needs to be looked at in the Islamic world. Prior to the modern era, the centers of communication in the Islamic world were primarily the mosques, especially during the daily and Friday congregations, and the meetings in the marketplaces, public squares, as well as the religious schools and colleges. The mosque not only served for daily prayers but also for the spreading of news and opinion and as a forum for political decision-making. This form of communication, called *khutbeh*, was largely based on the Islamic tradition of combining political and religious discourse. For example, during the month of Ramadan - a religious month for fasting - theological students and members of the religious profession customarily held meetings to present current topics and issues.

However, between the 13th century and the modern era, however, the Islamic world fell short in adopting new communication technologies due to internal and external political, economic and social factors. The European invention of the Gutenberg press in the middle of the 15th century heralded the birth of the print culture and a tremendous quantitative jump in the output of human information. However, in the Islamic societies, one mode of communication did not supersede another but rather the development of oral and written communication occurred simultaneously and came to complement technological forms of communications in the modern era. Hence, the growth of communications in the Islamic world was characterized by qualitative rather than quantitative jumps. During the 16th to the early 19th century, when a more or less formalized council of ministers came into being in a number of Islamic countries such as Iran and Turkey, the official government news writer occupied an important place. Occasionally the government news - or *akhbar* as it came to be called - was also read to the public from the stairs of mosques. The official governmental report continued to function as a successful medium for dissemination of news until the introduction of modern journalism. Printing presses were introduced into Islamic countries such as Egypt, India, Iran and Turkey as early as the 17th century. During the late 18th century and the first half of the 19th century, the printing press facilitated the establishment of various newspapers throughout the Islamic world. This early period of the press was not only responsible for the importation of modern nationalism and secularism from Europe, but also played an important role in the spread of the 19th century Islamic movement as well as in the campaign against European colonialism.

The early growth of the modern mass media in the Islamic world was associated first with the intervention of the state in the production and distribution of the press and, secondly, with the influence of both secular and religious leaders, who were seeking the use of the press for socio-political reforms. Thus, during the last two decades of the 19th century, two types of publications were emerging in the Islamic world: the press were led mainly by Western-trained and educated elites who were promoting European ideas of secularism, liberalism and modern nationalism; and the press pioneered by religious leaders and Islamic reformists such as Sayyid Jamal al-Din (known as al-Afghani) who was campaigning for a unified Islamic community throughout the Middle East, Asia and North Africa. Sayyid Jamal al-Din's influence was strong in most Islamic countries, especially Iran and Egypt. He and his followers published a number of newspapers including the famous *Al-Urvatul Vosgha* which was circulated in many Islamic countries. By the turn of the century, the new tool of journalism was in widespread use in the Islamic world, from Indonesia to North Africa.

The early years of the twentieth century witnessed the great struggle between nationalism, Islamic movements and imperialism - which was reflected almost continuously in the media of the Islamic world, from Indonesia and Malaysia to Turkey and Morocco. The press in Egypt, Iran and Lebanon achieved wide circulation. In other Islamic countries, the first decades of the 20th century were pinpointed as the period when journalism and modern communication media began to develop and expand in Syria, Iraq, Palestine, Central Asia and the Indian subcontinent.

With the revolt of the Young Turks against the Sultan in 1908, there developed a sudden upsurge in the number of papers being published in the Arab-speaking provinces of the Ottoman Empire. Of the three great media (of propaganda) in the Iranian Constitutional Revolution of 1905-06 - the omnipresent political pamphlets, the secret and revolutionary societies and the press - it was the last that made the greatest impact. Anti-colonial movements and the struggle for independence in India, Indonesia, Morocco and Algeria led to the growth of the press, political parties and a number of ideological movements ranging from Islamic radicalism to communist socialism.

Thus, the 20th century marked the rise of modern mass communication in the Islamic world. The process of decolonization of a number of Islamic countries in Asia and Africa, coupled with delineation of economic classes, and the recognition of the nation state system, elevated the communication media to a new frontier in which the state played a major role. In the Central Asian republics where the former Soviet Union's models of media became dominant, Islamic institutions of communication such as mosques and *madrasas* remained under the control and supervision of the state. In North and West Africa, communication media of the newly established independent states were developed along the lines of the Francophone and Anglophone models.

Today, many Muslim nation-states proudly include the words 'democratic' or 'socialist' (or any number of other descriptive political adjectives) in their official names, which have little or no relevance to their society. In fact, regardless of what type of government they claim to be represented by, almost the overwhelming majority of those states are dominated by a small number of political elites who are highly uncharacteristic of the general population and are indifferent to Islamic political and cultural values. These elites are generally supported by monarchical, tribal, ethnic or military regimes and rely almost entirely upon Western ideologies (i.e. beliefs, ideas, values and emotions) and the media to legitimize their existence.

THE STATE AND COMMUNITY

Politics is a cultural activity. The major crises facing the Islamic countries is that, with a very few exceptions, their political systems and their governments are inconsistent and incompatible with the core of their cultural systems and values i.e. that of Islam. The political tone of the Islamic countries since the beginning of the twentieth century was distinctly dominated by two streams of political forces: the politics of modern ideology and material interest. The prominence of modern ideological politics can be last seen in the constitutional movements and the ideas of European liberalism in Iran, Egypt and the Ottoman Empire at the turn of the century, in the rise of Arab nationalism during World War II; and in the movements of national socialism and the development of military governments in a number of Islamic countries after World War II.

This ideological flood which had its course in modern political parties, secular intellectuals, and the officers corps was paralleled by the system of material politics, which was rooted in traditional monarchy, inter-tribal coalitions and competition, and most recently in the growing sector of industrial and transnational infrastructure. This resulted in an attempt to alter the political and economic segments of society in order to meet the requirement of a global market system. The elites and the so-called modern institutions and groups using the diffusionist power of the media pursued their material interests with disregard to society as a whole and often without any accountability, thereby increasing the crisis of identity. However, both the politics of modern ideology and the politics of material interests were counter-productive in Islamic societies because they were inconsistent with the principles and precepts of the politics of *ummah* (Islamic community) which were perceived as the core of Islamic identity and as the doctrine of both spiritual and temporal powers and authorities.

For example, the one issue which today is causing the greatest instability in the Middle East is the fact that the very basis upon which the modern political structure of the region is built (i.e. the nation-state) is a concept which is alien to and in many ways diametrically opposed to the fundamental principles of Islam. Historically, the great Islamic empires which began their expansion in the seventh century were in no way related to those concepts which are integral parts of the modern nation state. Rather, they were based primarily on the precepts of the Islamic faith which helps to explain the great diversity and viability characterizing Islamic societies in the past. However, as almost inevitably occurs throughout history, the Islamic empires eventually eroded and were encroached upon by newly expanding powers. Thus, beginning with Napoleon's invasion of Egypt near the turn of the eighteenth century, a political system was imposed upon the Middle East which was not the result of an indigenous evolution but rather was a system which had grown to meet the needs of feudal Europe. The imposition of this concept of government (and with it an entirely new way of thinking) has been one of the primary causes of instability in the Middle East for the past two hundred years.

In many current analyses great confusion arises from the failure to make a distinction between a nation-state and an Islamic state. It should be emphasized that while the nation-state is a political state, the Islamic state is a *muttaqi* or religio-political "God fearing" state. The foundation of the Islamic state is based on the *Quran*, the *sunnah* (tradition), and the *Shari'ah* (Islamic canonical law). Whereas in a secular nation-state system, sovereignty rests in the people, in an Islamic order the sovereignty of the state rests in God and not in thrones, individuals, or other groups of people. Where the state does not acknowledge the sovereignty of God, religion becomes a private affair for the citizens. In Islam, religion is not a private affair; it is a public affair. The spiritual and temporal powers are not separated but are united.[1] When Islam appeared as a world power in the seventh century A.D. the concepts of the nation and the state as we know them today did not exist. Instead, Islam developed the concept of the *ummah*: the community of the faithful who professed to believe in both the spiritual and temporal dimensions of Islam.

To see the effects of grafting the Western political mind set onto a region for which it is not suited, one need look no further than the chaotic turmoil of the modern Middle East. The region is littered with the remnants of regimes which relied directly upon imported Western values and ideals and the media as the primary justification of their existence. Both the Shah of Iran and the former monarchs of Egypt had very little if anything to do with the historical processes of Middle Eastern political development and everything to do with seeing modernization along Western lines as the only viable option in a secular world. Even today, the majority of the governments in the region follow the same pattern.

THE SYNDROME OF NATIONALISM

As part of the nation-state system, one of the most destabilizing of the imported ideologies in the Islamic world has been that of nationalism. In Muslim countries, attempts to create a sense of loyalty to an entity which is for all practical purposes foreign, has led to seriously destructive consequences. The peoples of the Islamic world are divided, more than ever before, along the lines of ethnicity, language, and the possession of geographic territory due, largely, to the instigation from those in authority. Islam has thus not been used in its assimilative capacity to form a cohesive Islamic identity, which had made it the unifying force behind one of the greatest political powers the world has ever known. Islam has been subordinated to the powerful ideology of nationalism and has created a dependency upon the West for the understanding of the basic rules of both domestic and international policy-making.

The so-called 'decolonialization' under the nation-state system drew political frontiers in the Islamic world where none had existed before. It created competing national leaderships among a people with a long common history and, like Arabs, even a common language and culture. Decolonialization from imperialism and imperial powers became the beginning of the recolonialization process under the banner of nationalism. In the discussion of polity and society as one Western scholar observed,

> *"if the subject of government in Muslim society has been left almost until the end, that is because it was never, or almost never, anything other than superimposed; never, or almost never, the emanation or repression of that society. It is in its solidarities at the individual level that the true social coherences and structures of Islam are to be found, not in the princes, their soldiers, and their tax collectors."*[2]

Historically, the political and administrative institutions of the Muslim world were among the most highly developed in the world; but beginning with the dynastic systems, citizens were obliged to submit to the governors rather than to maintain the idealistic models of government which characterized the polity of Islam during the early period after the death of the Prophet.

The crisis of identity in the Islamic world was further reinforced by a series of humiliating events during the last four decades immediately after World War II. They included the failure of secular democracy in Turkey, Pakistan and Indonesia; the defeat of the Arabs in the Six Day War with Israel in 1967 and later in 1973; the Pakistani war with India in 1971; the Israeli occupation of Lebanon in the early 1980s; the Soviet occupation of Afghanistan; and most recently the devastating Persian Gulf War and the massacre and genocide of Muslims in Bosnia-Herzegovina. The Islamic revolution in Iran for many Muslims was a landmark and a watershed in their campaign against illegitimate governments in their own countries.

Arab nationalist discourse has tried to replace the term 'Islamic' with 'Arab' in an attempt to influence the population and eventually to change the backdrop of the analysis of political and social facts. However, the fact that Islam is not recognized as an important element of Arab nationalism characterizes two contradictions in its ideology. In the first place, the Arab nationalist movement emphasizes the unity of all Arabs based on history, language, interests and blood ties. However, the Arab nationalist movement is contradicted in geographic terms when it appeals to Arabs of the 'homeland' from the Persian Gulf to the Atlantic. Not only does this disregard other Arabic lands, it overlooks the fact that the notion of the homeland comes from Islam. In the second place, Arab nationalists are contradicted again in their view of Islam as a social growth, since it was also the motivating factor for the spread of the Arab homeland. Nationalist thinking recognizes certain uniting factors such as language, common history and heritage but ignores Islam because of nationalism's secular foundation. Ironically, it was Islam which united the warring tribes of Arab pre-history and created a true Arab identity. Arabic language and culture are a result of Islam, not vice versa. In reality, Arab nationalism reflects ideas of Western origin even though the movement's name implies that it is anchored by Arab culture and thought. Secularism, the defining idea of the nationalist movement, is Western.

THE PARADIGM OF DOMINATION

The penetration and the intrusion of the major European powers in the affairs of the Islamic lands had profound impact on the relationship between the state and communication institutions. It must be recalled that this direct incursion of the European powers in the affairs of the Muslim world signaled the beginning of both colonialism and the spread of modern communication technologies including navigation, telephonic and telegraphic systems, transportation and railroads. The introduction of the European powers in the Middle East, beginning with the Portuguese attempt of hegemony over the Persian Gulf in the sixteenth century and continuing later with the Dutch, the British and the French penetration into Islamic lands from Egypt to India, had two important consequences. In the first place it reduced the authority of the state in the Islamic Middle East, subjecting it to the political and economic will of colonial interests. Second, this colonial influence established communication dominance over the affairs of governments in the region and controlled channels of modern communication whenever possible.

Introduction and adoption of the nation-state system in Islamic countries created an atmosphere of crisis in which foreign intervention was succeeded by concealed control. Internally, political power was shifted from community and religio-political leaders to army and bureaucratic elites. In short, the nation-state system introduced other aspects of modern Western ideologies and institutions. In general, the public considered modern leaders and elites either agents of foreign powers or elements through which new systems of colonialism and ideological politics were imposed on society. Thus, each victory of the modern nation-state system in such countries as Turkey, Iran, Pakistan, Egypt and Indonesia, towards modernization, was overtaken by a new crisis of economic and social fragmentation. In short, a crisis of identity grew beneath a modernizing culture.

Internally, a divisive force in Islam sprung out of the ascendancy of Muslim rulers who valued the political authority of the state more than their religious duties. From the seventh century of the Christian era, beginning with the Umayyad and the Abbasid dynasties until the demise of the Ottoman Empire at the end of the World War I, the Islamic state gradually became separate from its original concept. Power became divided between the rulers who issued laws under their jurisdictions and the *ulama*, or religious scholars and leaders, who announced verdicts under the *Shari'ah*. Thus, two lines of communication were established in Islamic countries often in an adversarial position and which gradually evolved into conflict.[3] The situation is well captured by an Islamic observer of the eleventh century, Abul Malli, who said that "we obey the King in matters of State, but in matters of religion the King must consult us,"[4] and in time, contradictions between the state and religion ensued. The system of *caliphate* as a governing body gradually lost its authority yet attempted to retain its communication dominance resulting in repressive measures.

The changing nature of the Islamic state during this period resulted in the alienation and separation of the community from the state. In many cases, there existed only the community and its leaders, but the state as such had no place in their scheme of things. The rulers were more preoccupied with repressing disorders and reestablishing themselves against rebellion. In short, the state authority was not evenly effective throughout the territory or the communities claimed by it but tended to assert itself forcefully only in the immediate surroundings of the ruler. The separation of the *ummah* and the state characterizes the current crisis of identity in almost all Islamic countries.

For example, while the state attempted to centralize the institutions of communication by controlling the traditional channels such as the mosques and traditional schools of education, the community, under the leadership of the religious scholars, the *ulama*, maintained competing channels of communication which challenged the conduct of the state. The seventeenth and eighteenth century political systems in a number of Middle Eastern countries, including Iran and Egypt, were characterized by the proverb: "If you see the *ulama* at the gates of kings, say there are bad *ulama* and bad kings. If you see the kings at the gates of the *ulama*, say there are good *ulama* and good kings."[5] Thus, the contradiction between Islamic domination and secular power spurred further antagonisms within the Islamic world throughout this period.   With the public denouncement of the state, the *ulama* were pressured to act independently of the state.   This type of conflict is best illustrated by the Constitutional Revolution (1906) and the Islamic Revolution (1979) in Iran.   The resistance of the *ulama* to becoming mere instruments of the state and the correlating division between Islamic and secular leadership triggered these eventual revolutions.

The power of the state and the *ulama* was further distinguished by their relationship to foreign actors.   The government tended to yield to the influence of outside courtiers and ministers, whereas the *ulama* held a clear concept and practice of authority and despite restrictions they resisted outside pressures.   The steadfast quality of the *ulama* nurtured a close relationship with the community through the mobilization of traditional communication channels while the state typically ignored its subjects and used modern communication channels and the emerging mass media systems to maintain its legitimacy, collect taxes or recruit soldiers.   Hence, the *ulama* became an intermediary channel of communication between the people and the state, acting on behalf of the *ummah* as well as the nation, however, it must be noted that the foremost loyalty of the community remains towards Islam rather than the state.   Muslim disfavor of both the state and imperialism was proclaimed in an Islamic, rather than a nationalistic, framework.

The contacts between the Islamic world and the West in the nineteenth and twentieth centuries increased the absorption of many Islamic countries into quasi-secular political entities ranging from hereditary monarchies to modern Western and/or military style republics.   This also resulted in pronounced conflicts between modern secularism and the Islamic tradition of *Shari'ah* which, until the nineteenth century, provided the main if not the complete legal underpinnings of social and economic conduct in Muslim societies. The intimate contact between Islam and modern Western industrial countries, coupled with the process of colonization of substantial parts of Asia and Africa introduced a number of Western standards and values to these societies. Thus, at the beginning of the twentieth century and with the introduction of modern means of communication, transportation and technologies, the fields of civil and commercial transactions proved particularly prominent for change and new methods of conduct.

THE MEDIA AND MODERNITY

The crisis of identity was further enhanced by a number of conceptual as well as policy developments during the post-world war period. It should be recalled that with the triumph of romanticism and secularism following the French Revolution, naturalism came to occupy and dominate the world-views of the West. In the Islamic view of the natural and transcendent orders, it is the latter that governs the flow of the former. A large part of the law of Islam deals with the social order and, today, it is not the state of 'modernization' but the state of transformation that Muslims are concerned with. The most important difference between transformation and modernization is that the former is out of time (since time is a category of understanding) and the latter is in time.[6] Under the slogans of modernization, economic development and technological progress, the Islamic countries were deprived of the right to recognize their own unique and distinct civilization and culture. For the sake of convenience in terminology and world political hierarchy, they were merely lumped together with less industrialized countries under the vague category of the 'Third World'. As has been demonstrated by numerous studies during the last several decades, the process of modernization became a one-way traffic from the West. Soon, even the dichotomy of 'Occident' versus the 'Orient' was pushed aside, since the world wide diffusion of modernization which was now creating the new world of the so-called 'globalization' had rendered 'East' and 'West' irrelevant.

'Political stability' as a prerequisite for 'economic development' not only was a justification for keeping repressive regimes in power, but also the dominant world economic and political systems by now had claimed the right of access to valuable natural resources in Islamic lands. It was the economic and not the political infrastructure of such countries as Iran, Indonesia and Saudi

Arabia that had become vital for the well-being of the industrialized countries.

Identity, as a social-psychological concept, refers to how people perceive themselves in the environment and in relation to others. It is based on shared cultural assumptions that are historically rooted in a given community. In the contemporary Western writings and literature on social and political thought, the concepts of identity and anxiety have often been viewed as two sides of a coin. The advent of the alienated person is the theme which lies behind 'modernity' and has been the subject of intellectual discourse and among the ears of social malaise.[7]

In short, industrialization, rapid social change, secularization of thought and life and, above all, the media have produced not only a breakdown in morality and traditional beliefs, but have also devitalized the foundation of political community such as the modern nation state and have crippled normal mechanisms of cohesion and power in community. The contemporary return to religion in many Western communities is by and large a pragmatic attempt to establish a sense of comfort, mental health and morality or, in the language of Freud, an attempt of the ego to make up for the lack of the superego. The question of identity can also be observed in the politicization of gender and other social and biological groups.

While the print and electronic media in the Islamic world have helped to concentrate power in the hands of political and economic elites and have contributed to the centralization of modern state apparatus, the oral modes of communication largely have remained in the hands of traditional and religious groups who often have attempted to decentralize and diffuse the power of the state and establish a counter balance to authority. Led by traditional authorities, such as the *ulama*, the resurgence of Islam and revolutionary movements in the 20th century within the Islamic countries are examples of the potential use of oral media such as mosques.

Nevertheless, one of the most interesting and contemporary phenomena in the Islamic world has been the integration of modern communication technologies with the traditional media of communication, which have contributed to the legitimization of the centers of power and acceleration of the process of political and social change. In the 1978-79 Islamic Revolution in Iran, Ayatollah Ruhollah Khomeini and his followers used modern means of communication such as telephones and cassette tapes along with traditional channels to disseminate their messages throughout the country. In such countries as Indonesia, Malaysia, Pakistan and Egypt the use of personal computers and facsimiles for the diffusion of Islamic ideas have become widespread. Information about Islam has become more accessible to the layperson through databases on the *Qur'an* and *hadith*.

In the closing decades of the 20th century, three important developments have had the most profound impact on the nature and contents of information in the Islamic world:

(1) the Islamic Revolution in Iran and the subsequent political movements in other Islamic countries, setting the tone for the Islamization of the media and creating a new ecology of communication in a number of regions;

(2) the disintegration of the Soviet Union and the emergence of newly independent states in Islamic regions such as Central Asia and elsewhere contributing to the potential expansion of a greater Islamic communications network;

(3) the growth of national and international telecommunications through satellites and its possible effects on the integration of the Islamic regions and its impact on political and economic development. Hence, the Islamic world has developed its communication media with a new awareness of global change and, at the same time, a large sense of history together with an Islamic identity. An illustration of the new media and its impact on Muslim identity can be shown by the following example.

ISLAMIZATION OF TELEVISION IN IRAN

Islamization of the mass media in Iran, in both content and operation, has been undertaken since the Islamic Revolution in 1978-1979 and its full impact on society and polity is only recently starting to be recognized. Nowhere is this more visible than in the institutionalization of the broadcast system, particularly television, within the framework of the Islamic Republic of Iran.

Television has penetrated into Iranian society as a pervasive medium of communication technology not only because of its vastly growing audiences and organizational network, but more importantly due to cultural factors that give it legitimacy. Iranian television derives its legitimacy by being a "Voice and Profile of the Islamic Republic of Iran," relying considerably on the traditional sources of religio-political authority in society and asserting itself as a medium of public service. In an Islamic society, and yet geographically diverse country like Iran, where political and social legitimacy have historically been contested and influenced by religion as well as various ethnic, cultural and linguistic groups, television attempts to combine the rich, indigenous written and oral forms of communication into a unified framework. Hence, the popularity of television depends on its subordination to Iranian culture and tradition. Indeed, one of the major problems facing Iranian television prior to the Islamic Revolution was precisely its isolation from the mainstream Iranian culture and tradition and its excessive reliance on royal patronage, secularism and its dependence on foreign and imported programs. In short, the trends and characteristics of Iranian television can be summarized in its attempt:

(1) to Islamasize the medium.
(2) to integrate television within the existing traditional channels of communication.
(3) to create a state-community system of public broadcasting.
(4) to incorporate this institution with the principles of Islamic ethics.
(5) to be self reliant in the wake of globalization.

The importance attached to television as a means of Islamic propagation and cultural transmission is well recognized and documented in the constitution of the Islamic Republic of Iran. By proclaiming that "Freedom of publicity and propaganda in the mass media, radio and television shall be insured on the basis of Islamic principles," the 1979 constitution gave television an independent organization outside any single ministry placing it under the joint supervision of the judiciary, legislative and executive branches. Under the revised and supplementary constitution, adopted a decade ago, the radio and television organization remained under the supervision of a council composed of two members from each of these branches, and the power of the Leader of the Revolution to appoint the director of the organization for radio and television was confirmed. According to the constitution, the Leadership or *Vilayate Faqih* (guardianship of the jurist) is the highest spiritual and political position of the country and revolution. The special provision of the constitution not only emphasizes the vital role television can play in Iranian society, but it gives particular attention to this form of public broadcasting through its organization and regulatory apparatus. All other means of mass communication - including newspapers, magazines, radio and cinema - are regulated, and in some cases licenced, through the Ministry of Islamic Culture and Guidance.

The concept of public broadcasting in Iran is distinct in that there is no separation between religion and state; and the notion of civil society under Islamic tenets and jurisprudence does not make the same distinctions between the state on the one hand and the public on the other, as would be the case in Western secular settings.

News, information and documentaries are prepared within the Islamic community framework. Commercial advertising is common but subject to specific rules and regulations including the time framework to prevent the fragmentation of programs. The emphasis on entertainment and information is on their social functions and not determined by their commercial aspects. Serious educational and current affairs programs are allocated a large segment of television time. Locally created historical series also command large audiences. The amount of foreign produced materials broadcast on television is the lowest in the Middle East, which requires not only a very careful selection of internationally produced materials but also a fairly heavy burden on the production of local programming. There has been a vast increase in domestic programming and, hence, a considerable reduction in dependency on foreign materials. In 1991, eighty-five percent of all television programs were produced domestically. Before the revolution for every program produced domestically three imported programs were broadcast on television. Programs for children and adolescents currently constitute 16.4 percent of the domestic TV program production, while social and cultural programs occupy 14.9 percent with current news programs being 14.4 percent.[8]

Television programming and production are required to abide by the framework of Islamic ethics. For example, romantic dramas are featured but there are no explicit physical and sexual scenarios. Violent and aggressive programs usually associated with Western movies, dramas and soap operas are also excluded. All imported programs are closely monitored and reviewed for their compatibility with the Islamic social etiquette.

Unlike the United States and many industrialized countries, where television viewing mainly has become a single person entertainment, social activity, group listening and the viewing of broadcasting is a common occurrence in Iran. This practice has more of a cultural and social underpinning than one based on economics and the lack of access to radio and television sets. Extended families beyond immediate relatives and their interactions, in forms of home visits, all play a crucial role in social communication, making television viewing in Iran a group activity. Iran, since the Islamic Revolution, has fought the encroachment of Western dominated programming and has sought to maintain its autonomy through a comprehensive communication policy of investment in expansion of locally produced programs. The result has been a fair degree of success in that the Iranian television industry has become a prolific producer of programs and has strengthened its local infrastructure. Television in Iran illustrates a fascinating communication problem in many Islamic countries: how traditional culture can be synthesized with contemporary electronic media and how television can be employed in ways that better suit the mood and styles of the country's history.

The explicit and implicit policies carried out in Iran, with regards to television, underline the importance given to this medium by the leaders of the country and their perception of its power in national and international affairs. These policies are based on a further assumption that the process of individual selectivity and audience power is very much dependent on the quality of the public's education regarding the media. Indeed, the role of television in Iranian society has been a source of major debate among the people since the revolution. The assumption is that the direct involvement of the public in the discourse taking place in the media on this issue is a prerequisite to the kind of society they want to have.

The recognition and visibility of social communication within an Islamic setting and the reconstruction and changing of political and cultural public space in Iran, in particular relating to television, is based on two principles or concepts. In the first place, a principle guiding the ethical boundaries of social and public communication in Islam is the doctrine of *"amir bi al-ma'ruf wa nahy'an al munkar"* or "commanding towards rightness and prohibiting the wrong." Implicit and explicit in this principle is the notion of individual and group responsibility for preparing the succeeding generations to accept Islamic precepts and to make use of them. Muslims have the responsibility of guiding one another and each generation has the responsibility of guiding the next.   The Qur'an points out the responsibilities of Muslims in guiding each other, especially those individuals and institutions who are charged with the responsibilities of leadership and propagation of Islamic ideals. This includes all the institutions of social communication such as the press, radio and television as well as the individual citizens of each community. Thus, a special concept of social responsibility theory is designed around the ethical doctrine of "commanding towards rightness and prohibiting the wrong."

The second fundamental concept which has a direct bearing on the notion of public space, particularly as it might relate to the political life of the individual and Islamic society, is *ummah* or community. The concept of *ummah* transcends national borders and political boundaries. Islamic community transcends the notion of the modern nation-state system and is a religio-economic concept that is only present when it is nourished and governed by Islam.   The notion of community in Islam makes no sharp distinction between public and private, what is required of the community at large is likewise required of every individual member.   Intercultural and international communication (the emphasis here is on nationality and not the nation state) are the necessary ingredients of Islamic *ummah*. Every citizen in the Islamic 'state' is required to offer his best advice on common matters and must be entitled to do so.   These two concepts, therefore, over the years have gradually become the guiding doctrines of television content and are highly emphasized and publicized by the state and community leaders. Today, in the Islamic society of Iran, the modern systems of mass media have been, to a large extent, well integrated within the classical and traditional systems of social communication. The result has been a high level of social mobilization and organization, making the process of political, cultural, economic and military participation extremely effective.

The amplification of the human voice in Quranic recitals by microphones, radio and television as well as the production of such recitals on cassettes - distributed along with other public affairs materials - have brought new dimensions of communication into Iran. In addition, through a combination of traditional channels and television, community leaders and various groups have maintained their ability to voice their opinions to the public. In short, Iranian television, in general, serves to diffuse Islamic culture in pursuit of state legitimacy but refrains from the diffusion of propagation of anti-Islamic practices.

Traditionally in Iran, print and electronic media helped to concentrate power in the hands of political and economic elites and contributed to the centralization of modern state apparatus. By contrast, oral modes of communication remained largely in the hands of traditional and religious groups that had often attempted to decentralize and diffuse the power of the state and establish a counterbalance to authority. One of the most interesting contemporary phenomena in post-revolutionary Iran has been precisely the integration of modern communication technologies with traditional media - a process that has contributed to the legitimization of central power and the acceleration of political and social change.

Prior to the revolution, the commercial intrusion into the public arena of the state represented only one side of the coin. The other side of this process was the absorption, by the state, of a large portion of popular culture and its diversion into a sphere that was regulated by the state itself. A television model under consideration in Iran over the last two decades attempts to overcome this dilemma by creating what may be termed a state community perspective of television where the state is considered both in terms of its overreaching interests of those who compose it and the community of *ummah*, which stands for larger social groups and a variety of audiences.

In summary, the development of television in Iran has been propelled by several factors including the rise of the Islamic Revolution, the religio-political and cultural identity, and the expansion of communication technologies as instruments of social and political mobilization. The expansion of television has added a new dimension to a traditional means of communication in Iran. As stated, one important feature of television, in Iran, is that it is being integrated into the vast and complex system of traditional and oral channels of communication. Television, in Iran, achieves the power and penetration of traditional channels of communication when it serves as a social, political and economic tool. Political development, including the resurgence of Islamic identity, has had considerable influence on the regional, and even international, dimensions of Iranian television broadcasting.

The development of Iranian television has been unique in that it has not only tried to meet technological, organizational and production challenges but it has also taken the responsibility of creating and framing its operation based on an Islamic ethic. By rejecting both the commercial model of television broadcasting and the strict government-controlled system, it is striving towards a new model of state-community perspective. Its concept of public broadcasting rests on the Islamic principle of public service with a strong emphasis on public mobilization, social integration and (an) Islamic identity.

ISLAMIC IDENTITY AND THE INTERNATIONAL MEDIA

As regards to the question of Muslim identity and the world media, it has been demonstrated by numerous studies that until the Islamic Revolution in Iran, in 1978-79, the international media paid little or no attention to the Muslim world or to any subjects associated with the Muslim world. On the contrary, the coverage of Islamic countries in the Middle East and elsewhere, including Asia, was concentrated on national political institutions and the current secular leaders of the time. For example, the Arab-Israeli questions always dominated the news as did Arab nationalism and its confrontation with the West. American observers borrowed the label of "fundamentalism" from the history of Christianity when reporting on the revival of Islamic fundamentalism in Iran and elsewhere.

Another classic example, conveying this idea, is the coverage of Iran in the decade before the Shah's fall. Almost all the elite media of the West mislead their readers and viewers. They represented the Shah as a modernizing monarch, a benevolent dictator whose power at home and friendship with the West was quite secure. Only during the Islamic revolution did any analysis of the bankruptcy of the shah's regime and recognition of the far reaching influence of Islam and the Ayatollah Khomeini begin to appear in the media. In fact, there was little analysis of the nature of the Shi'ite branch of Islam until the Israeli invasion of Lebanon and the resistance movements of the Lebanese Shi'ites. Even then, the event seemed to draw coverage mostly because it was associated with terrorism and fanaticism.

Over the last two decades, beginning with the Islamic resurgence in the world, the Muslim identity has been mainly covered under two major themes. One is Islamic fundamentalism and violence and the other is the portrayal of Muslims as an ethnic group. The crisis in Bosnia provides us with an insight into the latter theme. In an endless system that makes the nation state the departing point for any discourse, the Serbian leaders strategy, in the media has, since the outbreak of the Bosnian tragedy, benefitted from the vocabulary used by the dominant global media and political elites. A major socio-linguistic bias which has, unfortunately, been copied and repeated throughout the crisis refers to the Balkan conflict as a war between the "Bosnian Serbs" and the "Bosnian Muslims." Notice that in this description of confrontation, the natives or the Bosnian Muslims are introduced by their religious affiliation whereas the non-Muslim residents of Bosnia are described by their nationality, as "Bosnian Serbs" and not by their religion such as the Christian or Orthodox church. In short, instead of branding the Bosnian Serbs as Orthodox Christian Bosnians versus the Muslim Bosnians, the international media simply call them Serbians. For the Muslims, the international media makes Islam a basis of ethnic identity, something quite contrary to the basis of Islamic tenants; for the Christian Serbs, it is nationality and geographical location that receives the media's attention. And what about identifying Bosnian Muslims as Europeans? Are Bosnian Muslims also Europeans or just the remnants of the Ottoman Empire in Europe who have now suddenly decided to ask for an independent country and government? Using this type of labeling, some 200,000 Spanish Muslims were persecuted and killed during the Inquisition against the Islamic influence in Western Europe. In the current crisis in Kosovo, for a variety of reasons that are not yet clear, the international media has retreated to the old concept of ethnic identity. This time the majority of the people of Kosovo, who are Muslims, are identified simply as ethnic Albanians thus ignoring their Islamic identity.

From the Islamic revolution to the Persian Gulf War and from the occupation of Afghanistan by the Soviets to the ethnic cleansing in the Balkans, numerous research and analysis has shown us that the mainstream international media have contributed more than their share to the already confused state of public opinion about Muslim identity in the West with their adverse publicity and propaganda waged against Islamic movements.[9] In the Islamic world the collapse of communism, combined with the social malaise and the economic and political stagnation in the West, has reaffirmed the long and historical perception of the Muslim peoples that Islam is, now, the only alternative to their present political structures. In the West, the resurgence of Muslim identity has been ignored by many writers and media analysts because of the emphasis they put on the analysis of formal political institutions such as the state, political parties, bureaucratic institutions and modern governmental infrastructures, simply because Islamic movements have become the major obstacle and resistant force to the existing international political system.

ISLAM AND THE INTERNET

Internet sites provided by computer technologies offer new channels for the dissemination of information about Islam. A user trying to find information on various concepts and issues relating to

Islam is confronted with varied and often biased information. Faced with such myriad viewpoints, Internet users need to be conscious and critical of the information they are receiving. For example, a site maintained by the Christian World Evangelization Research Center concerning Islam and China displayed the following:

> *"Pray against the spirit of Islam that has kept the Hui bound for many generation...Ask the Holy Spirit to soften the hearts of these Muslims so that they will be receptive to the Gospel."*[10]

This suggests that the Chinese government actually favours Islam, a point many Hui and others would disagree with. Alternatively, sites such as the Cyber Muslim Information Collective's Dunya features various Qur'anic translations, an Islamic bookshop and a "Virtual Sufi Lodge." It also needs to be mentioned that many Internet sites provide such voluminous information tied with a high quantity of commercial data that makes the collection of information, on specific topics very time consuming.

One of the benefits of the Internet is that it is an excellent source of immediate access to the media and issues in Islamic countries. For example, various countries specific on line newspapers such as 'The Turkish Daily News', Malaysia's 'Daily Star', 'The Singapore Straits Time', and the Pakistani Newspaper 'Dawn' can be used to provide perspectives on events and issues within Muslim contexts alongside other on-line news resources such as CNN, TIME and Reuters.[11]

Various governmental agencies, interest groups, academics and scholars are using the Internet to promote their specific understandings and approaches towards Islam both in Muslim majority and minority countries. For example, an Islamic server has been developed by a Singaporean government agency which maintains a site called the Islamic Gateway to Singapore, operated under the auspices of the Islamic Religious Council of Singapore.

It is now clear with the proliferation of the media and information technologies around the world, from conventional media to the Internet, that the information and news about the Islamic world will multiply and expand. However, the impact of such coverage will be determined on the reliability and accuracy of the information provided by the institutions and the individuals. Eventually, the process of political image making that distorts the political, cultural, and social realities of the Islamic world will continue to colour the perceptions of individuals and institutions both nationally and internationally unless two fundamental changes occur. The first would be the ability of Western individuals, the media and policy makers to see the developments in the Islamic world not from their own historical perspective but from the perspective of Muslim identity. The second change would be an internal political restructuring of the polity of Islamic countries that would be compatible to Islamic social and religious beliefs. Without these two conditions, the image of Muslim identity will continue to be distorted.

Endnotes:

1 Ayatollah Imam Ruhollah Khomeini, *Islam and Revolution: Writings and Declarations of Imam Khomeini*, (Translated and annotated by Hamid Algar), Mizan Press, Berkeley, CA, 1981; and Ayatollah Imam Ruhollah Khomeini, *Islamic Government*, (Translated and annotated by Hamid Algar), Islamic Foundation Press, Malappuram Dist., Kerela, India, 1988.

2 Claude Cohen, "Economy, Society, and Institutions," in *The Cambridge History of Islam*, Vol. 2, ed. P. M. Holt, H. Fisher, A. Lambton, & B. Lewis, Cambridge: Cambridge University Press, p. 530.

3 Hamid Mowlana, "The New Global Order and Cultural Ecology," *Media, Culture and Society*, (Special issue of Islam and Communication), Vol. 15, No. 4, 1993, pp.9-27.

4 Quoted in Altaf Guahar, "Islam and Secularism," in *The Challenge of Islam*, ed. Altaf Guahar, Islamic Council of Europe, 1978, p. 306.

5 Hamid Algar, *Religion and State in Iran: 1785-1906*, University of California Press, Berkeley, CA, p. 22.

6 Hamid Mowlana & Laurie J. Wilson, *The Passing of Modernity: Communication and Transformation in Society*, Longman, White Plains, NY, 1990.

7 Examples include Karl Marx' essays on "alienation," George Simmel's concerns in "The Metropolis," Graham Wallas' work on, "The Great Society," Eric Fromm's conception of the "Automation," David Riesman's "Other Directed," and of course George Orwell's often cited book "1984." Indeed the search for community in the history of the West is an attempt to assert the condition that would eliminate the probability of such anxiety and create a source of identity. W. H. Auden's "The Age Of Anxiety," and Albert Camus' "The Century of Fear," are in comparison with the seventeenth century as the age of mathematics, the eighteenth as the age of physical sciences, and the nineteenth as that of biology. Although their characterizations are not logically formed and that fear is not a science, Camus traces the negative functioning of the scientific and technological age to the deterioration of individual personality and the destruction of the community. Franz Kafka's novel "The Castle" is another illustration of Western Alienation in modern community and the search for a new identity. Kafka's hero is driven, "by a need for the most primitive requisites of life, the need to be rooted in a home and a calling, and to become a member of a community." But the governors in the castle remain uncommunicative, authoritarian, and inaccessible. In the sociological and political scene Robert Lynd's studies of "Middletown" in America and Paul Tillich's work in Europe respectively demonstrate the emergence of the awareness of anxiety and identity in urban centers and communities, and the description of the situation in Europe when German fascism developed. In the area of philosophy and religion the questions of anxiety and identity are among the central subjects posed in the thought of theological Reinhold Nieluhr and existentialist Martin Heidegger who have experienced in their own lives the cultural crisis of Western society. See W. H. Auden , *The Age of Anxiety*, New York, 1947; Franz Kafka, *The Castle*, New York, 1930; R. S. Lynd and H. M. Lynd, *Middletown*,

New York, 1920; *Middletown in Transition*, New York, 1937; Paul Tillich, *The Protestant Era*, University of Chicago Press, 1947; Eric Fromm, *Escape From Freedom*, New York, 1941; Reinhold Niehuhr, *The Nature and Destiny of Man*, New York, 1941; and Sigmund Freud, *General Introduction to Psychoanalysis*, American Edition, New York, 1920.

8   See, Mowlana, H (1997). "Islamicising the media in a global era: The state-community perspective in Iranian broadcasting," In Programming for people: From cultural rights to cultural responsibilities, Kevin Robins (Ed.). United Nations World Television Forum, Report presented by Radiotelevisione Italiana (RAI) pp 205-210.

9   See, Said, E. W. (1981). *Covering Islam: How the media and the experts determine how we see the rest of the world.* New York: Pantheon Books; Mowlana, H., Gerbner, G., & Schiller, H. I. (Eds.). (1992). *Triumph of the image: The media's war in the Persian Gulf: A global perspective.* Boulder, CO: Westview Press; Mowlana, H. "Muslims and Genocide in the Balkans." *Peace Review* 6(3), pp 373-381; Kamilapour, Y. R. (Ed.). (1994). *The U.S. media and the Middle East: Image and Perception.* Westport, CT: Greenwood Press.

10 Quoted in Bunt, G. R. (1997). Islam in cyberspace: Islamic studies resources on the Internet. *Muslim World Book Review*, 18(1), pp. 5.

11 See Bunt, G. R. (1997). Islam in cyberspace: Islamic studies resources on the Internet. *Muslim World Book Review*, 18(1), pp. 3-13.

Mass Media and the Changeable Identity of the Youth

*Hadi Khaniki**

THE QUESTION

The striking progress of communication and information technology in recent decades has exerted an extensive influence over cultural, social and political settings across the world. The appearance of ruptures in the former orders and systems and the emergence of various cultural and social processes and discourses have been the immediate outcome of these changes. Culture, which, in a sense, is the manifestation of the content of the network of social relations, is affected more - and earlier - than anything else by such developments. Mass media and communication technology disseminate the achievements, the solutions, the codes and signs of different cultures throughout the world with increasing speed and ease of access. When decoded in another culture, these signs are often accompanied by disturbances and crises in the cultural coherence of people and nations. This is the process that is nowadays referred to by such terms as the "Globalization", "Universalization", "Cultural assault", "Westernization", "McDonaldization" and "Americanization" of the cultures of the world.

Certainly, these cultural trends are not the only dominant trends in the contemporary age; rivalling them, are the tendencies to

* Department of Communications, Allamah Tabatabai University, Iran

revive religious, national, ethnic, lingual and gender identities. Today, religion and spirituality are becoming the sources of some of the major developments of our age, as vibrant and influential forces on the road to achieve independence and freedom. Such attempts by women and youth in search of identity have, in many societies, assumed a meaningful form.

Clearly, in the context of such a process, questions about the cultural future of society and the world as a whole, the destiny of these diverse and conflicting processes, and the meaning of "cultural identity" in an ever changing world of communication, are not merely of academic interest and concern. They are serious and vitally important issues in everyday life. Indeed, how can one define the religious and national bonds between generations that are subjected to different forms of communication and to overwhelming changes and, moreover, discern the role of the media in giving rise to these changes?

The concept of "identity" and discussions about its essence, substance and dimensions are mainly of concern to societies and peoples in the process of transition. In traditional societies, identity is not a new issue. There, Man's existence and destiny are, to a large extent, stable, immutable and predictable. His identity comes from an authoritative system of "guiding traditions" and perpetual rituals and, sometimes, mythological beliefs. Man occupies a place in a symbolic system which is not only quite familiar but also sheds light upon, and shows the possibilities and directions of, life. An individual is born as a member of a certain clan, tribe and family system. He belongs to a section of social life that is confined within a clearly demarcated and stable, social and cultural setting and can hardly ever escape his pre-determined destiny and situation by occupying a new place or attaining a new status. In such societies, individuals are not able to transform their identity in a fundamental way and, therefore, it is meaningless to speak of the notion of identity crisis in such societies (Ahmadi, 1377 pp. 39 & 40). "An individual is either a hunter or a member of the tribe, that is all." (Kellner, p. 141).

From a sociological point of view, the identity of Man in a traditional society is easily discerned since it is based on past history (Giddens, 1990, p. 378). It is the "past" that rules over the present and it is through the logical and comprehensible continuation of the "past" that the "present" and the "future" come into being. In fact, the concept of identity takes shape independently of individual and collective experiences.

On the contrary, in societies in transition, there is room for change. An individual living in such a society, even though having roots in traditions, is strongly susceptible to the influences of modern life. And in modern life, the concepts of "self-leadership" and "other-leadership" are more active than "tradition-leadership". "Man has become self-thinking because he cannot think of his identity as being the same as the identity of the past." (Ahmadi, 1377, p. 40).

Identity in modern life is a contradictory concept because both society and the individual are notions which are subject to continuous alterations and are rooted in changeable and unpredictable situations. Within the individual, himself, there are various identities in conflict with each other; those which he has chosen and those to which he is subjected. Each of these identities deprive the others of their core and the conflict is reflected not only in society, but also within the individual.

Clearly, it is not possible in such a process to identify the individual's actions, wishes, demands and thoughts according to any one of his connections or interests because few dominant and decisive identities exist under the conditions of transition. In fact, one's cognizance of one's own interests and situations does not depend on a single element and is not yet a certain and specific matter, rather, cognizance is a changeable and dynamic phenomenon and for this reason, can hardly be contained in one particular context. In a sense, modernity is an un-ending process of internal cleavage (Harbe, 1991, p. 12), as it is a decentralized form without any specific and orderly foundation and joints and one which does not come into being by any specific cause or according to any specific law (Laclau, 1990, p. 12). It is for this reason that, in the modern age, identity is defined as something unstable, plural, unclear, unspecified and un-particular. Identity is something perceivable but dependent on conditions and relations that are rarely stable. The rules and norms that create the modern identity are a great deal more receptive to theoretical and pragmatic changes than the system of values and norms of traditional societies. Because of this, modern frontiers of identity are continuously undergoing change and everyone seeks a new identity for himself by adopting new modes of living and new cognitive horizons. What is known as the identity crisis in modern society is, in fact, a part and parcel of the process of change which has displaced the centralistic structures of society. Modern identity is based on change and diversity, it comes to the fore in the absence of stability. Although, in appearance, it has a private and personal reality, in essence, it is a social and psychological relationship. It takes form through a process of continuous interaction with the cultural world.

"Social identity", as a concept, provides a bridge between personal and social worlds. It takes form in the quest for cultural identity and through attempts at the coordination of the notion of "we". The process of the search for identity has continually become more complex, more varied and more prone to the influence of various social factors. The current meaning of identity implies a dependence on both the perception of "self" and the attitude toward the "other". At the same time the concepts of "self" and "other" are undergoing rapid change and inevitably, where the dimensions of the change is wider, as in the world of the young, explanation of the connection between these two proves more difficult. Identity is connected both to ontology and a common conception of life and the world, as well as to a personal and individual approach to the world. In this way, identity is a combination of cohesion and individuality (Ahmadi, 1377, p. 81). Therefore, understanding this concept within modern society and the ever-changing world of the young requires greater effort.

Man enters the twenty first century while talks of the "power of culture" and "culturally based developments" are in vogue. In the context of new culturally based development strategies, as mentioned on the agenda of UNESCO's International Governmental Conference on Cultural Policies for Development, choice of an appropriate cultural guideline for development is no longer a purely ethical or academic recommendation; rather, it is an inevitable necessity for the survival and progress of the contemporary world. Without doubt, paying attention to the concept of "identity" has a special and central place in cultural development and naturally, the concept of identity in the world of the young is open to more diverse interpretations and perceptions.

Among the factors that have come to play very significant roles in the transmission of this concept and in the presentation of these interpretations are the mass media which impart an accelerating tempo to the process of communication and cultural transmission.

MASS MEDIA - CONSTRUCTIVE AND DESTRUC-TIVE ROLES

Among the most important social roles which the mass media have assumed in societies in transition is the manner of their participation in the process of national development in general, and of cultural development, in particular. The mass media can, according to the policies and strategies they adopt in conformity to, or in breaking with, the objectives of national developments, contribute to stability or change with regard to cultural values and norms. The culture of work, the culture of consumption, and the culture of leisure time are all influenced by these values and norms and in societies such as Iran, where development is taking place in a condensed and cumulative way, the influence is even more intensive.

Unlike the culture of the elite, the culture disseminated by the mass media has characteristics such as disorder, a lack of homogeneity and a lack of cohesion, as unstable, partial and dispersed inputs are more extensively involved. Because of this contrast within the culture of the elite - which relies more on traditional or formal education - the media culture traverses a far broader field of changeability. On that basis, the role of the media is one that leads to the emergence of a confused and prismatic culture which is composed of different and overlapping cultural elements belonging to all times and places. On their own, however, the media are neither the source of pain nor the fountain of remedy. Just as they are able to deprive society of the power of creativity and innovation against the on-rush of rapid and increasing social and industrial changes, they are equally able to teach it how to ponder about time. The link between the past, the present and the future, the link between various elements within the culture, the link between sub-cultures, the link between generations and between society and the world, are all among matters that lie within access in the framework of the media roles. That means that the media can call society to a cultural re-discovery and re-moulding, to a return to itself and in this way, bring up a dynamic and selective audience just as they can raise a passive audience by promoting the role of the "futuristic" requiring submission before the onslaught of technology. Thus, one ought to look at the media in their double roles of construction and destruction in the process of the cultural and social education.

The destructive role of the media is mainly visible in conditions where society suffers from a lack of cohesion in the process of an unbalanced development with severance of the links between various sectors of society, elimination or weakness of intermediary links and polarization of society, emergence of a multiple structure as the basis of legitimacy, cultural fragmentation, appearance of a gap between modernism and tradition, weakness of the process of national integration, crisis in individual identity and confusion over the definitions of "self" and "other". The constructive role of the media comes into being in the framework of the expanded capacity of society to arrive at higher levels of order.

In societies like Iran, where - under the influence of new social and cultural factors such as the Islamic revolution and the emergence of democratic processes such as various elections - the breadth and depth of public participation has undergone striking changes and the process of urbanization, communication, change in population structure and educational fabrics have undergone new changes, the media have assumed a new role especially because the Iranian society of today is a "young" society.

A young society is more inclined to obtain an identity and identity cannot be defined in a static and isolated manner. Discovery and reconstruction of identity is the characteristic of a society in action, one engaged in construction and for this reason, such a society is continuously challenging "the other" and trying to discover its *"self"*. "Self" assumes a meaning in connection with "the other" and identity is the product of "communication." This is why in Iran's social endeavours today, as well as in the process of the efforts of the younger generation in search of identity, the "mass media" have a fundamental part to play.

SOCIAL DEVELOPMENT AND CHANGING CONCEPT OF IDENTITY

Before being influenced by the mass media, the concept of identity is more significantly influenced by those social variables that the media, in one form or another, reflect. In communication research, it is usual to attribute to the media the role of acting either as an impetus or an impediment in the process of national development; they are even described as the products and the outcomes of underdevelopments or development of society. Society's breaking out of the traditional shell and arriving at a new arena of change naturally bring everyone to a new visualization of the concept of identity. This is a fact that most developing societies experience. Deep social and cultural revolutions impart even greater impetus and intensity to this process just as the Islamic and revolutionary society of Iran is now experiencing such a process under the light of the Islamic revolution and the changes born out of it. The new perception of Islamic and Iranian identity that took shape in the light of the thoughts of the late Imam Khomeini (God's blessings be with him) was based on a divine school of thought and the brilliant, but unknown, capabilities and power of the Iranian and Islamic society in the present-day modern world. Naturally, this new attitude and determination, which found most of its followers among the young, led to a great revolution at many ideological and cultural levels in the Iranian society and the Islamic world. The Islamic, Iranian and revolutionary identity found a definition in various processes of return to "self", defence against the "other" and dialogue with "the new world".

Apart from this cultural development, we can refer to some of the new social factors that have been influenced by the Islamic revolution and have had an impact on the process of new quests for identity:

Increased Urbanization and Higher Level of Literacy

In the wake of the Islamic Revolution, the Iranian society was a semi-urban and semi-literate one. According to the census of the Statistical Centre of Iran, carried out in Aban 1355 (1976), only 47 percent of the population of the country lived in urban areas and 47.5 percent of the total population was literate. Findings of the 1370 (1991) census show that over 56 percent of the population were not living in urban areas and almost 80 percent were literate. The proportion of literate to total population of women over these two decades has risen from 36 to 74 percent. For women in urban areas, the ratio is about 82 percent while it is 62 percent for women in rural areas.

Growth of Higher Education

In 1375 (1996), over 1.5 million Iranians had a university degree and if we added the number of university students to that figure, we arrive at the figure of 2.7 million. In other words, for every 10 Iranian households, two persons have a university degree or were engaged in university studies. It is interesting that according to the 1375 census, 137,823 persons living in rural areas had university or post-diploma degrees, which meant that, on average, there were 2.29 university graduates in each Iranian village.

Table 1: compares figures for the population distribution of Tehran according to gender and level of education for years 1359 and 1375.

	1359		1375	
	Male	Female	Male	Female
Higher education	8.2	4.4	13.7	9.1
High school	15.9	10.3	28.1	30.7
Guidance school	15.1	20.4	23.3	19.2
Beginning	36.8	34.4	27.7	28.8
Illiterate	16.2	30.6	8.2	12.1

Obviously, the growth of urbanization, literacy and higher education has meant the expansion of the scope of the influence of both written and unwritten mass media. With this, comes an expansion of the scope of information and communication access and, ultimately, greater participation and power of selection in individual and social life creating new patterns of consumption, production and presence in social arena. Naturally, these changes affect the concept of "identity", especially of the young who are the main elements in this change and this turns "identity" into a concept in need of refining. This is especially the case because active participation of the educated classes in Iran is a phenomenon that is more visible during particular phases such as the Islamic revolution, the sacred defence and the seventh presidential elections on 2nd Khordad, 1376.

Women's Greater Social Activity

The removal of social impediments to women's participation in, and greater acceptance of women's presence at, social activities resulted, in part, from their presence on the scene of the revolution. Influenced by a new understanding of religion, Imam Khomeini's courageous *fatwa* on the subject of women's social activity, and the protection offered to women by wearing the *hijab* and upholding religious standards in society, a raising of women's social and cultural status, and the possibility of their rising to higher levels of education and responsibility, have been made possible. This phenomenon implies the need for a new look at the concept of identity in the Iranian society today. Table 2 shows the increasing growth of women's participation in higher education courses.

Table 2: The number of applicant and accepted people from 1370 through 1377.

Year	Number of the Applicants				
	Female	Percent	Male	Percent	Sum
1370	317666	38.22	513489	61.78	831155
1371	357430	39.18	554821	60.82	912251
1372	397424	39.01	621354	60.99	1018778
1373	456653	41.04	655934	58.96	1112587
1374	521419	43.58	674948	56.42	1196367
1375	545768	46.25	634161	53.75	1179922
1376	607873	49.32	624527	50.68	1232400
1377	729955	51.40	689743	48.60	1419698

Year	Number of the Accepted				
	Female	Percent	Male	Percent	Sum
1370	25410	30.21	58688	69.79	84098
1371	41324	34.27	79277	65.73	120610
1372	45092	34.39	86035	65.61	131127
1373	46210	37.35	77528	62.65	123738
1374	48494	40.19	72169	59.81	120663
1375	62382	47.76	68227	52.24	130609
1376	67354	49.40	68991	50.60	136345
1377	72681	52.10	66755	47.90	139436

Employment

The rapid growth in the number of self-employed people in the private sector during the past two decades, which was realized despite slow growth of total employment in that sector, indicates the emergence of a new factor of selection in social developments. During the twenty years 1355 to 1375, private sector employment grew by around 37 percent while numbers of the self-employed in the same sector almost trebled (from 182,229 in 1355 to 527,510 in 1375) (Razaee, 1377, p. 133). During the same period, the numbers of wage and salary earners in the private sector and the number of independently employed persons in the sector grew by 189 percent. This signifies the entry of a large number of professionals into the arena of decision-making who, due to their employment independence, enjoy greater choice as regards their way of life, consumption pattern and political and cultural choice which, directly or indirectly, makes an impact on society's values and norms and, ultimately, its identity structure.

New Civil Institutions

In societies in transition, like Iran, many of the civil institutions have been, and are undergoing change, either being weakened or strengthened. The implications of the weakening or strengthening of these institutions for the process of identity changes, especially as they concern the young, are clearly visible. For example, in Iran, the institutions of the press and of academia have taken on special cultural and social functions in the absence of political parties and other political and professional bodies. The growth of the press and the increase in the number of professional and specialized publications naturally has an impact on the emergence of new identities. This is particularly so because the growth of this section of the press, both in number and quality of publications, has been considerable in recent years.

Table 3: The numbers of current publications in 1377.

Kind of publication	Number	Percent
Local	193	22.9
Scientific	340	40.3
Cultural	120	14.2
Newspaper	35	4.2
Political	43	5.1
Women	16	1.9
Sports	62	7.3
Children	31	3.8
Other	3	3
SUM	843	100

New Discourse

Undoubtedly, changes in the current discourse, both at the national and international levels, tend to influence the concept of the identity of the young. The Islamic revolution in Iran was, according to Imam Khomeini's interpretation, an "explosion of light" and opened up new ideological horizons in society and in politics. In recent decades, the culture of dialogue, sympathy, consensus, law-abiding participation and toleration has assumed the form of the dominant culture and the concept of identity has been affected by these discourses. Moderation has become the essence of attractive discourses that have been well received by the younger generation. What happened in the 1376 presidential elections was, to a large extent, the result of the growth of the discourse that reduced the polarization of Iranian society to a great extent (Abdi, 1377, p. 103).

Challenges

We must also take account of certain challenges and technological changes of influence to the indigenous social and cultural variables at the international level that affect the subject of individual and social identity. Among the most important of these factors are:

Growth of Localism and Nationalism Versus Globalism

The new society is faced with growth in the levels of cultural self-determination and autonomy against the most forceful and diverse impact of globalism and uniformity. The result of this contact has been the emergence of a new concept which does not equate globalization of culture with westernization of culture and intends to acquire an equitable share of participation in the construction of the global culture. In this formation, the narrow casting against the broadcasting of the mass media is interesting to note as they influence the process of the formation of a new identity.

Growth of Spiritualism Versus Cationalism

Just as modern societies have turned to some kind of rationality and self-criticism, when faced with social issues, they have, in a notable way, turned to spirituality and metaphysical outlooks. The combination of these two require an updated supply of religious and cultural heritage and sources and an increase in the power of religion to supply appropriate answers. In fact, presentation of an effective portrayal of religion in the modern world can fill the gap between these two tendencies and end the current cleavages between this-worldly and other-worldly subjects. Thus, the identity defined in such an arena will be free from the usual fractions between justice, liberty and religion and will have the power to regulate and harmonize the demands and ideals of the young at the beginning of the twenty first century.

Networking of Communications

The growth in network communications has, in effect, undermined the existence of concentrated power in the cultural structure and, by presenting various information services through networks, will organize cultural, scientific, economic and politically complex entities. In these networks, new identity-building structures and institutions shall appear in the fields of management, culture and politics. These networks are able to alter educational, work and leisure models quite easily.

Bilateral Communication

The modern communication industry is based upon the notions of active, selective and initiative audiences. Thus, the individual's identity takes shape not by monologues or one-way addresses, but in the process of dialogue and bi-directional exchanges.

Activation and Convergence of Media

Today, national borders are easily violated by the world media. Dynamic media using temporal extensions such as voice and moving pictures and static media using spatial extension such as static pictures and texts have, in effect, intermingled in the content of multi-media systems and have created a convergent and effective system in mass and inter-personal communications.

Solutions

Against these challenges and technological changes, various solutions have been proposed for the preservation of cultural identity in the modern world. Some of the main solutions include:

Diversity and Search for Multiplicity and Variety of Cultures Versus Homogeneity of Cultures

This concerns the question of whether it is natural for all individuals to be identical, as regards ideas and attitudes and consumption of goods, or whether diversity and variation is a natural phenomenon. In the multi-cultural notion, being different in cultural interests and tendencies is viewed as a right and as such, is considered natural while according to the uni-cultural view, all individuals must adapt themselves to, and adopt a single and uniform attitude.

Confrontation Versus Coexistence of the Existing Value Systems

This concerns the question of whether value systems emerging from religious, national and ethnic cultures are in conflict with those coming from the trans-national ones or whether some form of coexistence can be arranged for them. In this context, a confrontation between animosity and friendship, "we", "not-we", "self" and "not-self" assume valid connotations. In the context of the coexistential idea, differences emanating from contractual relations replace natural and objective differences. Needless to say, both views cover a wide spectrum of ideas.

Open Versus Closed Information Society

Whether it is possible to make use of special instruments and policies to prevent free dissemination of information or whether modern communication technology has eliminated this option.

Privacy Versus Public Encroachment

Whether it is possible to preserve the privacy of individuals, despite modern communication technology, or whether we must give up some of our rights to privacy in the interest of public observation.

Cultural Participation Versus Monopoly

Whether all individuals can, and must, be involved in the process of production and consumption of cultural goods or whether culture is to be under the monopolistic control of a particular elite or ideological group. Participation requires the creation of institutions and mechanisms intended to involve individuals continuously in the fields of culture whereas a monopoly of culture implies the perception of culture as a luxurious and superfluous phenomenon.

Cultural Creativity by Relying on Past Elements by a New Reading of Cultural Heritage

Whether cultural creativity based on the sole use of cultural elements and institutions left to us from the past is possible, or whether neglecting the cultural heritage and clutching at other cultures, or recreating a novel presentation of what is left to us as our past heritage from the two new cultural ways, is to be used for the definition of identity.

Competition Between National Cultural Organizations and Regional and International Cultural Organizations at the National Level Versus Competition at The International Level

Whether national cultural institutions are obliged to compete with regional and international institutions or whether competition should also take place between these institutions at the national level, as well as between indigenous cultural institutions and international institutions at an international level. These form the two ends of the spectrum of ideas in this field. This challenge results from two kinds of interpretation of identity. According to one, national identity gains in strength in competition with others; in the other interpretation, identity is a political phenomenon.

Strengthening a System of Emission and Reception at the International Level Under Centralized Ownership Versus Sectoral Diversity of Independent and Numerous Emission and Reception Systems

Whether media activists must be restricted to the confines of nation-states or must go beyond. In the first outlook, the limit of the coverage by the media is set by the nation-state. In the second approach, the media face no restrictions except their technical capacity.

Passive versus Active Audience

One-way media, particularly radio and television, keep the audience passive while other information networks and highways as well as cable communication bring about the possibility of two-way communication. Today, the media looking for passive audiences and those in search of active audiences are gripped in a serious challenge. The users of the second method enjoy greater freedom of choice of cultural and artistic products but they must also be prepared to take a greater part in the process.

Mediacracy/Manipulating of Opinions

Whether the media themselves shape the cultural and artistic tastes of the public or whether they can only give expression to them.

CONCLUSION

Today, Islamic societies face the outlook of responding to the increasing needs of the young who wish to live as Muslims in the twenty first century and of having an Islamic identity and being able to leave this - their culture and civilization - as a legacy to the following generations their culture and civilization. On the one hand, they have observed the unbridled utilization of their religious sources and assets under the pretext of safeguarding traditions and identity and, on the other, they have witnessed the consequences of infatuation with and submission to the dictates of the modern world. Neither do they consider retrospective approaches to signify "originality" nor are they dreaming about being totally absorbed and annihilated in the modern industrial civilization. The rationale of this generation is dialogue, a logical understanding of the modern world and an updated protection of its religious heritage. It is this need that leads the generation to a free choice in the modern world; a choice based on the pure essence of Man and on lasting religious values. Freedom of thought, power of reasoning, dialogue and law and order in collective behaviour is the outcome of such an approach.

The experience of Islamic Iran has shown that it is possible to define the identity of the young within this context and in order to give it meaning, the production of thoughts and cultural organization is more important than any other factor. Thoughts generated at various centres of thinking, whether at seminaries or universities, must arrive at optimal richness, fruition and effectiveness and then be propagated by the mass media using the appropriate language. As long as the centre of thinking is centred in the media, the result is simply a stronger collective culture and not the deepening of a lasting culture. But when the media come to act as the conveyers of thoughts that are generated in their original centres, this leads to real and realistic expectations from the media in the creation of identity. In that case, the constructive role of the media in the process will include the:

1. Re-creation of the indigenous culture and an overcoming of the symptoms of historical cleavage.
2. Establishment of a link between the world and society (cultural exchange).
3. Reduction of force of intra-sector and inter-sector fragmentation and the resolution of social conflicts (traditional and modern cultures, national and sub-national cultures, generation gap, gap between social groups etc.).
4. Elevation of civil life and identity and the strengthening of the culture of participation, competition and dialogue.
5. Safeguarding of elements that impart solidarity to social and cultural sectors in the rapid process of development (religion, language, history etc. As against cultural assault).

6. Creation of a balance between stable components (for example, education) as "intermediaries" or "interpreters between society's sectors and generations."
7. Reduction of the gap between technological advancements and the traditional structure and system of communication.

References:

Farsi
Abdi, Abbas, "The Hidden Dimensions of the Recent Elections" in *Entakhan-e-no* (*New Choice: Sociological Analysis of the Event of the Khordad the Second*).

Ahmadi, Babak, *Me'mari Modernite* (*The Construction of Modernity*) Tehran, Markaz Publications, 1377.

Foucault, Michel, *What Dreams Iranians Have in Their Head?* Translated into Farsi by Hussein Ma'sumi Hamedani, Tehran, Hermes Publications, 1377.

Irans Center for Statistics Report No. 1330 and 1331.

Razaie, Abdolali, "The Full Part of the Glass" in *Entekhab-e-no*.

UNESCO's manual of the Inter-Governmental Conference on Cultural Policies for Development, Tehran, 1377.

English
Giddens, Anthony, *The Consequences of Modernity*, Cambridge, 1990.

Harvey, D., *The Conditions of Postmodernity*, Oxford, 1990.

Kellner, D., "Popular Culture and the Consumption of Postmodern Identities", in S, Lash and J. Friedman, *Modernity and Identity*, oxford, 1992

Laclau, E., *New Reflections on the Revolution of Our Time*, London, 1990.

Index

n = footnote; t = table

Abideen, Zayn-al, Imam 145
Abraham 98, 128
Abu Bakr, Caliph 84
action, theories of 127, 129–32
Adam 4
Adelkhan, Fariba 206
Adorno, Theodor 128
al-Afghani *see* al-Din, Sayyid Jamal
Afghanistan 247, 261
Africa 54, 243
Agha Khan 83, 87n
Ahmad, Nazir 211
Ahmed, A. 160
Ahmed, Kemal 228
Akhtar, Shabbir 99
Alaqsa Mosque 224
Ali, Caliph *see* Mu'mineen, Amir-al, Ali bin Abi Tabib
alim see ulama
Ameli, S.R. 28–9
American Muslim Council 230
Amnesty International 198
An-Na'im, Abdullahi 201
Andereesen, Marc 221
Ansari, K.H. 27
Anthias, Floya 55–8, 69n
anti-Islamic attitudes
    in Asia 74, 195
    on the internet 228, 229–30

in Western media 238, 239, 259–61, 263
in Western popular culture 94–5, 164–5, 168, 198–202, 230
AOL (America OnLine) 229–30
apostasy 201
Arab conquest of Asia 71
Arabic, use of 52, 99, 247
Araki, Mohsen, Ayatollah 26
Arendt, Hannah 59–60
astronomy 106, 121n
Ataturk, Mustafa Kamal Pasha 107, 195, 229
Auden, W.H. 264n
Al Azhar University 229–30
al-'Azm, Sadiq Jalal 210

Baab, Seyyed 107
Bahmanpour, Mohammed Saeed 28
Bakhtiari, Bahman 30
Bangladesh 72, 90, 212–13
Bao'an people 81
Barber, Benjamin 61–3
Baudrillard, Jean 161–2
belief systems 105–6, 107–8, 124n
benefits, provision of 174, 180, 185t
Berger, P., and Luckmann, T. 159
Berlin, Isaiah 123n
Bernerslee, Tim 221
Beyer, P. 156, 159–60
Binsa'id, Sa'id 211
Biruni, Abu-Raihan 106
Bonchek, Mark 227
Bosnia 247, 260–1
Bourguiba, Habib 195
Buddhism 75, 84, 127, 133

Bulaç, Ali 210–11
business practice 29, 171
    Islamic *vs.* non-Islamic, study of 174–83, 185–8tt

Caliphate 84, 249
Camus, Albert 264n
capitalism 115, 127–8
carnal desires (*vs.* reason) 140
Castells, Manuel 1–2, 3, 29, 49, 69n, 166, 220, 223, 227, 231
Central Asia 71, 74–5, 238, 243, 253
China, Muslims in 27, 74–86
Chinggis (Genghis) Khan 79
Christian World Evangelization Research Center 262
Christianity 97–8, 113, 161, 164, 260–1
Church of England 89
civil society 105, 166, 207, 209
    compatibility with Islam 27–8, 111–20, 211
Cohen, Claude 264n
Cohen, J.L., and Arato, A. 112, 121–2n
colonialism 72, 73, 195, 196–7, 241, 248
    opposition to 66, 242, 246
communication technology *see* information technology
Condorcet, Émile 145
conversion to Islam 93–4, 97–9
Copernican system 106, 209, 213
Coulson, N.J. 18–19
Council of American Islamic Relations 230
Council of Guardians 16, 17
Crimea 5
cultural imperialism *see* globalization: cultural

da'wa(h) (propagation of the faith) 93, 212

DERVISH (website) 228
diasporas 26, 53–61
    African 54, 60
    Jewish 53–4, 59–60
    Muslim 51, 65–8, 90–1
    see also minorities
Dillon, Michael 27
DILP (Ahlu Bayt Digital Islamic Library Project) 226–7
al-Din, Sayyid Jamal ('al-Afghani') 242
divergence of Muslim teachings 82, 85, 105–6
diversity of Muslim cultures 2, 52–3, 71, 72, 77, 82–6, 90, 153,
        193, 227
Dongxiang people 81
Durkheim, Emil 154–5

e-mail servers 225
East-West relations 2, 4–6, 24–5, 48, 65, 108, 163–6, 230, 248,
        250–1
economics 52, 171–3, 212, 251–2
    Islamic ethos of 10, 20–1, 29, 173–4, 182–3
    see also business practice
education 30, 205–14
    and identity 86, 100, 110–11, 166
    media-based 225–7, 255
    statistics 208, 274–5t, 276t
egalitarianism 1
Egypt 5, 171–2, 174–5, 212, 243, 244, 245
Eickelman, Dale 30, 221
Einstein, Albert 220
employment 172, 276
Enayat, Hamid 5
Eriksen, T.H. 159
Etzoini, Amitai 222

European Union 50
existentialism 107
expediency, policy of 8

fascism 128
Fatima (daughter of the Prophet) 83, 84
fatwas (religious edicts) 14, 168, 200–1, 226, 275
Featherstone, Mike 156
Feng Jinyuan 83
fiqh see jurisprudence
France 5
Frankfurt school (of philosophy) 128, 130
French Revolution 238, 251
Freud, Sigmund 252
fundamentalism 23–4, 69n, 165, 207, 260
    see also traditionalism

G7/G8 groups 197
Garvey, Marcus 57
GATT (General Agreement on Tariffs and Trade) 197
Gedimu sect 84–5
Gellner, Ernest 1, 111, 160–1
Giddens, Anthony 155–6, 162
Gilroy, Paul 54, 60
globalization 23–5, 155–6
    cultural 2, 25, 61–5, 156–8, 167–8, 251, 267
    economic 66, 156, 168, 173
    political 49–51, 156, 168, 251–2
    religious 167–8
    vs. cultural/spiritual identity 157–8, 159–63, 164–5, 251–2,
        278, 279–82
Gonzalez-Quijano, Yves 211

Gorbachev, Michail 74
government use of media 228–9, 253–5
Graham, Billy 211
Gray, John 111
Grossman, Lawrence 222–3
guilds (in Muslim cities) 113–14, 122n
Gülen, Fethullah 211
Gulf War 94, 247, 261

Habermas, Jurgen 123n, 129–32, 134
hadith (ahadith) (sayings of the Prophets) 16, 41, 44, 141, 226,
       253
Hafiz, S.G.M. 123–4n
hajj (pilgrimage to Mecca) 4, 63
Hallaq, Wael 209
Halliday, F. 91
Hamas 31, 228
Hanafi school of thought 82
Hart, H.L.A. 117
Hassan, Adnan 228
Headley, Lord 98
Hegel, Friedrich 115
hijra(h) (migration) 1, 40–1
Hinduism 133
Hisham ibn al-Hakam 136–41
history of Islam 4–6, 71, 73, 74–5, 82, 98, 107–10, 152–3, 163–
       5, 240–3, 244–5, 248–51
   education in 225–6
Hizbollah 31, 228
Hobbes, Thomas 116
Horkiemer, Max 128
Hui (Huihui) people 75, 77–8, 262
human rights

in civil society 117
in Islamic thought 29, 193–5, 201–2
secularisation of 195–6, 197–201
violations of 29–30, 195, 196–7
Western tradition of 196
Huntington, Samuel 47, 52, 207
Hussein, Saddam 94
Huwaidi, Fahmi 198–9

ibn Ja'far, Abu'l Hasan Musa 136–41
Ibn Sayghal, Hasan 135–6
identity
    as cornerstone of Islam 1, 37–9, 44–5, 152–3
    of Muslims in UK 27, 91–3, 94–7, 99–100
    nature of 28–9, 55–7, 105, 123n, 149, 151–2, 158–9, 161,
        193–4, 220–1, 252, 268–70
    problems of 27, 32, 166, 167, 240, 282–3
    reshaping of 91–2, 100, 108–9, 213–14, 225, 230–1, 269–70,
        277–8, 283–4
    social *vs.* individual 39–43, 117, 268–70, 272–3
    types of 29, 163–7
    vs. globalization 24, 159–63, 251–2, 278, 279–84
ijtihad (independent thinking) 15, 199
Ikhwani school of thought 82
Imam, role of 7, 8, 21, 43
IMF (International Monetary Fund) 172, 197
India 5, 72, 247
Indonesia 173, 247, 251–2
information technology
    global advances in 1, 156, 267, 279
    impact on Muslim world 30, 111, 213–14, 235n, 238–9,
        252–3
    see also internet

inheritance, laws of 174, 197
Inquisition 261
al-insan (the human being) 194
Institute of Islamic Studies 1
integration with non-Muslim cultures 91–2, 96–7
interest, borrowing/lending at 174, 175–6
internet 30–1, 118, 156, 219–33
    education on 225–7
    history of 221
    impact on Muslim identity 220–1, 223, 225, 230–1
    political expression on 227–30, 261–3
    religious materials on 223–5, 226–8, 261–3
    user statistics 222, 230
    see also e-mail servers; websites
Internet Islamic Lobby 230
Iqbal, Muhammad 205–6
Iran 5, 195, 243, 251–2
    Cultural Revolution (1906) 106, 109, 242, 250
    education in 274–6tt
    and the internet 228–9
    Islamic Revolution (1979) 1, 14–18, 22–3, 94, 109, 247, 250,
        253–4, 259–60, 261, 273–8
    media in 31–2, 253–9, 271, 272, 277t, 278
Iran Freedom Movement 228
al-Islami, Jimmat 109
'Islamic books' 211–12
Islamic doctrine, foundations of 3–4
Islamic Encyclopedia Foundation 225
Islamic Voice 224
IslamicConnection 224
Israel 200, 247, 259–60
i'tiradh (objection) 39–41

Jacobson, Jessica 166
Jamaat-e Islami (Pakistan) 31, 228
James, William 231
Jeddah 63
Jesus Christ 97–8
jihad (holy war) 39, 61–3, 200
Jordan 172
jurisprudence in Islam *(fiqh)* 52, 106, 151, 226
    theories of 5–23

Kafka, Franz 264n
Kamaluddin, Khwaja 98
Kant, Immanuel 119
Kasravi, Ahmad 107
Kazakh people 77, 79–80
Kazakhstan 78, 79–80, 85–6
al-Kazim, Imam 136–41
Khamenei, Saiyyid Ali, Ayatollah 17, 228
Khan, Maulvi Inayat 98
Khaniki, Hadi 32
Khatami, Mohammed, President 228–9
Khomeini, Ruhollah, Imam 15–18, 20, 21, 22, 66, 94, 168, 228,
    253, 260, 273, 277
Koran *see* Qur'an
Kosovo 261
Kuhn, Thomas 107
Kuwait, Iraqi invasion of 94
Kyrgyz people 80

languages of Muslim communities 52, 72, 75, 77, 78, 79–82, 85,
    86, 99, 247
Larijani, S. 114–15

law-making, process of 15–18
law(s)
    conflicts between 13–14, 117
    expressed *vs.* non-expressed 7–8, 10–12, 17
    mutability of 10–14, 92, 94
    non-specific nature of 11, 13, 19
    social order, focus on 238, 251
    see also shari'a
Lawyers' Committee for Human Rights (New York) 198–9
leadership, role of 26, 41, 43–5, 269
learning from experience 110, 143–5
Lebanon 5, 199, 247, 260
Lerner, Daniel 207
Lewis, Bernard 114
liberalism 114–16
'linguistic imperialism' 99
literacy 1, 274t
Liverpool 97
Lynd, Robert 264n

Ma Tong 83
MacIntyre, Alasdair 111
Mahfouz, Naguib 212
Malaysia 173
Malcolm X 57
Malli, Abdul 249
Mannheim, Karl 205–6
Mao Zedong 27, 75
Marcuse, Herbert 128
marriage, Islamic laws on 10, 22–3
Marx, Karl 107, 115, 154–5, 264n
Masjed Net 224
Massignion, Louis 113–14

Mawlana, Hamid 25, 31
McLuhan, Marshall 156
'McWorld' 25, 26, 61–3, 156, 267
media
early use of 241–3
global development of 128, 157
in Muslim world 31–2, 111, 209, 210–11, 213–14, 238–9,
240, 242, 252, 277t, 278
role in society 271–3, 282, 283–4
in West 166, 238, 239, 259–61
see also television
meditation 133, 135–6
Mesbah, M.H. 123n
mindfulness 142–3
Ming dynasty 83
Ministry of Islamic Culture and Guidance (Iran) 255
minorities, Muslim, in non-Muslim states 27, 29–30, 72, 74–7,
86, 91–3, 152–3, 163, 164–6
missionaries 82
modernity (of Islam) 1, 6, 23, 213–4, 248
Modood, T. 95
Moghul Empire 5
Mol, H. 159
Morocco 172
Mosaic (software program) 221
Moses 98
Moslem Brotherhood (Egypt) 31, 220, 228
mosques, social role of 240–1
Muhammad, the Prophet 3–4, 7, 17, 20–1, 31, 84, 97–8, 120,
124n, 135, 193, 211
mujtahids (authorized lawmakers) 8, 13, 14
Mu'mineen, Amir-al, Ali bin Abi Tabib 26, 37–8, 83, 84, 136,
143–5
al-Munajjid, Muhammad Salih, Sheikh 226

Murad, Khurram 93
Muslim Internet Community 219
Muslim Parliament of Great Britain 93
Muslim Students' Association 220
al-Muslimun, Ikhwan 109
Mutahhari, Murtedha (Murtaza), Ayatollah 12–14, 107
mysticism 28, 119–20

NAFTA (North American Free Trade Agreement) 50
Na'ini, Saiyyid Muhammad Husayn, Allamah 6–9, 10, 11, 12,
     35n
Naipaul, V.S. 87n
Napoleon 5, 244
Nasr, S.H. 121n
Nasser, Gamal Abdel 212
Nation of Islam 152, 164
nation states
    concept and evolution of 47–8, 239, 242–3, 248–9
    conflict with Muslim ideology 31, 49, 51–2, 237–8, 239–40,
         244–5, 249–50
National Islamic Consultative Assembly 8, 16
nationalism 58, 241, 242, 243, 245–7, 278
Negroponte, Nicholas 223
NGOs (non-governmental organizations) 49–50
Nielsen, J. 95
Nisreen, Taslima 200–1
Nuri, Fadhlullah, Shaykh 6–7

Oklahoma City bombing 228
Omar, Caliph 84
Online Islamic Propagation Team 223–4
Orientalism 28, 49, 94

Orwell, George 264n
Osman, Caliph 84
Ottoman Empire 5, 65–6, 243, 261

Pahlavi, Reza Shah 195, 245, 260
Pakistan 72, 90, 247
Parekh, B. 164
Paya, Ali 5, 24, 27–8
Pfeifer, Karen 29
Piscatori, James 31, 221
pluralism *see* diversity
Polanyi, Michael 119
Popper, Karl 123n, 132
population statistics 219–20
post-modern culture/society 153–5, 160–1
press *see* media; printing, development of
printing, invention of 241
protest activity 172

Qadiani, Gholam-Ahmad 107
Qajarid dynasty 5
al-Qaradawi, Yusif, Shaykh 210
al-Qasim, Faysal 210
Qianlong, Emperor 76
Quillium, W.H. 97
Qur'an 92, 120, 245
    core doctrines of 3–4, 121n
    on human dignity 194–5
    and the internet 220, 230, 231, 253, 262
    on leadership 43–4
    on legislation 6, 8, 14, 19
    on mindfulness 142–3

readings from 258
on reason 124n, 128, 134, 135, 141, 145
reinterpretation of 198–9, 201, 209–10
on social identity 39–42
on social responsibility 257
on women 69n

Ramad(h)an (month of fasting) 4, 241
rationality/rationalization
    compatibility with religion 134–42, 145–6, 149
    theories of 28, 126–32, 133–4
reason, Muslim view of 120, 122n, 125–6, 134–45
    elements ('troops') of 146–9
refugees 51
religion
    and the media 212–14 (*see also* internet)
    questions of 109, 133–4
    restructuring of 205–7, 209–11
revivalism 2, 84, 260
Robertson, Roland 155, 161–2, 164
rules *see* laws
Rushdie, Salman 94, 164, 168, 200–1
Russia/Soviet Union 5, 74, 238, 243, 247, 253, 261

al-Sadiq, Ja'far, Imam 134, 135–6, 145–9
Sadr, Mohammed Bakir, Ayatollah 20–1
Salar people 81
salaries 179–80, 186–7t
Saudi Arabia 230–1, 251–2
Sayyid, S. 25, 26
Schmitt, Carl 48
School of Islamic and Social Sciences 225–6

'Search for Common Ground' (Helsinki symposium) 199–200
Shah of Iran *see* Pahlavi, Reza Shah
Shahrur, Muhammad 209–10, 211
shari'a(h) (Islamic holy law) 1, 6–7, 8, 9, 12, 25, 84, 194, 226,
    245, 249, 250
Shari'ati, Ali, Dr 107
Shi'ism 2–3, 6–14, 20–1, 82–3, 84, 106, 107, 226–7, 260
Siddiqui, Kalim 93
Sijzi, Abu Sa'id 106
Singapore 235n, 262
Sistani, Ayatollah 228
Sister Net 224
Six Day War 247
social change (in Muslim world)
    adaptation to 6–9, 15, 19, 25, 110–11
    impact of 4–6, 16, 32, 108–9, 153–5, 161–2
social contract 116
socialism 115–16, 154, 243
Sorbonne 107
Soroush, Abdul Karim 30, 211
Soviet Union *see* Russia
subjectivity (in Muslim world) 51, 65
Sucarno, President 73
Sufism 2–3, 77, 82, 83–4, 133, 228, 262
Suharto, President 73
sunna(h) (way of the Prophet, tradition) 3–4, 6, 8, 14, 92, 194,
    195, 245
Sunnism 2–3, 6, 23, 82, 83, 84, 106

Tabatabai, Sayyid (Seyyed) Muhammad Husayn, Allamah 9–12,
    14, 15, 107
Taha, Mahmud 201
Tajik people 81–2, 83

Taliban 229
taqwa (piety) 41–3
Tatar people 80–1
tax 174
Taylor, Charles 206
television (in Iran)
   government use of 253–5
   program content 255–6
   social role of 31, 256–9
   see also media
'three worlds' (of human consciousness) 132–3
Tillich, Paul 264n
Timimi, Azzam 29–30
traditionalism 28, 114–16, 118, 210
   see also fundamentalism
Tunisia 172, 195
Turkestan *see* Xinjiang
Turkey 195, 210–11, 229, 242
Turner, B.S. 113, 160–1, 165
Turner, Tina 160

ulama (sing. *alim*) (religious scholars) 6, 12, 14, 15–16, 23, 31,
    249–50, 252
umma(h) (worldwide Muslim community) 2, 6, 9, 27, 58, 90–1,
    92, 257–8
   defined 26, 51–3, 65–8
   vs. nation state 49, 51–2, 244, 249, 250
UNESCO 270
United Kingdom 5, 27, 72, 89–100
Universal Declaration on Human Rights 198
USA 225–6
Uyghur people 77, 78–9, 83
Uzbek people 80

Wahhabi Islam 2–3
Waliy Amr (Infallible Imam) 8, 11, 21
war 48, 66–7, 128, 247
Warner, Michael 214
Waters, M. 156, 162
Weber, Max 113, 126–8, 129, 131, 142, 154–5
websites 31, 219, 223–30, 232–3, 262
Webster, Richard 201
welfare organizations 174
Westphalian model (for nation states) 47, 49–51, 57, 61, 67
wilayat-e (vilayate) faqih (supreme authority of senior jurisprudent)
        11, 15–18, 21–2, 255
Wittgenstein, Ludwig 119
Woking Mission 98
women
    attitudes towards 179, 197
    laws relating to 22–3, 174, 275
    role in Muslim society 22, 69n, 206, 210, 224, 275, 276t
World Bank 197, 228
World Islamic Network 224

Xidaotang sect 85
Xinjiang (East Turkestan) 74, 75, 76, 77–82

Yoga 133
young people 2, 86, 167, 220, 225, 231, 268, 271, 272–3, 277–
        8, 282–4